A PEDAGO
OF POSSIBILITY

# A PEDAGOGY OF POSSIBILITY

*Bakhtinian Perspectives on Composition Studies*

Kay Halasek

SOUTHERN ILLINOIS UNIVERSITY PRESS

*Carbondale and Edwardsville*

Library of Congress Cataloging-in-Publication Data

Halasek, Kay, 1959–

A pedagogy of possibility : Bakhtinian perspectives on
composition studies / Kay Halasek.

p.     cm.

Includes bibliographical references and index.

1. English language—Rhetoric—Study and teaching.   2. Bakhtin,
M. I. (Mikhail Ivanovich)—Views on rhetoric.   3. Report
writing—Study and teaching.   I. Title.

PE1404.H33   1999

808'.042'07—dc 21

ISBN 0-8093-2226-9 (cloth : alk. paper)                        98-8354

ISBN 0-8093-2227-7 (paper : alk. paper)                        CIP

The paper used in this publication meets the minimum requirements of
American National Standard for Information Sciences—Permanence of
Paper for Printed Library Materials, ANSI Z39.48-1984. ⊗

FOR SHARON CROWLEY,
MELISSA, ELIZABETH,
AND ROGER

# CONTENTS

# PREFACE

When I began this project several years ago, I was guided by the prospect that Bakhtinian writings might offer composition studies a guiding voice for theoretical and pedagogical reform.[1] The students in our graduate program here still chuckle good naturedly when I preface my remarks in seminars, colloquia, examinations, and meetings with, "Bakhtin has something relevant to say about this point in *Dostoevsky's Poetics*. . . . " It was when I realized that readers and students of other theorists respond similarly in their daily intellectual lives that I stepped away from my advocacy of Bakhtin and toward my concerns as a teacher and admitted that Bakhtin simply provides me a productive way of engaging many of the questions currently debated in composition studies. At the same time, I am acutely aware that I run the risk of presenting myself as an advocate for Bakhtin. I do not believe—and I want to make this clear early on—that Bakhtin is the only theorist (or even the best, for that matter) whose work can illuminate work in composition studies.

However, I am encouraged by the reception of work on Bakhtin and composition studies, and I continue to believe that his work is important to the discipline since Bakhtinian terms, concepts, and insights bring a new perspective to our field. As I wrote *A Pedagogy of Possibility*, I became convinced of the need to explore the (in)congruities between Bakhtinian theories and theories of writing instruction, and I became increasingly dedicated to the project of examining and reinfusing our understanding of composition studies on disciplinary and discursive grounds. The central purpose of *A Pedagogy of Possibility* is to examine and rearticulate the central elements of composition studies and to frame our discussions at every level of the discipline in Bakhtinian terms. My goal is not to promote Bakhtin as *the* theorist for composition studies, but rather to examine the preconditions, assumptions, and implications of a Bakhtinian philosophy of composition studies. Like bell hooks who writes that her "goal as a feminist thinker and theorist is to take . . . abstraction and articulate it in a language that renders it accessible—not less complex or rigorous—but simply more accessible" (*talking back* 39), my goal is to make Bakhtinian work useful to scholars investigating alternative theories for composition studies, as well as to make it accessible to writing teachers as they construct and teach their writing classes. With this said, I must also acknowledge that the Bakhtinian necessarily loses something in the translation. In applying Bakhtinian constructs to composition studies, I not only take them out of their cultural, intellectual, and disciplinary contexts, but I also take liberties with them, "reaccentuating" them, to use a Bakhtinian term, with my own intentions. Bakhtinian ideas have been freely appropriated across disciplines for over a decade now, but many scholars—most notably Bakhtin's own students in the former Soviet Union—are protective of his writings. Acutely aware of this and the entire scholarly enterprise *A Pedagogy of Possibility* represents, I have struggled for some time with the appropriations I make of Bakhtinian thought, going so far as to acknowledge at one point that

> [a]s a teacher and theorist of composition (and, by extension, as a rhetorician), my work with Bakhtin is guided by a desire to apply his work in composition studies. To meet this end, I have at many points in my writing (here and elsewhere) become less concerned with interpreting Bakhtin than with formulating useful approaches to applying this work to student texts and composition pedagogy. Admittedly, my work will probably never be of consequence among Bakhtin scholars, but I hope that my work will reach teachers and researchers of composition eager to engage his voice in their investigations. The polemic and parodic rhetorics about which I write here serve as a case in point. . . . To view students' expository writing as informed by competing rhetorics, competing voices and languages is to claim for them a status as texts worthy of interpretation, not simply evaluation. ("Starting" 8)

My comments in "Starting the Dialogue" prove particularly helpful in clarifying my concerns about appropriation. Bakhtin commends novelistic discourses for their ability to represent the dialogized heteroglossia of a given epoch. Extending that discussion to student texts, arguing as I do that "[t]o view students' expository writing as informed by competing rhetorics, competing voices and languages is to claim for them a status as texts worthy of interpretation, not simply evaluation." Such an extension does not *negate* or undermine Bakhtinian comments on novelistic discourses but amplifies them and allows us to redefine novelistic discourses outside the confines of the literary-artistic linguistic stratum to which Bakhtin confines them. This move is a critical one, for me and for composition studies, as it illustrates the corrective nature of some of my appropriations of Bakhtin.

James Berlin argues in the opening chapter of *Rhetorics, Poetics, and Cultures: Refiguring College English Studies* that English departments over the past one hundred years have tended to valorize the study of literary texts and vilify rhetoric: "[A]ll that is important and central in the study of discourse," Berlin writes, "falls within the domain of literary texts and all that is unimportant and marginal falls within the realm of rhetoric" (3). Although his *motives* for privileging novelistic discourse differ, I would argue similarly with regard to Bakhtin; he valorizes novelistic discourse and marginalizes rhetoric. For me, personally, the results of Bakhtin's marginalizing of rhetoric have been palpable. I have spent a great deal of time examining the consequences (for rhetoric and writing instruction) of Bakhtin's prejudice against rhetoric, seeking not to justify it but to work around and against it, defining it as a point of conflict.

For rhetoricians and compositionists generally, the consequences of Bakhtin's privileging of the novel are also damaging. If we are to take Bakhtin at his word, rhetoric is monologic, combative, confrontational, authoritative, and bears no resemblance to the dialogized novel. To continue along with Bakhtin in his privileging of novelistic forms without working to rearticulate our own understanding of novelistic discourse and moving beyond Bakhtin's representations would mean marginalizing rhetoric further. As Berlin points out, training students only in the "aesthetic and putatively disinterested interpretation of literary texts"—regardless of their role in the subversive discourses of an era—and *not* in the eminently more important production of "political texts that would enable them to take their rightful place as leaders in their communities" is to deny our responsibility for educating them and encouraging their ideological becoming (*Rhetorics* 3). I have little hope that in the near future we in composition studies will see a significant change in the political position of composition in English departments. The prospects of dethroning literary interpretation as the valued activity in English departments are dim, for like the literary forms about which Bakhtin writes in "Discourse in the Novel," the possibility of unseating powerful hegemonic linguistic forms or literary enterprises is dependent upon larger cultural movements:

> The resistance of a unitary, canonic language, of a national myth bolstered by a yet-unshaken unity, is still too strong for heteroglossia to relativize and decenter literary and language consciousness. This verbal-ideological decentering will occur only when a national culture loses its sealed-off and self-sufficient character, when it becomes conscious of itself as only one among *other* cultures and languages. (370)

The political climate and nationalist culture in the United States today continue to feed the myth of self-sufficiency, as evidenced in the renewed vigor of such initiatives as the English Only Movement and tightened immigration and public policy laws, such as those in California and Arizona. The "rhetorical text," Berlin suggests, "has been relegated to the limbo of first-year composition, a course offered only because of the alleged failure of the high school to do its job in what is now designated a 'lower' level of study" (*Rhetorics* 3). If we simply accept a Bakhtinian hierarchy of novel/rhetoric, rhetorical texts would remain in the subordinate position. But by revising, rewriting, even denying the privileged position of the novel by treating student texts as novelistic genres in their own right, we begin the process of resituating composition studies in the English department. To resituate composition studies (and by extension rhetoric) not as the *center* of English departments but as a vital, viable, acknowledged *presence* in those departments is to redefine it as I do here—as the site at which students (1) examine the implications of their various rhetorical proficiencies, (2) survey the discursive possibilities available to them, and (3) produce discourse from positions informed by their active and purposeful engagement with cultural (e.g., literary) texts.[2]

*A Pedagogy of Possibility* provides an overview of portions of the Bakhtinian canon that are relevant to composition studies, explores the implications of this work for the teaching of writing and for current debates about the role of theory in composition studies, and provides a model of scholarship that strives to maintain a "dialogic" balance between practice and theory, between composition studies and the Bakhtinian. As a result, the study ranges broadly across the field, at one point painting in broad strokes a new picture of the discipline, at another focusing on the fine details of the rhetorical situation, and at yet another point examining the efficacy and ethics of academic discourse, student resistance, and critical and conflict pedagogy. If compositionists are to consider a Bakhtinian influence in composition studies, they must understand not only how his thought parallels and illuminates similar work in the field, but also the implications of a Bakhtinian philosophy of composition for their classroom teaching. As these premises suggest, a book-length study like *A Pedagogy of Possibility* presents a special set of problems, not the least of which is knowing where to begin. The organizational principle to which I finally turned situates this project squarely in composition, rather than in Bakhtinian, studies. Of course, applying the Bakhtinian to composition studies requires that I examine the notions central to his work, such as dialogue, heteroglossia, interanimation, answerability, and the philosophy of the act. But rather than simply explicate these terms as they function within the Bakhtinian corpus, I use them as tropes for revisioning the field and as the terms from which I develop a larger argument to which the Bakhtinian is only secondary.

Accordingly, *A Pedagogy of Possibility* is organized around three central questions that guide scholarly discussions in the field:

1. What is the disciplinary status of composition studies and how might we reframe our constructions of it?
2. What do we gain by reexamining (through Bakhtinian notions) discursive representations of the rhetorical situation and their function in composition classrooms?
3. What alternative ways of thinking about the teaching of writing do Bakhtinian perspectives on pedagogy offer composition teachers?

Far from these questions existing as separate debates in the discipline, however, I argue that to reconstruct composition studies as an integral and dynamic field of inquiry, we must move methodically through each of these discussions—from disciplinary to discursive and finally to pedagogical concerns. Composition studies, invigorated by the Bakhtinian, takes on a renewed disciplinary purpose, one more fully engaged in working with students toward what Bakhtin calls "ideological becoming." To state these premises in different terms, I argue that by addressing pedagogical concerns about such issues as plagiarism and the academic essay without first questioning the construct of the student writer or examining our representations of the discipline itself, compositionists have addressed local needs without first examining disciplinary and discursive structures that inevitably undermine the goals of their pedagogical choices.[3]

My work has been guided by an overriding concern with those less immediate, but nonetheless important, large-scale issues, including the ways that composition historians and theorists construct the discipline in their scholarship and the implications of these constructions on pedagogy. In this ongoing inquiry, *A Pedagogy of Possibility* represents both the development and culmination of my scholarly efforts. Very early in my career, my objective in examining scholars' constructions of composition studies was guided by a desire to disclaim the validity of literary representations I felt were detrimental to the continued growth of the field.[4] That does not mean, however, that I believe composition studies should dismiss work in literary studies. Clearly, the interdisciplinary nature of the discipline demands that scholars in the field examine and critique relevant scholarship and research in other fields. A great deal of debate has swelled around the issue of bringing literary theory into the college writing classroom, with proponents arguing that the very nature of rhetoric and writing instruction welcomes (perhaps even necessitates) interdisciplinary approaches. Others, however, have argued—very convincingly at times—that constructing composition studies as a discipline dependent upon or informed by literary studies is to ghettoize, or at least subordinate, composition to literary studies once again.

Compositionists have also spent quite a lot of time brooding over the purity of theory in the writing classroom, wondering, for example, if it is possible to implement a truly poststructuralist or deconstructivist writing pedagogy. Our allegiances should be with the writing classroom, with improving the quality of our students' education and their writing abilities, so for me the terms of the debate are not as simple as "Should we or should we not?" look beyond composition studies proper for intellectual arguments, constructs, or models. Rather than question whether we should "forage,"[5] we must question the results of the foraging. Borrowings from cognitive psychology in the 1970s and 1980s, for example, produced an entire cottage industry in quantitative research that continues to define a great deal of the discipline's understanding of writers and writing (e.g., Flower and Hayes), and, more recently, ethnographic methods based largely on anthropological methods inform recent studies in the field (e.g., Chiseri-Strater, Moss).

It seems to me that foraging is an inherent characteristic of all academic inquiry and to argue against its efficacy or value is to argue in vain. Nevertheless, compositionists must be critical of the borrowings that take place, especially when those borrowings come from literary criticism, a field that is valorized in many of the same departments that vilify composition studies. We must examine and evaluate the work of philosophers of composition on these terms: Does the work represent nothing more than a template imposed on the discipline, with so much jiggling and shuffling needed to make the pieces fit? If the answer is yes, then the application does little in the way of advancing composition studies and instead maintains its subordinate position to the literary theory applied. Stephen North suggests that the tendency to "treat such [foraged] claims as 'facts,' not premises" is more likely to occur with work imported from the sciences, "but," he continues, "it can happen with borrowings from any method, and the error is the same, violating the fundamental tenet of dialectic: No premise is unassailable" (102–3). Foraging, then, must be accompanied by a keen sense of self-reflexivity—or dialogism—with regard to the borrowings. That is, we must trust that composition studies has as much to offer cognitive psychology or Bakhtinian scholarship, for example, as they have to offer composition studies. I strive to achieve such a reciprocity of influence in this text.

# ACKNOWLEDGMENTS

To write is to collaborate, and the collaborators in this project are many, for the final manuscript of *A Pedagogy of Possibility* represents much of my intellectual work since 1987, spanning my years as a graduate student at the University of Texas at Austin and faculty member at Ohio State University. Although little remains in this book from my dissertation, I still owe (and wish to acknowledge) a debt of gratitude to those people in Austin who contributed to my education. I thank Rick Penticoff for introducing me to Bakhtin's work and Shelli Fowler for offering her insights on feminist and cultural studies, very few of which, I must admit, have made it into these pages. For a decade of friendship and camaraderie too dear to name, I thank Nancy Peterson and Kristi Hamilton. The members of my dissertation committee—Linda Brodkey, Lester Faigley, James Kinneavy, John Ruszkiewicz, and Ramón Saldívar—provided both direction and freedom, and they each remain for me models of scholarly integrity.

I acknowledge the financial and professional support of the Department of English and the College of Humanities at Ohio State University, which provided me a Special Research Assignment to work on this manuscript. To my colleagues at Ohio State who have read drafts and provided support over the years, I thank you. These people include Brenda Brueggemann, Sara Garnes, Nan Johnson, Kitty Locker, Andrea Lunsford, Beverly Moss, Frank O'Hare, Jackie Royster, Jim Phelan, and Amy Shuman. I would be a far poorer person without their scholarly and collegial presence. Graduate students in my spring 1996 seminar on Bakhtin and composition—Natalie Herdman, Michael Lohre, Vic Mortimer, Pat Schutjer, and Rebecca Greenberg Taylor—deserve mention for their commitment to writing instruction and their attention to and comments on portions of the manuscript. Nels Highberg and Tara Pauliny, my research assistants during the final months of manuscript revision and preparation, brought to the project keen eyes and a sharp pencil—both of which made the final product much better. Thanks, as well, to Tracey Sobol-Hill at Southern Illinois University Press, whose advocacy of this project I greatly appreciate.

To Don Bialostosky I owe particular recognition for his gifts of time, insight, collegiality, and friendship. For many years he has read and supported my work with dedication. Sharon Crowley's influence on my career cannot be overstated. I came to know and work with her by coincidence, yet my years as her student, colleague, and friend in Flagstaff were formative and remain among the most significant. She taught me well and has tried her best to make a rhetorician and writer out of me. I can only say, I think I'm getting there.

Thanks, Roger, for your patience and good humor over the years. I can't begin to tell you how much I respect, admire, and love you. It's a good life we have.

The decisions for what is included and omitted in this book are my own. Despite the influence of the colleagues listed above, I have no doubt committed errors and inaccuracies. They remain my responsibility.

Grateful acknowledgment is made to Caroline J. Hudak, Rebecca G. Taylor, and Chris Zawodniak for permission to publish their writing. For permission to reproduce sections of the CUE (Committee on the Undergraduate Experience) document, I thank Martha Garland, Vice Provost, Ohio State University. And for writing by Barbara Smith and Eunsook Koo from *A Community of Writers: A Workshop Course in Writing* by Peter Elbow and Pat Belanoff (New York, 1995), grateful acknowledgment is made to McGraw-Hill. Reproduced with permission of the McGraw-Hill Companies.

# A PEDAGOGY
# OF POSSIBILITY

# INTRODUCTION

## *A Compositionist Reads Bakhtin*

Mikhail Bakhtin was born in Orel, near Moscow, in 1895. Schooled in classics at Petrograd (Petersburg) University, his work was influenced by Nietzsche, Kant, Hegel, Buber, Kierkegaard, and Cassirer, among others. Yet the theoretical concepts for which he is most known are perhaps equally a result of the political, religious, and intellectual turbulence of revolutionary and postrevolutionary Russia. Like many intellectuals after the Bolshevik Revolution, Bakhtin moved from province to province, sometimes of his own volition, other times in exile. Although Bakhtin's work did not reach publication until late in his life, he was a prolific writer and member of a group that has come to be called the "Bakhtin Circle." Bakhtin and his colleagues formed a transient intellectual community—convening and reconvening in several cities over many years—that gave birth to the ideas that appear in Bakhtin's work and now inform current scholarship in linguistics, discourse theory, and literary theory. Among his colleagues in the "Bakhtin Circle" were Valentin Volosinov and Paul Medvedev, around whom swells the debate of the disputed authorship of several texts. Volosinov and Medvedev were, during their lifetimes, the generally acknowledged authors of *Marxism and the Philosophy of Language* and *The Formal Method in Literary Scholarship*.

Bakhtin did not lose his life during the purges, but neither did he escape unscathed. He was arrested in 1929 on religious and political charges, among which was the Socratic crime of corrupting youth through his teachings. Nor was Bakhtin's physical life an easy one. He and his wife Elena barely subsisted for many years on meager disability pensions and the earnings from his occasional lectures and tutorials. Despite his chronic ill health (he suffered all his adult life from osteomyelitis and later from emphysema) and his habit of drinking strong tea and chain smoking, Bakhtin lived until 1975, by which time he had gained recognition and acclaim for his work.

Of all of the work Bakhtin produced over his fifty-year writing career, he

1

is most lauded for his work on the novel. His texts have drawn the attention and commentary of such scholars as Wayne Booth, Paul de Man, and Julia Kristeva. Don Bialostosky, Katerina Clark, Caryl Emerson, Michael Holquist, and Gary Saul Morson have also brought Bakhtin to the attention of North American literary scholars. By discussing and applying Bakhtin's work in semiotics and literary and linguistic theory, these scholars provide important explications of difficult and sometimes seemingly inaccessible thought.

## REACCENTUATING BAKHTIN

The preceding section presents a rather conventional introduction to a literary figure. As such it valorizes, even heroicizes Bakhtin, focusing on his hardships, trials, and triumphs. His is an intellectual success story set against the backdrop of social injustice. Bakhtin is immortalized, preserved, and passed down from one intellectual generation to the next. Yet, the "Bakhtin" that we call upon in this or any other narrative is not the Bakhtin of Moscow in the 1960s or even Kristeva's French Bakhtin of the 1970s. Bakhtin's work and image, like the "great novelistic images" he writes about at the close of "Discourse in the Novel," "continue to grow and develop even after the moment of their creation; they are capable of being creatively transformed in different eras, far distant from the day and hour of their original birth" (422). By working with Bakhtin's ideas as they might be applied to composition studies, I reaccentuate Bakhtin for my own purposes, focusing not upon Bakhtin as literary theorist, but instead upon Bakhtin as possible contributor to the theory and practice of expository writing instruction. As I first undertook this study, I was concerned about using Bakhtin in this manner, but his own words on the inevitability of dialogue and of creative transformation and reaccentuation mollified my concern. I began to ask not, "Is it appropriate to use Bakhtin?" but rather, "Why, how, and to what ends should I use Bakhtinian ideas?"

One might begin to make a case for considering Bakhtinian contributions to composition studies by noting their influence in other areas of English studies. Bakhtinian texts inform research in linguistics (Schultz), business communication (Cross), literary criticism (Bialostosky, *Wordsworth*; Gardiner), feminist criticism (Bauer; Bauer and McKinstry; Finke; Hohne and Wussow; Longfellow), film (Longfellow; Dunne), performance theory (Sabatini), the essay (A. Hunt; R. Hunt; Bellanca), African American literary theory (Hale; Henderson; Mason), Asian American literary studies (Souris), English education (Lensmire), theory of ethnography (Quantz and O'Connor), the popular press (Glynn), detective fiction (Mason), popular culture (Hoy), and poetry (Richter, "Dialogism"; Shapiro). We might also note Bakhtin's growing recognition as "one of the giants of 20th century social and cultural theory" (Aronowitz 22), a figure of such stature that to "ignore Bakhtin . . . is to deny rhetoric an important influence" (Schuster, "Mikhail Bakhtin" 594). We cannot afford, we might argue, *not* to examine his relevance to a field increasingly concerned with cultural studies.

Moreover, applying Bakhtinian principles to composition studies is timely, even crucial, given the renewed interest in social learning theory, collaborative learning, the concept of knowledge as socially constructed, and the problematic relationship between speaking and writing. Like many composition theorists and practitioners, Bakhtin emphasizes the centrality of language use in the development of and changes within social structures and cultural institutions. Like social constructivist pedagogy, which C. H. Knoblauch describes as "aim[ing] above all to situate students self-consciously within the objective social realities that impinge upon them, cause them to be what and who they are, and, in some circumstances, account for their domination" (135), Bakhtinian theories of language establish a similar goal for any user of discourse; each must bear a self-conscious awareness and understanding of language and its power, its ideological assumptions, and the purposes revealed by his own languages.[1] The potential importance of the Bakhtinian canon to composition studies leads Gregory Clark to argue that "for people studying rhetoric and composition . . . Bakhtin's work provides perhaps our most comprehensive explanation of the process through which social knowledge is constructed in a cooperative exchange of texts" (8). It also prompts Jon Klancher to suggest that compositionists can use Bakhtinian constructs to rethink the very function and nature of writing education and pedagogy, a call answered by Martin Nystrand, Stuart Green, and Jeffrey Wiemelt as they define and argue for a Bakhtinian theory of composition.

## POINTS OF CONTACT: THE APPEAL OF THE DIALOGIC

Bakhtinian meditations on dialogue, varied as they are, form the basis for much of the recent surge in the writing-as-dialogic metaphor in composition studies, and for this reason alone Bakhtin's work demands scrutiny among compositionists.[2] In her introduction to *Literacy, Ideology, and Dialogue*, Irene Ward rightly identifies a growing body of research in composition studies that espouses dialogic principles and practices. This move to embrace the dialogic is not surprising, Ward suggests, given the increasing acceptance of student-centered pedagogies, growing emphasis on multicultural education for an increasingly diverse student population, and poststructuralist understanding of language. The dialogic—as metaphor, as philosophy, and as practice—has been elevated to the level of a "god" term in the discipline, and as such, it has become at once ossified, transparent, and irrecoverable. The meaning of the term, however ambiguous, is infrequently interrogated; it has achieved, at least at this moment, both denotative and connotative purity, as well as an unquestioned position within composition studies.

In this respect, dialogue has replaced writing as a process as a defining metaphor for the discipline. And like the process metaphor, the dialogic eludes definition in the scholarship except in application. (We know a writing as process pedagogy when we see one, just as we know a dialogic pedagogy when we see one.) Some scholars have gone so far as to claim, for example, that "all effective writing teachers know instinctively (even if they have never heard of Bakhtin) that the writing classroom must be dialogic" (Middendorf 35). These are, however, superficial observations with dangerous implications; conflating a philosophy of composition (writing as a process, writing as dialogic) with particular classroom practices, or arguing that *all* effective writing teachers subscribe to a dialogic philosophy of composition diminishes, even elides, the value of the dialogic.

Regrettably, many applications of the dialogic in composition scholarship overlook the complexity of dialogue as it is characterized by Bakhtin. To gain a better understanding of the dialogic as a controlling metaphor in writing instruction and at the same time reap the greatest benefit from the Bakhtinian canon, we would do well to review the constructions of the term. In *Marxism and the Philosophy of Language*, *Freudianism*, and in the essays of *The Dialogic Imagination*, Volosinov and Bakhtin establish the bases from which we might begin to think about the implications of a Bakhtinian reconceptualization of composition studies. In these works, Volosinov and Bakhtin define discourse theory and the elements of the rhetorical situation in terms of a socially constructed reality and a socially defined individual. Meaning, knowledge, and reality are constructed through language and between ideologically bound individuals within historically situated language spheres. Bakhtin maintains that the individual exists in and relates to the world only insofar as language and his way of seeing and constructing the world allow. Consequently, an individual's languages, discourse, and rhetoric are conditioned and defined by complex, fluctuating social relationships.

At the core of a socially constructed reality and knowledge lies "dialogism." As Sidney Monas and many others, including Paul de Man, suggest, the concepts of dialogue and of dialogism are central to the Bakhtinian canon, informing discussions of linguistics, psychology, and criticism. The definitions of "dialogism" and its cognates "dialogue," "dialogic," and "dialogization" vary according to the context in which they are discussed. At first glance, readers might be inclined to associate dialogism or dialogue with the give and take of conversation or the alternating lines given to characters in a drama, and this is not an entirely misplaced response to the term in Bakhtinian work. Bakhtin views this responsive element of dialogue as one of the most important forms of discourse and verbal interaction. Implied in such a literal example of dialogue is the cooperative sharing of texts. Dialogue is a constructive activity that leads to a new and heightened understanding of the issue at hand. The Bakhtinian tenet that all knowledge is created dialogically has been taken up time and again in the existing scholarship on Bakhtin in composition studies (e.g., Comprone, Cooper, Middendorf, Ward, N. Welch), and the implications for writing instruction are far reaching. Such an understanding of dialogue, for example, informs Middendorf's commentary on Bakhtin and basic writing as well as Nancy Welch's contention that teachers responding to student texts might work to "promote conversation rather than allegiance" by requiring students to attach letters outlining the students' readings of their own work or writing logs that set out students' comments on the reception of their work by peers and the instructor (500). Teachers who ask students to work together composing and/or revising their work believe (on both theoretical and practical levels) that such cooperative activities will not only improve the texts under review, but also lead students to a more complete and long-term understanding of textual production.

An actual cooperative verbal exchange between two speaking subjects serves as another appropriate analogy for dialogism. In this sense of dialogue, all utterances take part in a conversation. As each of us contributes our own ideas to a subject, teaching writing, for example, our communal understanding of that subject grows. We are actively involved in socially constructing a body of knowledge about writing instruction that could not have been possible had we not engaged one another's ideas. According to Kenneth Bruffee in his essay "Social Construction, Language, and the Authority of Knowledge," this understanding of dialogue, also taken and applied as a pedagogical method, informed the movement in writing classrooms away from lecture to whole and small group discussions. Teachers devoted to class discussion formats often cite the communal "coming to know" as a motivation for engaging students in discussions of texts. Discussions offer students the opportunity to contribute to the communal understanding of an issue, text, or topic. It is important to remember, for example, that as we speak or write about pedagogy, we each reveal something of our own world views—world views that Bakhtin claims are also constructed dialogically: "Words carry with them their own histories, their own previous and potential significations" (Schuster, "Mikhail Bakhtin" 597).

So we in composition studies must not be satisfied with simply understanding the dialogic as manifested in classroom practice. We must recognize the inherent dialogism within the word and among utterances. In composing this introduction, for example, I write in response to and in anticipation of the words of others. That is, my utterance encounters, assimilates, rejects, tests, evaluates, analyzes, and transforms what others have said about the Bakhtinian corpus and writing instruction and what I anticipate still others will say in response to my discussion. I am involved in a diachronic dialogue that extends retrospectively from me to Bakhtin (and beyond), and prospectively from me to my readers and their potential responses (and beyond). In the end, the Bakhtinian metaphor of an utterance as "one link in a continuous chain of speech performances" is insufficient for describing the interactive nature of discourse (Volosinov, *Marxism* 72). The late-twentieth-century constructs and metaphors developed by chaos theorists and hypertext technologists might be more helpful in characterizing the dynamism of discourse. This web of interindividual and intertextual dialogue forms a complex network of statement, response, and restatement, one that, among other things, complicates our understanding of audience and acknowledges the inherent "addressivity" of all discourse.

As this short example reminds us, dialogism is not restricted to interindividual discussion or sharing of texts, for at the most elemental level of Bakhtinian sociological linguistics lies dialogism. Every word has its own internal dialogism; like a musical score, the dialogized word is composed of many voices. In listening to a score, one can discern or foreground one voice, letting the others continue at an aural distance. Similarly, every word contains not only many denotative or connotative meanings but also the tones and colorations of various voices, generations, professions, classes, eras, and cultures. The word has a history and a memory. In selecting and using a word, a speaker often unconsciously de-emphasizes or ignores some voices and attends to others, but all the voices remain present because all are part of the linguistic and ideological genealogy of the word. Each time a person constructs his discourse, he decides which voices to acknowledge, which ideologies to privilege.

The linguistic battle within the word, then, is a battle on two fronts. On the first, as structuralist linguists have theorized, a word cannot exhaust the essence of the thing it names. The concept or object struggles against the word(s) that attempt to define it. On the second front, however, rages an even more critical battle. Here, Bakhtin writes,

> any concrete discourse (utterance) finds the object at which it was directed already as it were overlain with qualifications, open to dispute, charged with value, already enveloped in an obscuring mist—or, on the contrary, by the "light" of alien words that have already been spoken about it. . . . The word, directed toward its object, enters a dialogically agitated and tension-filled environment of alien words, value judgments and accents, weaves in and out of complex interrelationships, merges with some, recoils from others, intersects with yet a third group: and all this may crucially shape discourse, may leave a trace in all its semantic layers, may complicate its expression and influence its entire stylistic profile. ("Discourse" 276)

This understanding of discourse has broad and significant implications for the teaching of writing, not the least of which is a mandate that we revisit our demand that students have *original* ideas about a topic or that dissertation writers make an *original* contribution to the field. No one person, Bakhtin, reminds us, owns a word; he merely reaccentuates the word, making it his own while it remains always someone else's as well. No work is ever original in that it is always already part of a complex set of discursive relationships. By asking students to understand discourse in Bakhtinian terms, we demand that they become self-conscious about and attentive to the language they use.

Because the verbal arena into which a speaker steps is "always marked by [undeniable] social and ideological implications" (Cobley 324), to construct a self-consciously dialogic utterance a speaker or writer must recognize and respond to these implications. And herein lies a most compelling motivation for engaging Bakhtinian thought in composition studies: a philosophy of writing instruction based on Bakhtinian precepts entails that educated language users "recognize and respond to" the ideological implications of their own and others' discourses. According to Charles Schuster in "The Ideology of Literacy: A Bakhtinian Perspective," without this basic understanding of the life of discourse, writers are doomed to a discursive life, a life of illiteracy, in which they never acknowledge the intertextual nature of all discourse. Student writers and writing instructors alike must understand that classroom expository essays are not immune to this dialogism although they often actively discourage it. Just as speeches, declarations, and rebuttals enter into an ideologically motivated dialogic relationship with other utterances in a conversation, so do expository essays. Dialogism is reflected, then, in the style of the prose, but unlike the easily discerned lines of conversation or argument, the languages and the discourses of the student (or anyone writing) cannot be neatly parceled out, for the influences of previous discourses leave "trace[s] in all its semantic layers . . . complicat[ing] its expression and influenc[ing] its entire stylistic profile" (Bakhtin, "Discourse" 276). The discourse of college writing classrooms, like the dialogized language of the novel, is interanimated ideologically and stylistically by the discourses of others. More than the novel, though, the college writing classroom is a site of lived immediate response, full of immediate addresses and answers, and marked by a certain restlessness, even a discomfort, over meaning. Novels represent a certain textual heteroglossia, a representation of the dialogic tension in a heteroglossic world, and for this reason they are the privileged genre in the Bakhtinian corpus. Writers in a college writing classroom who contend with readings and argue about meanings and representations *enact* that same heteroglossia.

In a writing classroom based on a Bakhtinian understanding of language, students and teachers recognize the intertextual nature of discourse and its implications for action. "Intertextuality," defined by Tzvetan Todorov as the exchange between related utterances, artistic and non-artistic alike, is a term borrowed from Julia Kristeva who interprets the intertextual nature of all discourse as "a mosaic of quotations" (37). Like Bakhtin, Kristeva posits that all texts are constructed from preceding and anticipated texts. Every utterance encounters and negotiates the discourses of its listeners and of those who have already contributed to the subject at hand. An utterance encounters and analyzes the texts of multiple others. But others' utterances are not immediately or necessarily interanimated or dialogically coordinated; only when a speaker is able to "regard one language (and the verbal world corresponding to it) through the eyes of another language" has he constructed a dialogic utterance (Bakhtin, "Discourse" 296). Any speaker speaks a variety of languages, and in that sense he is, to some extent, polyglossic. But only when that speaker begins to understand the variety and dissonances among languages, and that each language carries its own slant on the world, can he begin to situate himself linguistically (and ideologically) in the world.

## POINTS OF CONTACT: THE HETEROGLOSSIC WOR(L)D

Heteroglossia, like the dialogic, is another Bakhtinian term that serves as a barometer of the climate in composition studies and suggests that Bakhtin's work is particularly relevant to the discipline. Both Middendorf and Ewald, for example, note Andrea Lunsford's keynote address for the 1989 Conference on College Composition and Communication in which she characterizes the discipline of composition studies as Bakhtinian in nature. The significance of dialogism and heteroglossia to composition studies, however, reaches beyond their value as methods of characterizing the state of the discipline or in describing the state of language in Bakhtin's linguistic scheme. Dialogism and heteroglossia name the very processes by which people come to know through language. Dialogism is, very simply, "the characteristic epistemological mode of a world dominated by heteroglossia" (Bakhtin, *Dialogic Imagination* 426), that is, a world that recognizes the viability and necessity of existing social, economic, and national languages. Through the concept of dialogism, Bakhtin establishes the critical need to sustain dialogue in the unending quest to maintain difference and diversity, hallmarks of intellectual growth and health, or what de Man refers to as the "heterogeneity of one voice with regard to any other" (102).

At the core of this notion of dialogue and diversity rests both unifying and disunifying linguistic and ideological forces. From the "irreducible diversity of . . . voices" comes heteroglossia, the inevitable complexity of languages that exists within and between utterances. Heteroglossia, closely related to dialogism, is in essence a "diversity of languages," and each of these languages is accompanied by a set of ideological elements and is informed by certain "ideological horizons" (Todorov 56). All national languages are stratified in terms of these various socioideological horizons, which are determined by such things as profession, age, social status, and genre.

Bakhtin further defines and places heteroglossia in relation to the struggle between decentralizing centrifugal language forces and unifying centripetal forces. The individual, immersed in the heteroglossic word, exists in and relates to the world only insofar as his language and his way of seeing and constructing the world allow him. The individual is not only a biological being, but also an ideological being who is the sum of the socioeconomic relationships in which he participates and, most elementally, a linguistic being determined by the languages that define him. Consequently, an individual's utterances, discourses, and rhetorics are constituted by complex and fluctuating social relationships, by the dialogues in which he takes part, by heteroglossia. By failing to note the multiple voices occupying an individual's languages, many compositionists and discourse theorists fail to address the assumption articulated by Faigley that an understanding of language use must proceed from a sociocultural perspective. Meaning and knowledge are constructed through language and among historically situated individuals who speak from their ideological horizons. Individual consciousness is, in its essence, a linguistic and ideological fact. All elements of the psyche—by virtue of their inception in and through language—are themselves socioideological.

Perhaps the most succinct way to define heteroglossia in terms of dialogism is to turn to the brief explanation given by Peter Buitenhuis in a review of a series of essays on literary theory and Canadian literature. According to him, both heteroglossia and dialogism are linguistic responses to a social and cultural breakdown of the dominant ideology, hierarchy, and ethnocentrism. Out of this cultural breakdown comes heteroglossia, "the multi-voiced condition of narrative discourse." "Dialogism," Buitenhuis continues, "is the name given to the formal principle according to which these narrative voices interact" (929). Heteroglossia is the natural chaotic state of languages as they exist in the world; dialogism is the organized manner in which these various languages interact. Perhaps of greatest import with regard to heteroglossia is its effect on dominant, monologic discourse, which conceives of itself as primary and privileged, and

> denies the existence outside itself of another consciousness with equal rights and equal responsibilities, another *I* with equal rights (*thou*). With a monologic approach (in its extreme or pure form) *another person* remains wholly and merely an *object* of consciousness, and not another consciousness. . . . Monologue is finalized and deaf to the other's response, does not expect it and does not acknowledge in it any *decisive* force. . . . Monologue pretends to be the *ultimate word*. (Bakhtin, *Problems* 292–93)

When confronted with heteroglossia, with the existence of myriad other cultures, languages, and conceptual horizons, a dominant monologue attempts to ignore and then deny their legitimacy. In the end, the dominant ideology is disempowered, stripped of its absolute authority. Monologic academic discourse is an excellent example. Through official and unofficial means, the academy historically has rejected the notion of the students' right to their own language in an attempt to marginalize and disempower women, minorities, and underprepared students. The degree to which this movement is conscious or unconscious is not easy to determine. By challenging this monologism, educational theorists have begun to question and challenge the monolith of academic discourse.

Bakhtinian heteroglossia, like dialogism, is defined contextually. That is, novelistic heteroglossia differs from social or linguistic heteroglossia. Within the novel, heteroglossia describes a mixing and interanimating of authorial and reported speech, the representation of *"another's speech in another's language,"* a double-voiced discourse (Bakhtin, "Discourse" 324). Heteroglossia functions in the novel most completely when it enters "in person" as a character whose discourse and ideology are represented, but heteroglossia may also remain outside the novel as a "dialogizing background." In either case, the novel represents the dialogized heteroglossia of popular low genres that ridicule, contest, and parody official genres of the dominant ideology. Heteroglossia in the novel is represented by means of stratification of discourse types. At any one time, various strata of discourses—determined by profession, age, geographical locale, and social status—exist in a culture. This stratification within the novel and within a society is not a state but a process, for "languages are continually stratifying under a pressure of the centrifugal force, whose project everywhere is to challenge fixed definitions" (Bakhtin, *Dialogic Imagination* 433). Depending on the social and cultural conditions, certain discourses will prove more powerful and influential than others in combating ideological dominance.

In a broader cultural (as opposed to aesthetic) sense, heteroglossia is the natural state of language. As long as people have been conversing about and living within cultural contexts, discourses have taken on differing ideological meanings and determined differing cultural horizons. Heteroglossia in the world is defined by Bakhtin as a diversity of socioideological languages. The rich diversity of ideological opinions represented within the strata of a given society's languages reflects a shifting dynamism, a liveliness that opposes the strict ethnocentrism and linguistic monologism of a dominant culture. The battle between centripetal and centrifugal forces, and between heterologic and monologic tendencies, does not only take place between and among discourses. It also occurs within an utterance itself, for the utterance is "a contradiction-ridden, tension-filled unity of two embattled tendencies in the life of language" (Bakhtin, "Discourse" 272). As a scene of linguistic and discursive tension, the utterance is a microcosm of dialogized heteroglossia.

Dialogue and heteroglossia together establish the terms under which we might begin to reconceive writing instruction from a Bakhtinian perspective. Bakhtin's work leads us, almost necessarily, to reexamine the object(s) of our instruction within the wider context of our students' lives through a pedagogy that privileges human consciousness and lived experience.

## BAKHTIN AND COMPOSITION STUDIES

Relatively speaking, Bakhtin came late to composition studies—in 1985, when Charles Schuster introduced him as a "rhetorical theorist." It is perhaps not coincidental that Bakhtin emerged as a rhetorician just as the discipline of composition studies was beginning to embrace social constructivism, collaborative learning, and the concept of knowledge as a social construction. Although Bakhtin's ideas and constructs are commonplace in articles in *PMLA*, *Papers on Language and Literature*, *Genre*, *Poetics Today*, *Communication Studies*, *ELH*,

*New Literary History*, and *College Literature*, relatively few articles (roughly twenty) attend to Bakhtin as a rhetorician or consider in any detail his contributions to writing instruction. Those that do exist take varying approaches to estimating his value to composition studies and speak to the range of current thought on Bakhtin in the discipline. Few scholars have examined the trends in Bakhtinian scholarship in the field, and most merely nod appreciatively toward one another's work.

One scholar who has remarked on the distinctions among scholarly works on Bakhtin, rhetoric, and composition, Marilyn Middendorf, simply observes in her 1992 *Journal of Basic Writing* article, "Bakhtin and the Dialogic Writing Class," that "[m]ost of the conference presentations and the growing number of articles on Bakhtin explicate his key concepts or interpret his ideas through the individual writer's philosophical or political filter. Yet, essentially Bakhtin remains outside the writing classroom" (35). Middendorf's description of the published scholarship is misleading, for by 1991, Don Bialostosky, Catherine Pastore Blair, Joe Comprone, Frank Farmer, Jon Klancher, Thomas Recchio, and Joy Ritchie had all published articles linking Bakhtin to issues of pedagogical importance. In fact, of the dozen or so scholars publishing on Bakhtin and rhetoric or composition, only three—Judith Goleman, R. Allen Harris and Charles Schuster—might be described as explicating and interpreting Bakhtinian thought "outside" the classroom. Schuster appeals for including Bakhtinian theory in discourse and stylistic analyses, and Harris extends Schuster's work by applying Bakhtin's concepts of the speaker, listener, and subject in a rereading of the *Phaedrus*. Goleman, on the other hand, interprets the pedagogies of Ann Berthoff, William E. Coles, Jr., Paulo Freire, and the ethnographic research of Shirley Brice Heath as "dialogics" of competing languages of home and alien cultures. We might ask exactly what "outside the writing classroom" means for Middendorf, whose comments imply the dichotomous foci of theoretical interpretation and pedagogical application.

Another of Middendorf's central observations—that many scholars interpret Bakhtin's work through their own "philosophical or political filter"—suggests a rather naive understanding of scholarship. As we read and interpret texts, we all work from within particular positions and through "philosophical or political filter[s]." This seems less a condemnation of the scholarship and more a statement of the reality of its production. Faigley looks to Bakhtin's poststructuralist moments; Gregory Clark to his pluralistic; Laib to his irenic; Lamb to his feminist. Lunsford and Ede seek from Bakhtin theoretical underpinnings for collaboration and their notion of plural authorship, while Ritchie seeks a method of relating individual and community voices. Dillon, Cooper, and Selfe find in Bakhtin ways of interpreting classroom behaviors and discourse conventions. Donahue and Quandahl, Kent, and Spellmeyer call on Bakhtin as a philosophical forebear to radical, externalist, and resistant pedagogies. Each scholar reaccentuates Bakhtin to meet his or her own ends.

Helen Ewald, in terms much more detailed than Middendorf's, reviews Bakhtin scholarship in composition studies, finding the field woefully unself-reflexive in its use of his work:

> Bakhtin has been invoked to promote various and sometimes oppositional approaches to composition studies. If he has been cited by advocates of a collaborative notion of authorship, he has also been quoted by those reasserting the importance of the single (although still socially-constructed) author. If he has been employed by those arguing against received forms in academic discourse, he has also been recruited by those rejecting the bipolar opposition of "exploratory writing" and "formal presentation" upon which the argument against received discourse seems to depend. Moreover, if Bakhtin has been helpful to those who seek to escape convention-driven pedagogies, he is becoming useful to those for whom there is no escape, no exit. (337)

Both Middendorf and Ewald overlook the dialogic relationship among these various scholarly essays. Rather than uncritical or unselfreflexive appropriations of Bakhtin, the various essays suggest the possible readings available to scholars with differing philosophical or political agendas.

As "philosophical" inquiry, the scholarship on Bakhtin and composition studies seeks to "account for, to frame, critique and analyze the field's fundamental assumptions and beliefs" (North 91). Despite the intellectual appeal of the category, the "philosophers" of whom North writes are not, in his mind, a privileged community. Rather than devote themselves to sustained intellectual inquiry, he writes, compositionists publishing philosophical scholarship do not "propose or account for some set of assumptions, but . . . urge them as *the* assumptions" (91). The "dominant strategy" of philosophers, North contends, is what he refers to,

> mostly without disparagement, as foraging. That is, the Composition Philosopher makes a foray into some field outside Composition itself, works to reach some degree of expertise in it, then returns ready to work out an argument about the nature of doing, learning, or teaching writing on the basis of the foraged premises. (102)

Those scholars who have published on Bakhtin and composition studies fulfill North's requirements, but so do most scholars in the field. North himself suggests that philosophers are not a very stable group; compositionists make short forays into philosophical inquiry, often to address and resolve particular pedagogical questions, and then retreat to other methods of inquiry.

I do not intend to launch a critique of North's representation of philosophical inquiry; his estimation of it seems convincing enough. I am concerned, however, with the image of the philosopher that North creates for us: the proselytizer, arguing heatedly for the intellectual conversion of readers, abandons dialectical inquiry in favor of the impassioned conversion narrative. Although North acknowledges that the philosophical "search for a foundation, for some first principles, seems to have become both more self-conscious and more reflexive" over the past thirty years, he is clearly disappointed with the outcome of much of philosophical inquiry in composition studies (95). North takes philosophers to task on several counts, among them their proselytizing and unselfreflexivity. Although some philosophers (e.g., Ann Berthoff, Janet Emig, and Richard Young) have "become more careful and critical about what contributions from elsewhere might entail" and have "turned their attention inward, as it were, trying to see what Composition already *is* before looking to see what it might become," the majority of philosophical inquiry does not meet North's conditions (95). Rather than establishing the "preconditions of those understandings which might allow us to decide what to do," philosophers often make the mistake of telling practitioners in the field what should be done (101).

Because of the relatively recent nature of work on Bakhtin in composition studies, the bulk of the scholarship on the subject (excepting Ewald) is what I call first generation philosophical inquiry—inquiry that North describes as "first offerings—arguments, that is, that are not responding to positions previously spelled out by other members of the community, and so not framed yet in deliberately dialectical terms" (106). The scholarship carries with it a dialogized backdrop, a dialogism that is not characterized by an immediately recognizable tension or argument. North proposes the following argumentative form—reminiscent of problem identification and solution as it is used in business, interpersonal relations, or human resources—as characteristic of this type of philosophical inquiry:

1. identify the problem—some gap in the current collective knowledge of Composition, suggesting the deleterious effects that ignorance has on practice, research, scholarship, or all three;
2. identify criteria for adequate solutions to the problem, suggesting what sort of knowledge we need to fill the gap;
3. establish some premises by offering the foraged knowledge;
4. make arguments based on those premises, outlining some new way of looking at all or some part of Composition; and
5. conclude by indicating the new positions' implications, and suggesting areas for further inquiry. (105)

Despite North's grudging acceptance of philosophical inquiry in composition studies generally, he has described in clear and fairly accurate terms the methods of the types of inquiry characteristic of compositionists working with Bakhtin. Schuster's 1990 essay, "The Ideology of Literacy: A Bakhtinian Perspective," serves as an example of first generation philosophical inquiry into Bakhtin and composition studies. Schuster begins (as North suggests philosophers of composition generally do) by identifying the problematic nature of two strands of literacy research: one that grants too much validity to the notion of "educational deprivation" of institutional complicity in a political struggle to maintain an undereducated working class, and a second that equates literacy with "intellectual power."

Schuster continues by identifying criteria for a fuller understanding of illiteracy, which he illustrates through a discussion of Cassandra. Like Cassandra, those in American culture deemed illiterate are those whom the dominant group names illiterate and refuses to hear, and therefore to whom it refuses to grant sovereignty over their own agency. Like Cassandra, whose prophecies are disbelieved, the illiterate of America are literate in their own communities but are nonetheless "doomed to a solipsistic existence, despite the power of language" they possess ("Ideology" 227). Bakhtin's social constructivist views of language, responsive understanding, addressivity, and answerability provide the premises on which Schuster bases his argument for a richer understanding of literacy and illiteracy, the crucial third and fourth steps in North's methodological description. In concluding, Schuster does not make explicit suggestions for further inquiry, but he does close the essay by noting that if we are to combat illiteracy we need nothing short of a "social transformation in which persons discover a means to engage one another meaningfully through language[s]—not as antagonists, not on the basis of class differences, not through racism or sexism or commodification but through a shared identification of self with other" (231).

Describing the methodology of philosophical inquiry as North does is a useful enterprise, but merely setting out the movements of the argumentative form elides the dialogic nature of this type of inquiry. Although Schuster's essay conforms to the argumentative pattern described by North, it also illustrates the four discursive functions necessary for what I refer to as dialogic scholarship. The essay *clarifies*. Schuster provides information on literacy and Bakhtin, summarizing and testing our own understanding of the topics. By establishing a common ground through clarifying definitions, concepts, and goals, Schuster begins the work of constructing a dialogic enterprise, which he continues as he *reacts* against the notions of literacy held by Kozol and Pattison. Here, the conversational (or argumentative) nature of the essay is perhaps most apparent. Schuster enters into a charged debate regarding the very definition of literacy. In many respects, Kozol and Pattison serve as representatives of positions on literacy more than direct contestants, yet the most crucial dialogic elements of Schuster's essay are found in its philosophical contribution when bringing Bakhtin's work to bear on the conversation.

In this sense, the essay *initiates* a new way of thinking about literacy. It is not enough, from a dialogic perspective, for Schuster merely to critique Kozol and Pattison for their misunderstanding. Schuster has a responsibility to contribute to the conversation, and he does this by proposing an alternative way of thinking about literacy with a new model based on Bakhtinian thought. In this sense, then, the essay *generates*, that is, it provides a point of departure for compositionists not only through a reading of literacy informed by Bakhtinian ideas, but also by means of an introduction to the ways that Bakhtinian work might inform our thinking in other areas of composition studies. Rather than bemoan, as Middendorf does, the paucity of scholarship that introduces

Bakhtin to the writing classroom or, like Ewald, recoil from the explosion of scholarship on Bakhtin and composition studies, we might look to the scholarship to determine more broadly the generative nature of its enterprise and seek to construct scholarship that clarifies, reacts, initiates, and generates.

## (RE)CONSTRUCTING COMPOSITION STUDIES

Since the mid-1980s, the field of composition studies has increasingly moved away from the process/product division that dominated disciplinary discussions of pedagogy in the 1970s toward a triadic construction developed between 1982 and 1988. If Bakhtin had lived another ten to fifteen years, and had he taken an interest in the field of American composition studies, I imagine he would have immediately recognized the terms that the discipline has employed in constructing itself during this period. Objectivist, subjectivist, and social schools are terms with which Bakhtin is intimately familiar, for they inform a great share of the work of the Bakhtin Circle in literary criticism, linguistics, and psychology. I also imagine he would have found the application of these terms appropriate and well-conceived. For as the discussion that follows demonstrates, James Berlin and others take considerable care in constructing the framework on which they base their discussions of composition studies, and that framework is informed by and defined in terms of many of the same schools of thought that inform Bakhtinian work in *Marxism and the Philosophy of Language*, *Freudianism*, and *The Dialogic Imagination*. Although the Bakhtinian triadic paradigm has not been applied to composition theory directly,[3] similar frameworks exist in the taxonomies of James Berlin, Lester Faigley, and C. H. Knoblauch.

These recent taxonomies of composition mirror Bakhtin's triadic paradigm in that they establish three schools of thought vying for dominance in a particular historical period. As taxonomies, Berlin's writings intend not to relate rhetorics to one another so much as they intend to distinguish them. A taxonomy by its nature classifies and therefore establishes categories whose relationships appear static, or at best, dialectical and evolutionary. Nevertheless, both Bakhtin and Berlin privilege the transactional (social) over the objective and subjective. For Berlin, social-epistemic rhetoric is superior to the others, and for Bakhtin, the social reigns as that most conducive to heteroglossic tendencies in language. Both social rhetorics and social linguistic schools refute many objectivist and subjectivist premises, while at the same time relying on them for professional dialogue and academic growth. Like Berlin who seeks to discuss only those "three rhetorics that have emerged as the most conspicuous in classroom practices today" ("Rhetoric and Ideology" 477), Bakhtin engages the most prominent linguistic schools of his day.

Berlin has been largely credited with introducing the objective-subjective-social triad to composition studies, some scholars arguing, for example, that Faigley's work is derivative of Berlin's, "[r]elying on . . . Berlin's discussions of the present rhetorical scene" (Gradin 2). Certainly, the discipline cannot ignore Berlin's contribution to and influence on historiography in composition studies, but publication history tells us a slightly different story regarding the development of the triadic paradigm. To suggest that Berlin is the sole author of this triadic construction or to imply that the triad sprang fully formed from Berlin's earliest pedagogical and institutional histories of composition studies elides differences among his various taxonomies and overlooks the important contributions of other scholars to the developing paradigm. In his earliest taxonomic essay, "Contemporary Composition: The Major Pedagogical Theories," Berlin establishes four categories—classicists, current-traditionalists, expressionists, and new rhetoricians.[4] In his later monographs on the history of nineteenth- and twentieth-century college writing instruction, however, the categories shift. In *Writing Instruction in Nineteenth-Century American Colleges*, Berlin discusses classical, eighteenth-century, current-traditional, and romantic rhetorics.

Only in the closing chapter, "Postscript on the Present," does Berlin begin to articulate "three contemporary approaches to teaching writing"—classical, expressionistic, and epistemic rhetoric—that, "consciously or unconsciously, reflect rhetorics of the nineteenth century," and serve as a corrective or "alternative to current-traditional rhetoric" (86). Not until 1987, with the publication of *Rhetoric and Reality: Writing Instruction in American Colleges, 1900–1985*, does Berlin articulate a triadic paradigm of the field whose rhetorical categories include objectivist (current-traditional and behaviorist); subjectivist (expressionistic); and transactional (the "new rhetoric," which itself includes classicist, cognitivist, and epistemic rhetoric).

Even this brief overview of Berlin's developing paradigm might seem unnecessary until I note that at about the same time Berlin published *Writing Instruction in Nineteenth-Century American Colleges*, which still divided the discipline into four categories, Lester Faigley, Roger Cherry, David Jolliffe, and Anna Skinner posited in *Assessing Writers' Knowledge and Processes of Composing* three "theoretical positions on composing"—the literary, cognitive, and social (13). Their descriptions, although constructed as a means of examining the "array of theoretical positions" on composing available to researchers, no doubt sound familiar to readers acquainted with Berlin's work. The literary view of composing, like Berlin's expressivism, has its roots in a romantic (i.e., mysterious and inaccessible) notion of the self; the cognitive view, the authors argue, includes cognitivist scientists who work to "represent how people find solutions to problems" (16); and the social view of composing "argues that a writer's competence includes something much broader which can be explained only in terms of a community connected by written discourse" (17). Indeed, in its last formulation, Berlin's paradigm resembles those of Faigley, Cherry, Jolliffe, and Skinner, as well as Faigley's earlier versions.

I do not intend to argue the origins of the triadic paradigm. Rather, I hope to use its nearly simultaneous and interdependent development by Faigley,

Cherry, Jolliffe, Skinner, and Berlin as a means of illustrating the rapidity with which it took hold in the discipline. Berlin's *Rhetoric and Reality* merely secured the position of the triadic paradigm as a defining disciplinary construct. The appeal of the triadic paradigm was so strong in composition studies, in fact, that it began almost immediately to inform the very terms of professional discussions in the field. Between 1985 and 1988, four major articles or monographs appeared that reaffirmed the position of the triadic paradigm in composition and pedagogy.[5] Like these compositionists, Bakhtin and Volosinov undertake the taxonomic enterprise as a means of making sense of their disciplines, mapping the movements and conflicts among various approaches to language study, and at the same time setting out their own agendas, creating the space for the ascendancy of their particular ways of seeing their respective fields.

### Implications of a Dialogic Paradigm for Composition Studies

As coincidental as they might be, telling similarities exist between paradigms articulated in composition (most notably in Berlin's *Rhetoric and Reality*) and the Bakhtinian (especially the work of Volosinov).[6] Both Berlin and Volosinov define three schools, the first of which is objectivist in nature. Informed by structuralism, objectivist schools claim that the material world and language systems exist independently of the individual, society, and ideology.[7] In addition to arguing vehemently against such foundationalist tenets, Faigley and Volosinov also critique objectivists on the artificial distinction they draw between the social and the individual.[8] By contrast, Berlin and Volosinov name the Platonic and romantic philosophical traditions as the intellectual roots of the second school, the subjectivist. Bound also to the individual psychology of Sigmund Freud and the idealism of Benedetto Croce, the subjectivists incur the rancor of Berlin and Volosinov by insisting upon individual autonomy and its preeminence over the social.[9] The third and privileged school, the social (or transactional) locates meaning at the confluence of writer, reader, and text— each of which is thoroughly social. Here, reality is constructed only through the interaction of these particular elements as they are set within a particular language's sphere and defined in and through one another.[10]

Berlin argues that transactional (social) rhetorics subvert and decenter objective and subjective rhetorics in the same way Volosinov suggests the sociological subverts and decenters the objective and subjective. Their paradigms, however, do little to promote dialogue among the categories they articulate. Transactional rhetoric or sociological linguistics replaces objectivist and subjectivist rhetorics or linguistics, earning transcendent positions through a dialectical, or an almost evolutionary, progression. Unfortunately, this does little more than reverse the positions of the three, undermining the intention of dialogue. Because these are taxonomies whose purpose is to divide and define, Berlin's and Volosinov's descriptions seek to resolve the problematic nature of the schools they dismiss. "[T]he function of dialogism," de Man reminds us, "is to sustain and think through the radical exteriority or heterogeneity of one voice with regard to any other" (102). These taxonomies do *not* work to sustain conversations about the nature of linguistics, genre, or composition pedagogy. Rather they seek to find an ascendant position for one school. The triadic paradigm as enacted by Berlin and Volosinov is a theoretical framework that, while ostensibly built on dialogism, promotes synthesis, not a continuing heterogeneity and diversity of or tension among voices. Volosinov and Berlin fail, as well, to meet the criteria of the dialogic set forth by Don Bialostosky, who, in "Dialogics as an Art of Discourse in Literary Criticism," characterizes the difference between the dialectic and dialogic:

> To read others dialogically, then, would be to read for an opening in the discussion or a provocation to further discourse. . . . Dialogic reading would not generally reduce others to consistent dialectical counterparts, or dwell on the inconsistencies in their positions, or transcend them in higher syntheses. Nor would it minimize others as rhetorical opponents by attempting to discredit them. (790)

Berlin's narrative places the social in a set of confrontational relationships with the objective and the subjective. Although Volosinov, too, finds the social preeminent, he avoids (but only to a small degree) the closure and opposition of Berlin's taxonomy. By placing the locus of the dialogic in language, a common element of all three positions, Volosinov forms a sociological-linguistic discourse out of the materials of objectivist and subjectivist discourses. He denies the validity of some premises of objectivism and subjectivism but also reshapes others in forming a sociological perspective. Volosinov, more than Berlin, it appears, recognizes the contingent nature of his own linguistics and poetics and its indebtedness to the earlier forms. In theory, a sociological poetics is simply another contribution to the conversation. In practice, however, it looks very much like the last word.

The fundamental similarity between Volosinov's and Berlin's taxonomies is their shared objective: to promote a socially oriented theory. Berlin and Volosinov consistently and unabashedly proclaim that they prefer the social-epistemic to objectivist or subjectivist schools. Berlin does not hide his allegiances; in fact, he states them quite clearly, as in "Contemporary Composition": "I am convinced that the pedagogical approach of the New Rhetoricians is the most intelligent and most practical alternative available, serving in every way the best interests of our students" (766). Volosinov's and Berlin's taxonomies, in valorizing the social, strive for resolution and solution, and in doing so, marginalize dialogue among the theories and pedagogies they describe.

## Pedagogy as Genre

Compositionists who embrace Berlin's taxonomy, like neoclassic critics, have insisted, albeit implicitly at times, on maintaining strict distinctions between genres and pedagogies, supposing a "pure" expressivism or social constructivism. We can, however, as Leith and Myerson note, "never [have] any 'pure' forms, even though in a given instance the characteristics of particular forms cannot be ignored" (44). Recent work in composition studies, such as that of Gradin, Nystrand, and Ward, suggests that the field is moving away from a strict neoclassic view of pedagogical genres and toward an understanding of pedagogy informed by Wittgenstein's notion of family resemblances, where genre is not defined in terms of a set of defined or marked characteristics but in terms of shared likenesses.

Berlin's work has received its share of critique, much of which reveals compositionists' resistance to categorization. Claiming that such a static description of the discipline obscures both similarities across categories and differences within them, some scholars argue that Berlin mistakenly defines composition studies in a "quotation." As early as 1987, compositionists began examining the efficacy of Berlin's categories in describing the field. Steven Lynn, for example, notes that despite the "masterful" analysis and value of Berlin's work, we might find it useful to "explore the potential of a different approach" in examining the ways that the writing process has been characterized (902). Lynn, rather than undertaking an exhaustive history, examines the presentations of the writing process in three textbooks, finding Maxine Hairston's objectivist in nature, C. H. Knoblauch and Lil Brannon's expressivist, and Ann Berthoff's "divided" between the two. Lynn concludes by stating that "[w]e need somehow to move beyond such either/or choices, into a realm of both/and where our writing instruction can self-consciously and coherently draw on or evolve out of conflicting pedagogies" (909).

Lynn's plea calls our attention to another of the functions of taxonomy—that of distinguishing among biological species. What Lynn overlooks, however, is the power of the construction itself. By working within Berlin's categories, by imagining Hairston's, Knoblauch and Brannon's, and Berthoff's work in terms of objectivist and expressivist orientations, his alternative reading remains embedded in Berlin's terms. If we are to reconceive the discipline in other terms and truly "explore the potential of a different approach," we must move outside of Berlin's constructions.

Unlike Lynn, Sherrie L. Gradin is obviously aware of the power of current constructions of the field. In examining the appeal of the objectivist/subjectivist/social construct, she quite explicitly states that, by invoking the categories, she is "guilty" of perpetuating the distinctions among scholars that are implied by them: she is "trapped by the language of category and dichotomy" (15). Nevertheless, she fails to recognize that it is *because* some compositionists "fall between the cracks of categorization" that we must work beyond and against the construction, "unbind [our]selves from the categories," and imagine a rhetoric that "more accurately reflects our actual theories and practices" (15–16). Gradin points to the inherent a(nta)gonism of taxonomies as one of their most inhibiting characteristics. Critics of expressivist pedagogies, for example, simplify expressivist theories, excluding what is valuable about them from their own theories. If expressivist ideas are embedded in their theories, they do not acknowledge them as expressivist in form and nature. Pointing to or even creating flaws in expressivist theories and pedagogies makes it easier for social-epistemic rhetorics to look superior in every way. Unfortunately, this tendency to create a straw man sets up a problematic system of categorization so narrowly conceived that it ignores what romantic theory contributes to the discipline and even to social-epistemic theories themselves. (11)

Gradin's comments point to what is critical in redefining pedagogical genres: we must understand that generic assumptions shape our expectations about a given approach and limit our own teaching practices. Social constructivists, as Gradin suggests, limit the value of their own teaching by denigrating the value of expressivist elements in it.

Irene Ward's discussion of the notion of the dialogic across epistemological and pedagogical boundaries in composition studies illustrates one of the ways compositionists have now begun to examine shared likenesses among pedagogical and epistemological schools. Motivated by the pervasive nature of dialogue in composition scholarship and pedagogy, Ward argues for a fuller understanding of the notion, one that recognizes and analyzes the various formulations of the term as it manifests itself across the discipline: in the expressivists' authentic voice, writing as a social act, peer criticism, Freire's problem posing education, and poststructuralist theories of language. She notes along the way that "compositionists are largely locked into a variety of ideological frames, and therefore their concepts of dialogic pedagogy are accordingly limited." Ward argues that only by bringing the various manifestations of dialogue into contact with one another through a "comprehensive dialogism," one that "would recognize that knowledge unfolds in the process of attempting to communicate with others," can compositionists begin to enact a dialogic pedagogy (201). Ward's work is also notable for its movement away from the triadic paradigm. Her work is informed not so much by Berlin's categories but by central movements and figures in the field. She eschews epistemology as the defining moment in pedagogy and relies instead upon the mandate set out by dialogism: we must recognize that our knowledge is constructed from multiple and conflicting knowledge claims. Dialogic approaches to composition studies and language allow us to compare claims and assumptions, as well as to engage alternative ways of seeing, freeing us from the confines of pedagogical, theoretical, or even epistemological consistency.

Introducing Bakhtin to the narrative of composition pedagogy offers it a linguistic and sociological (as opposed to epistemological) foundation. By turning to language, the single most constitutive element of the rhetorical situation, Bakhtin redefines the other elements—author, audience, and subject—in terms of a sociological dialogism, for each is constructed by and through language. Introducing Bakhtin to this conversation provides composition studies with a broader view of the dynamics among schools of pedagogy and their attendant linguistic assumptions. A dialogic paradigm serves as a model for a conversation among competing pedagogies that allows composition theorists and historians of rhetoric to investigate relationships among the centripetal and centrifugal pedagogies of the past century, without the added concern of reaching resolution or maintaining strict distinctions among opposing schools. The alternative of disregarding these pedagogies proves far more dangerous, and more difficult, than maintaining and promoting diversity, for if classical, cognitive, current-traditional, and expressive pedagogies continue to be powerful or inviting methods for practitioners, they must serve some pedagogical or political end. To stifle or abridge them is to stifle and abridge dialogism. Introducing Bakhtinian treatment of objective, subjective, and social linguistic schools to our current understanding of composition studies allows us to investigate the points of contact and conflict among educational goals, ideological diversity, and pedagogical interconnections. At the same time, Bakhtinian representations of all language as heteroglossic and dialogically arranged encourage us to look past the triadic as a rather false construction, one that inhibits, even denies, the dialogic nature of language and knowledge.

# PART ONE

---

# Reimagining the Rhetorical Situation

Bakhtinian discourse theory serves as a point of departure in part 1, as I reimagine the three primary agents in the rhetorical situation: subject, speaker, and listener. To examine each element separately, as I do here, is to risk abstracting the elements, decontextualizing them, and de-emphasizing their interdependence. Yet Bakhtin himself argues that the three components are autonomous. Although I take to heart R. Allen Harris's contention that to discern and abstract the traditional "parts" of the rhetorical situation from one another is to distort Bakhtin's understanding of heteroglossia, I also find the elements of the familiar rhetorical situation useful in constructing the discussion that follows. Compositionists are, moreover, inclined to emphasize the speaker and to consider the listener and (particularly) the subject of secondary importance in the life of the utterance. I. R. Titunik notes this as an understandable tendency, but still, as Harris notes, the dialogic relationship among all of the participants cannot be overlooked. Titunik writes that

> Each of the participants represents a context of discourse in active, dynamic relationship with the other two. The author's speech context is "dominant" in the sense that it coincides with the message as a whole, encompassing the other contexts and incorporating them within itself. But at the same time as presenting the context of hero [subject], the author establishes a relationship with that context through which he affects that context in some way or by which his own, authorial, context is affected. Likewise, at the same time as positing a listener, the author enters into a relationship with that latter's assumed or anticipated context of response whereby effects on the hero's context (listener-hero relationship) and/or on the author's own (author-listener relationship) are produced. (193)

All of this is to say that in the Bakhtinian scheme, speaker, listener, and subject are cast in new terms because each affects and is affected by the others, and the three together form an utterance through their interrelations and dialogism.

## A BAKHTINIAN THEORY OF COMMUNICATION

Bakhtin himself did not schematize his theory of the utterance, and in fact systematizing it, as Tzvetan Todorov attempts to do, essentially undermines the diachronic poststructuralist nature of Bakhtin's translinguistics. We would do well, before going any further, to heed Bakhtin's own advice about such static abstractions as Todorov's:

> What is represented by the diagram is only an abstract aspect of the real total act. . . . Such scientific abstraction is quite justified in itself, but under one condition: that it is clearly recognized as merely an abstraction and is not represented as the real concrete whole of the phenomenon. Otherwise it becomes a fiction. ("Problem of Speech" 69–70)

Any model that seeks to represent the phenomenon is an abstraction and not the "real concrete whole of the phenomenon." Todorov names three elements common to most models of communication—the object (referent), speaker, and listener. Because Bakhtinian language theory takes the utterance as fundamental, object, speaker, and listener are not isolated from one another as message, encoder, and decoder. Instead, the three elements are always situated in terms of the utterance, which is, in turn, defined by its intertextual relationship(s) with other utterances. Similarly, language is "something other than a code" or a static system with a "uniform relation with its object; it does not 'reflect' it, but it organizes it" (Todorov 55).

Abstracting the elements of the utterance in this fashion of course captures only the definition and not the essence of a linguistic act. The six distinct elements—object, speaker, listener, utterance, intertext, and language—are, in fact, never static. The role of speaker or listener is determined by the object, utterance, and intertext. As these change, so do the relationships between the speaker and listener. Object, utterance, and intertext, as well, are interrelated. The object of an utterance influences the formation and content of that utterance, and vice versa. Similarly, intertext affects both object and utterance just as they contribute to and change the nature of intertext. Language, as an entire ideological sign system, affects all but remains the element of least consequence. To diagram a Bakhtinian "model" of communication, admirable as such an undertaking may be, serves only to suspend in a two-dimensional plane a diachronic, multiplanar phenomenon that, at every point, struggles to free itself from the confines of space and time, the here and now. Always, the essence of the utterance (its intertextual connections to past and forthcoming utterances) has already been or has yet to occur, was previously spoken or is not yet uttered.

As one of the more influential discourse theories in composition studies, the work of James Kinneavy provides a point of departure for engaging Bakhtinian thought on discourse theory.[1] Bakhtin's *Speech Genres and Other*

*Late Essays*, in fact, leads directly to a dialogue between Bakhtin and Kinneavy. Its essays reveal a shared concern: the study of language in its social and cultural context. Like Bakhtin, Kinneavy warns his reader of the dangers of abstracting and interpreting this model, which is made up of "a person who encodes a message, the signal (language) which carries the message, the reality to which the message refers, and the decoder (receiver of the message)" (*Theory* 19). The model is not, he indicates, a complete objectification of the communicative act.

Unlike Bakhtin, who is concerned less with the production of discourse and its analysis than with describing its essence and with the ways that it is received, Kinneavy sets out to systematize and classify discourse. Kinneavy draws a systematic description of syntactics, semantics, and pragmatics. Syntactics studies the signal and its characteristics and is unconcerned with either the relation those signals have to referents or how they are put together by language users. Semantics, on the other hand, studies meaning, the relationship between sign and signified, between the signal and the reality it names or attempts to name. These two, syntactics and semantics, taken together constitute what Kinneavy refers to as "language as a potential tool"; they constitute the study of linguistics (22). Pragmatics, on the other hand, is discourse theory, the study of how people use language, the study of the production and reception of texts.

Volosinov, in contrast to Kinneavy, recognizes the traditional distinctions among the fields of linguistic study, but only long enough to comment that language as a social construct undermines such distinctions,[2] attacking their separation into distinct studies. As a "translinguist," one who recognizes a need for a socially based whole language theory, Bakhtin does not forego commenting on the traditional elements of linguistic study. Instead he covers all aspects of linguistics. As a translinguist, Bakhtin undertakes a study of the utterance within social and cultural contexts. For Bakhtin, all language study must be contextualized because all utterances are influenced by and constructed from within social and cultural relationships. Speaking more generally than Bakhtin, Kinneavy likewise includes along with social context such elements as psychological and social motivation, situational context, and "immediate . . . effects of discourse" (*Theory* 21), all of which are central to Bakhtin's work with speech genres and utterances.

More important for Bakhtin, perhaps, are those elements Kinneavy lists as having to do with cultural context, "the nature and conventions of which make the situational context permissible and meaningful" (*Theory* 24). Cultural contexts allow a theorist to inquire about the motivations for, taste in, and effects of literature, science, and politics. Bakhtin's implied objectives and basic understanding of communicative situations differ from Kinneavy's. Bakhtin names author, audience, and subject as among the necessary elements of any utterance, but in doing so he contends that an utterance is not the sole property of the speaker in any way—stylistically, formally, or evaluatively—and that language does not refer to a "reality" (Kinneavy's term) separate from language. Any written or spoken utterance is, instead, Volosinov writes,

> *the expression and product of the social interaction of three participants: the speaker* (author), *the listener* (reader), *and the topic* (the who or what) *of speech* (the hero). Verbal discourse is a social event; it is not self-contained in the sense of some abstract linguistic quantity, nor can it be derived psychologically from the speaker's subjective consciousness taken in isolation. ("Discourse in Life" 105; emphasis in original)

The dynamic relationships among these three elements inform the utterance. The traditional rhetorical triangle that depicts speaker, audience, and subject as points on that triangle does not adequately represent the utterance as part of an ongoing, complex, interactive web of discourse set within a social context, as Kinneavy and others warn. The speaker does not simply select language to fit a structuralist reality or signifier and signified. Choosing a subject and collecting the language to present it are intricate processes, for even these acts are replete with ideological implications. The subject of a discourse, suggests Bakhtin, becomes a "hero" with which the author must continually battle and compromise. The subject of the discourse is not an object to be acted upon, to be researched or described; rather, it becomes an important and controlling being, "as potent a determinant in the rhetorical paradigm as speaker or listener" (Schuster, "Mikhail Bakhtin" 595).

Moreover, the language of the speaker is itself a locus of heteroglossia, that point at which centripetal and centrifugal discourses battle. By suggesting that the subject of a discourse, its intended audience, its speaker, and the situational context alone shape an utterance, discourse theorists overlook the importance of intertextuality. In the end, Bakhtin's work extends and revises the Kinneavian model of the rhetorical situation by providing a poststructuralist notion of language within the context of an established discourse theory.

# ONE

# Redefining the Student Writer

Like any discipline, composition studies is defined by the metaphors it uses to describe itself and its projects. We constantly debate the nature of writing—is it an art or a skill? Each metaphor has its own distinctive consequences: If it is an art, can it be taught? If a skill, is writing debased as mere technique? Recent discussions in the field clearly recognize the power of the metaphoric, and scholars have examined the implications of many of the metaphors used to describe the act of teaching and the writing process. Much emphasis, for example, has been placed on the implications of coaching, facilitating, or empowering as metaphors for instruction and on transportation and club metaphors in basic writing scholarship. Although scholars have turned a critical eye to the discipline and its metaphors, these examinations have not been comprehensive, particularly with regard to the construction of the "student as writer." I address this issue by first defining and critiquing three prominent notions of the student writer in composition studies and then arguing that composition studies must go beyond its reconstruction of "voice" as polyphonous and begin examining closely its practice of naming students in first year classrooms as "writers." Several concepts from the Bakhtinian canon—most notably Volosinov's work in *Marxism and the Philosophy of Language* and *Freudianism*—provide points of departure for the latter portion of the chapter in which I articulate the colonizing motives that lie behind the "student-as-writer" metaphor in composition studies.

## WRITING AS A SOCIAL ACT, THE WRITER AS A SOCIAL BEING

I face an immense task if I am to argue that composition studies should examine and critique its own practice of defining students in writing classes as "writers." The task is complicated as well by the various and contradictory ways that scholars in the discipline themselves define "writer." Certainly, authorship and the characterization of writer are variously defined in twentieth-century rhetorical theory. As Berlin suggests in *Rhetoric and Reality*, objective characterizations of the writer were prominent through most of the first sixty years of this century, while expressive and social views of the writer were less common in classroom pedagogy. During the 1920s and 1930s, as Berlin argues, and again in the 1960s, subjective and social characterizations of the writer emerged and reemerged, culminating in an uneasy but effective alliance that shook the previous dominance of objective rhetorics and resulted in the ascendancy of alternative views of the writer and her ability to create.

Karen Burke LeFevre's *Invention as a Social Act* provides a helpful continuum from which to discuss how compositionists characterize the writer. LeFevre's work, while primarily concerned with heuristics and inventive practices in composition, offers a range of progressively more social understandings of the writer and her relationship to the writing process. Contrary to what Berlin suggests, LeFevre finds that a subjective concept of writer and invention dominates most current research. An introspective and individualistic approach to invention, this concept lacks an understanding of the writer as a social being and reinforces a notion of the writer as creative genius that distances it from the lives and work of students in first-year writing courses.

Like Volosinov, LeFevre suggests that subjective, individualistic psychology and linguistics fail to account for social influences on authorial choices, particularly with regard to invention. In describing the first perspective on invention, which she refers to as a Platonic view, LeFevre echoes the Bakhtinian description of subjective linguistics and psychology. The dominant Platonic version of rhetorical invention, LeFevre writes, depends upon "recollecting or finding and expressing content or cognitive structures that are innate" (52). For Volosinov, the subjectivist "self" assumes a similar individualized search for language, for linguistic subjectivism posits the speaking individual as the basis of language use: "The source of language is the individual psyche. The laws of language creativity . . . are the laws of individual psychology" (*Marxism* 48). These views of self and language, while still influential among classroom teachers, are less frequent among social-epistemic compositionists.

The second perspective on invention is a form of internal collaboration, a means of invention that rests on the psychological theories of Freud. Although characterized by a generative dialogue between self and an internalized other, this dialogue only nominally recognizes social influences and constraints because the "other" is constructed by the self for the expressed purposes of a mock or hypothetical dialogue.[1] Because the writer cannot step outside of her own preconceptions or ideology to understand fully alternative points of view, a constructed, internalized other can only approximate other perspectives. These forms of invention perceive the dialogue as an internalized exchange between one person's constructed voices, not an exchange between two people as members of designated social groups or ideological positions.[2] Internal collaboration may best be characterized as dialogue in the sense of debate or dialectic. In composition studies, the internal dialogic described by LeFevre takes many forms, particularly in rhetorical invention. Carl Rogers's listening with understanding, Donald Murray's "writers' dialogue," and Elbow's doubting and believing game are among the most recognized, according to LeFevre (52–53). Elbow's game in particular is reminiscent of the Bakhtinian and Vygotskian inner speech, yet because doubting and believing remain essentially individualized, they are only nominally social heuristic forms.

In the third perspective on LeFevre's continuum, interindividual collaboration, invention is characterized by persons interacting to generate, develop, and evaluate ideas for writing. Scientific research teams, business project groups, and collaborative writing peer groups all undertake collaborative work. In contrast to internal dialogues, which are characterized by imagining alternative ideologies and contrary and opposing positions or ideas, collaborative interaction places invention in the objectifiable world of group discussion and peer commentary. Collaborative groups often function as groups of individuals sharing common goals, methods of inquiry, and forms of arguing, organizing, and presenting knowledge. Kenneth Bruffee sets out to create within the writing classroom learning groups based on the premise that writing is an act of adapting, acculturating, and affirming communal bonds among knowledgeable peers. As such, Bruffee implies, the collaborative peer group models how decisions about meaning, proof, logic, and evaluation are made in the academy.

The collective perspective on invention is the last and most "social" category articulated by LeFevre. Collective invention is not a strategy or method for invention, as are the other forms. Social collectives are those institutions, sociocultures, organizations, or other establishments (abstract or concrete) that promote, encourage, hinder, or constrain invention. In contrast to internal dialogism and collaboration, where assessing and evaluating discourse rests with the individual or a finite group of knowledgeable peers, the social collective evaluates discourse through the institution(s) within which individuals and groups of writers are working. Academic genres, for example, are the products not only of a community of scholars but also of the society, of larger social collectives.

Of the recent scholarship in composition, the work of David Bartholomae, Patricia Bizzell, and Min-zhan Lu best recognizes academic genres as discourses defined by social collectives outside the academy. These scholars raise educational, economic, and ethical issues involved in leading students into the academic community. For example, Bartholomae argues that students gain entry into the academic community only by learning its discourse. Before adopting a discourse, students are urged to analyze assumptions in the academy regarding knowledge, meaning, and value. Still, at the heart of the work of Bartholomae and other leading scholars in composition studies lies the belief that students in our classrooms are most productively defined as writers. Despite LeFevre's realization that collective invention impinges upon and determines the writing that takes place in any given context, the discipline—by naming "writerly-ness" as a primary characteristic of students' roles in the writing classroom—continues to marginalize students from what and why they write. Three constructions of the student as writer serve as points of departure for examining in closer detail the ways that more specifically defined notions of "writer" have come to bear on composition studies. In each case, despite the power of the position stated, scholars continue to assume the question I am raising here as central: What are the implications of the metaphors we choose to describe writing and writers?

### VOICE AS A DIALOGIC OF DOUBTING AND BELIEVING

The work of Peter Elbow represents a long and powerful tradition in composition studies that defines "writerly-ness" in terms of individual expression, authentic voice, and stylistic independence. Of greatest interest to me in examining the construction of the writer in Elbow's work is doubting and believing, a form of inner speech that resembles (but is not analogous to) the Bakhtinian dialogue of centripetal and centrifugal forces at work within the psyche and the utterance.[3] While doubting and believing provide an interesting vehicle for internal dialogue, Elbow inadequately addresses the political ramifications of doubting and believing and overlooks the essentially social nature of all dialogues, including personal and internal ones. He uses dialogism as a means of giving social force to individualistic theories of the self and writing. Nevertheless, his work with inner speech, invention, and dialogue provides a useful starting point for a discussion of the writer in composition studies.

Unlike Bakhtin, Elbow posits the writer as an autonomous individual existing in a relatively stable social system for whom social forces prove only a minor disruption. For Elbow, a student having difficulty with writing needs to find more control over words, which, in turn, helps her gain control over her life generally. By finding the center of her writing, she becomes more adept at revealing and expressing her opinions to herself and others. The student must find her own voice through writing. It is here that Elbow and Bakhtin differ, for Bakhtin insists that only by denying the existence of individual voice and realizing that an utterance is generated by a multiplicity of voices can a writer come to understand the essence of language and communication and their various purposes.[4]

Elbow acknowledges social influences when discussing invention, and he also maintains a social element in his schema by recognizing what LeFevre refers to as a writer's "internalized social codes and values" (52). He recognizes, for example, that a student writer's opinions about nuclear weapons deployment are influenced by a range of individuals and institutions—family, friends, teachers, church, and so on. Yet to say that a student is *influenced* by society's values and codes is not enough. To imply that a student internalizes these codes, values, and assumptions, and from them creates an unpredictable and mysterious amalgam unique to her "real" self and expressed in her voice, greatly underestimates the generative and shaping power of the social on that individual's thought and language. By reading Elbow through a Bakhtinian lens one may make some deceivingly simple contrastive statements regarding voice. According to Elbow, a successfully crafted utterance reveals its writer's voice. Bakhtin posits a contrary opinion: An utterance is univocal only insofar as it is physically initiated and delivered by one person. Its success is not determined by its univocality, but by its orchestration of its many voices.

Although Elbow fails to recognize a "multivocal" voice, he defines an explicit dialectic between doubting and believing.[5] He synthesizes Aristotelian (agonistic, "doubting") and Rogerian (cooperative, "believing") approaches to inquiry, which then serve as a dialogic means of invention for a writer. Doubting and believing unite two ways of thinking previously considered antithetical. The two are also self-defining: believing entails leaving off with all criticism while attempting sincere understanding; doubting, on the contrary, disbelieves all, searching for error and logical fallacies. Yet, they function as neither knowledge generating, epistemic, politically nor ideologically motivated activities. As methods of inquiry, doubting and believing represent only one person's various perspectives on a subject. Elbow does not reach, in even his latest version of doubting and believing, a Bakhtinian internal dialogic, but he accomplishes what others have not—a useful relationship between the two methods of inquiry. Doubting and believing are no longer irreconcilable or contradictory methods of inquiry, means of testing and rejecting, or affirming hypotheses; they represent (as closely as possible within one person's psyche) various ideological stances.

In the end, Elbow's pedagogy remains, as Berlin argues, too individually oriented. Here, Volosinov offers the point from which to begin the critique:

> We shall never reach the real, substantive roots of any given single utterance if we look for them within the confines of the single, individual organism, even when that utterance concerns what appears to be the most private and most intimate side of a person's life. Any motivation of one's behavior, any instance of self-awareness . . . is an act of gauging oneself against some social norm, social evaluation. (*Freudianism* 86)

"Inner speech, too," writes Volosinov, "assumes a listener and is oriented in its construction toward that listener. Inner speech is the same kind of product and expression of social intercourse as is outward speech" (79). All writing is social in two ways: it is informed by social influences and it is interindividual. Carl Rogers, whose work so clearly influences Elbow's notion of believing, defines the goal of communication as an attempt to resolve differences between therapist and client through the awareness, development, and presentation of the client's own world view and self-understanding. Similarly, "[t]he writer's goal is to engage in some sort of cooperative activity with the reader" (Young, Becker, and Pike 171). Elbow, and others, to a lesser extent, preserves the psychologist's aims of a congruent self and effective communication.

Reading Elbow in *Embracing Contraries* through a Bakhtinian scheme of centripetal and centrifugal forces establishes a new forum for future discussions of Rogerian and Aristotelian approaches by uniting, in a dialogic relationship, the activities of doubting and believing as socially oriented activities. But to speak of "real" self or "real" voice is illusory, and in altering doubting and believing to accommodate centripetal and centrifugal forces I am neither faithfully representing Elbow's work nor maintaining his original intentions. Like Peter Berger and Thomas Luckmann, who write of the transformative nature of their endeavors into a sociology of knowledge, I do not claim to be undertaking exegesis or synthesis in my comments on Elbow's later work.

In constructing a pedagogy of possibility, I feel a need to recognize the generative effect of certain elements of previous theorists' work on my own thinking—particularly those like Elbow's doubting and believing—that prove helpful in articulating the goals of dialogic understanding and negotiated meaning. In other words, the basic difference between Bakhtin and Elbow on the self need not prevent composition teachers from using the latter's work when compiling strategies for a socially oriented pedagogy. Just as Bakhtin uses Freud's basic structure of the mind in constructing the official and unofficial conscious, so too can we revise and use Elbow's doubting and believing game as a heuristic in assisting students in the early stages of their reading and writing processes. To "socialize" Elbow's doubting and believing using centripetal and centrifugal discourses is to transform it into a Bakhtinian dialogic, emphasizing social relationships and external loci of evaluation. Reforming Elbow, of course, deconstructs doubting and believing, but at the same time it reconstructs them in an effort to reclaim Elbow's contributions.

When surveying Elbow's sense of self, a number of questions regarding voice, language, and writing also arise. How can a writing instructor be sure which style, which perspective is that of the "real" self as a student writes? Or, can we even equate "voice" with "self"?[6] Defining good writing entails more than determining honesty, integrity, or coherence in a student's voice. Claiming each writer has one voice is analogous to suggesting that she has only one writing process. Insisting that a writer has or even uses only one voice suggests that it, unlike other elements in writing, does not adapt to changes in rhetorical situations. By infusing Elbow's understanding of self and voice with the Bakhtinian, writing instructors may approach authorship differently. Like a volatile molecule, voice is made up of atoms held together by contextual forces. In the case of a molecule, those forces are electromagnetic; in the case of voice, the forces are social and contextual. To suggest that voice, unlike style, word choice, or organization, does not change with the context of an utterance is to deny the flexibility and inevitable variety of voice.

To determine the integrity or individuality of voice according to its degree of conformity, as some have, is also a grave error. Let me illustrate this point. Stewart, in a 1969 article, suggests that a student who wrote an essay entitled "Money Isn't as Valuable as It Seems" (which is reproduced in the text of the article) is dishonest, his generalizations inane. Stewart concludes this by arguing that the student unthinkingly and uncritically followed the popular belief that money won't buy happiness and instead breeds greed. His pedagogical strategy notwithstanding, Stewart states the brunt of the problem clearly: students do not select their language self-consciously. That this is a central problem in teaching writing is not a revelation, but addressing it from a Bakhtinian perspective is.

An incongruous, or—in Stewart's terms—a "dishonest," voice is, from a Bakhtinian perspective, not a false voice but one that has not yet placed itself consciously among the competing voices from which it emanates. This voice does not lack integrity; it lacks the ability to make alien discourses its own, to discern its place among the ideologically bound languages it uses. The same may be said of the students about whom Bartholomae writes in "Inventing the University." Student writers are more or less able to manipulate academic discourse according to their ability to place themselves comfortably or congruently within that discourse and its conventions. The problem is the same whether one subscribes to Stewart's or Elbow's explanations or to Bakhtin's: In creating an utterance, many students are unable to use language that distinguishes their thought from that of others. They often appear to mimic the style, form, and content of others' utterances, claiming that they, too, hold a particular opinion. To suggest that by finding a "real" voice they will achieve distinction, however, misdirects them, leading them to think that they must create an utterance by disregarding what others have said and how they have said it.

By emphasizing the social nature of all discourse, Bakhtin, on the contrary, asks the writer to align herself with some influences and dissociate herself from others, thus allowing her to make conscious choices about the language she uses in various rhetorical situations. How a person uses language reveals her relative position within her social, historical, and political time. Students who mimic and therefore perpetuate a standard discourse (or their versions of a standard discourse, as in the case of Bartholomae's students) are among those who seem to have little of their own "voices." The writing of these students reads to some as if it has no voice of its own, no style or flare. In effect, it is dominated by the voice of an unquestioned or mimicked standard discourse. In writing, these students recreate the dominant centripetal discourse, and in many university courses, that sort of imitation is rewarded. Genres are established by a discipline and perpetuated by students attempting to gain admission to that discipline. By asking them to venture on their own—in effect, to create subversive, centrifugal discourses—means far more than asking them to write honestly and with integrity. If nothing else, it asks them to place themselves consciously within, among, or against the myriad discourses of everyday life.

Elbow and Stewart, like many other compositionists, concern themselves with style as the most revealing sign of a student's failing to write with voice. Voice goes much deeper than style, however. Style and voice reveal ideology, but content even more so. The student who wrote that money did not matter wrote unconvincingly not only because of the way that he put language together, but also because he was writing about a topic within other significant social constraints—he was writing for a teacher in a composition class.[7] Stewart neglects the power of the teacher's opinion (or, more generally, that of the audience) over every element of the student's writing. By virtue of his position in the academy, Stewart has in effect coauthored the essay.

In the end, alerting first-year writing students to the political power and cultural significance of language may be all we can manage in first-year writing courses. Asking them to move beyond recognizing and writing centripetal prose to creating centrifugal discourse is asking them to consider, rearrange, and realign their positions with regard to disciplines, the academy, and society. That is a great deal to ask of them before they have completed three months of trial membership. Changing their discursive styles is neither a simple nor a politically neutral request. Holding on to safe and familiar styles or strategies (the five paragraph theme or following such rules as "Never begin a sentence with a preposition or coordinating conjunction") is less a sign of their linguistic immaturity than an indication of social or disciplinary conformity—both of which must be expected if not simply tolerated among novice writers. Standing with the dominant opinion on an issue reveals not conscious dishonesty, but ideological indecisiveness or naïveté. Only after student writers have been made conscious of linguistic and ideological positionings can they begin to have the power over words that will allow them to write from a more personally well-defined ideological perspective.

## THE WRITER AS A KNOWLEDGEABLE PEER

A Bakhtinian perspective reveals Elbow's emphasis on the individual writer apart from her ideological context, but the Bakhtinian also provides the basis for examining Kenneth Bruffee's work with peer groups and collaborative writing. Elbow and Bruffee certainly hold varying opinions about the construction of individual knowledge and social reality, as suggested by Elbow's emphasis on individual knowledge and Bruffee's emphasis on peer groups, community, and consensus. Despite the differences between the two, the resulting issues surrounding a writer's choices remain much the same and revolve around the Bakhtinian concern with centripetal and centrifugal discourse.

Unlike Elbow, who emphasizes the importance and primacy of an *intra*personal dialogue of doubting and believing, Bruffee promotes an *inter*personal dialogue among peers, that is, among students enrolled in a given writing course. While they seem to be only contrary pedagogical decisions, these two approaches disclose philosophical and, as Berlin suggests, epistemological differences about these theorists' views of the writer. In positing invention as introspective doubting and believing, Elbow constructs an author who relies on personal experiences, observations, and evaluations as the means by which she determines truth and reality. Doubting and believing do not extend outside the individual, even when used on interpersonal ground. As revision methods, doubting and believing do little more than shift the locus of evaluation from one individual to many. The result is not a community of writers, as Bruffee proposes, but a group of individuals retaining individual autonomy over their observations, decisions, and opinions despite their relationships as authors and audiences. Individual opinion remains eminent in doubting and believing, even though opinions inevitably differ among the members of a teacherless writing class. Differences are not negotiated among the class; the author evaluates others' comments about her writing based only on their presentation in the group and her own evaluation of their worth.

The peer groups devised by Bruffee are not immune to problems of conflicting individual opinion, but in theory, differences occur with less force. Collaborative learning pedagogies assume that any one individual will have greater difficulty enlisting the support of the group because the group as a whole strives to reach consensus by discussing and evaluating the opinions presented. That Bruffee emphasizes community and consensus is central to his philosophical difference with Elbow. Where Elbow valorizes the individual as the locus of evaluation and knowledge, Bruffee reifies the collective. In fact, Bruffee writes in *A Short Course in Writing* that only by setting aside "personal, unshared biases and preconceptions" can writers begin to make conscious and informed decisions about their writing (6). This seemingly innocuous statement, when closely analyzed, reveals the core of Bruffee's philosophy of the author. Personal opinions, when *unshared*, carry no authority within a given community. When *shared* by the community, personal opinions become worthy. Reaching valid decisions, in other words, entails community recognition and approval. An individual, as individual, carries no power or significance apart from the community and its consensus. Individual perspective must take on ideological design to gain authority: "We must try to see the world," Bruffee writes, "as other people seem to see it, or more precisely, as other members of the community we are trying to join seem to agree to see it" (6). Only after a writer begins to perceive the world as does a given community can she start to influence that group and its world view. The task, however, is much more difficult than Bruffee intimates.

Adopting a new knowledge paradigm requires far more than seeing the world from a different perspective. In the quotation above, Bruffee suggests that a writer seeking membership in a group need only adjust her own ideology to coincide with that of the community. Once she is in sync with that world view, and then recreates it and espouses it in her writing, she no longer runs the risk of unknowing or naïve idiosyncrasy, personal bias, or prejudice. I will not argue this particular point, because in theory, and in a limited and abstract sense, Bruffee's argument is logical. A member of a community who speaks in favor of a community ideal faces little opposition. Her views, because they promote and perpetuate consensual opinion, will not be considered, within that community, idiosyncratic or indefensible. Having convinced her community of the worth of its ideas, she does not necessarily carry authority outside that group. As she communicates with others who are not members of her community—particularly those who consider its ideals and actions ignorant, short-sighted, or reprehensible—she faces a much more complex rhetorical situation. No longer is she preaching to a congregation of believers, and she may encounter doubt, anger, or disbelief. Bruffee's notion of community also suggests that any defined group is bound by a set of consensual beliefs unique to that language community. I would argue that the flexibility of language and the nuances of words and their meanings allow for an individual *and* communal variation within communities not accounted for by Bruffee's comments. Dissensus, as well as consensus, exists within every group.

Still, college students will encounter new knowledge paradigms. Their world views—which are influenced by and perpetuated through their methods of argument, logic, and proof—may not coincide with those knowledge systems that dominate thinking within the academy. Their previously successful methods of studying, speaking, and writing, all manifestations of their ideological upbringing, may lack the rhetorical, analytical, and organizational characteristics of institutionally sanctioned academic discourses. Encountering new and strange discourses might not be dramatic or dangerous, but it can be damaging, for a student's survival in the university depends upon her ability to decipher and encode into her own discourse the language and rhetorical strategies of the academy. Put differently, she must accommodate academic discourse within (or against) her own dominant discourse, not simply exchange the latter for the former. At the same time, her own discourse is undeniably altered, and so, too, is the discourse of the academy.

Patricia Bizzell makes a similar argument for basic writers when she suggests that they suffer less from academic ill preparedness than from epistemological or ideological disenfranchisement. "Their difficulties," Bizzell writes, " . . . are best understood as stemming from the initial distance between their world-views and the academic world view, and perhaps also from the resistance to changing their own world-views that is caused by this very distance" ("What Happens" 297). To succeed in the university, students must learn its languages, its conventions, and its ways of thinking. At the same time, students' belief systems are challenged. Ways of constructing arguments, ordering proofs, using language, and stating opinions are all ways of seeing the world and one's place in it. When students change these strategies, they change themselves. Dissensus is not simply a result of differences of opinion that can be neatly worked out through negotiation within a community. At the heart of dissensus lies ideological difference, not random disagreement or idiosyncrasy. Asking students to reach consensus, as Bruffee does, is asking them to set aside previous priorities and beliefs in favor of a preferred, and perhaps alien, system.[8] It remains one of education's most ironic demands that a student who gains admission to the academy must lose, deny, or neglect her home knowledge in order to acquire the power to defend and argue for the validity of that same alternative world view. She must, to return to a Bakhtinian terminology, become adept at producing centripetal discourse while simultaneously seeking to create centrifugal discourse.

When discussing a basic writer's experiences with academic and home discourses, Bruffee refers to Richard Rorty's concepts of normal and abnormal discourse. Normal discourse, that which is "explanatory and argumentative" and seeks to "justify belief to the satisfaction of other people within the author's community of knowledgeable peers," should be the focus of writing courses and must be mastered before a student attempts abnormal (centrifugal) discourse ("Collaborative" 643).

However, what Bruffee overlooks is that, in producing the normal discourse of the academy, students are neither writing for nor seeking to justify their beliefs to peers. Instead, students are asked to attempt to "justify their beliefs to the satisfaction" of the academy and of their professors. If these students were writing to justify their beliefs to their peers, they would most likely turn to the quotidian discourses that they share, and have shared, before entering college. Normal discourse is, in more rhetorical terms, epideictic. It is, according to Aristotle, the discourse of "praise, blame, persuasion, dissuasion, and appeals to the hearer's indulgence" (*Rhetoric* 3.14, 222). And like the epideictic speech about which Aristotle writes, normal discourse praises the listener and enobles the community by maintaining the standards and requirements of that community. Normal discourse, in other words, is the hegemonic form tacitly agreed upon through continued use by a community. In asking students to construct academic discourse, we are in fact asking them to serve the academy's epideictic ends. Although Richard Rorty might take exception to my description, he notes similar goals for normal discourse in an educational setting:

> It seems to me that the normal division between secondary and tertiary education is and should be the line between getting in on the normal discourse of the tradition in the nation and the community to which you belong, and higher education is a matter of being told about all the alternatives to that tradition, to that discourse. But that isn't necessarily going to move you into one of these alternatives; it's just going to make it possible, if you have an imagination, for that imagination to work. (qtd. in Olson 234)

Bakhtin is much more suspicious of normal (centripetal) discourse than either Bruffee or Rorty, and perhaps understandably so given his political experiences. Because of its innate conservatism, normal, centripetal discourse promotes a community's dominant tradition at the expense of less powerful or less recognized alternatives. Academic discourse, as the normal discourse of the university, is itself dominant and latently hegemonic.

Bruffee, in applying to his writing pedagogy Rorty's notion of normal discourse along with other elements of social constructivist theory, makes several assumptions, the first of which is believing that students placed in a group constitute a discourse community. In first-year writing courses, these groups, however, are brought together in a forced alliance. The students in first-year writing classes do not necessarily have similar codes, tenets, or expectations for the course. Any points of similarity, for that matter, are most likely negative. All are required to enroll in and pass first-year English, or worse, none performed well enough on placement exams to be exempted from it. To suggest that this group of students constitutes a community of knowledgeable peers is to imply that they have in common a standardized or "normal" discourse form—an "explanatory and argumentative" discourse whose purpose it is "to justify belief to the satisfaction of other people" in that community.[9] The basis for a successful discourse community in the university must come from more than the uneasy partnerships created in a first-year writing course. Granted, students in advanced courses, electives, or professional preparatory courses are more likely to form more permanent communities of learners whose goals and aspirations reflect those of the course or their professions. This is not to say that biology and advertising majors cannot be members of the same language community, but it must be a community in which the biologists and advertising majors share a basic understanding of some body of knowledge and adhere to common strategies and conventions for attaining that knowledge.[10] Put differently, communities and their shared languages rest on fundamental similarities, something more enduring than enrolling in the same writing course or fulfilling a writing requirement.

Bakhtin, when writing about the social languages that exist within the novel, names several elements that may be helpful in defining discourse communities in quotidian and academic discourses. Stratification, or heteroglossia, within a single national language may occur according to genre, profession, class, or age. In addition, language systems, including those of students, vary "depending on social level, academic institution (the language of the cadet, the high school student, the trade school student are all different languages) and other stratifying factors" ("Discourse" 290). Students in a first-year writing course may have a common discourse at their disposal, yet this is a stratum of our national language whose power rests outside the academy. Theirs is the language of the high school, the family, social activities, or of a particular ethnic, religious, or social group, neither necessarily bound by nor related to the university. To assume that any group of young people will arrive at decisions based only on their interactions as members of an *ad hoc* community (regardless of the power of their previous languages) reflects a limited understanding of social constructivism and of human nature.

In addition to idealizing writing groups as discourse communities, Bruffee's pedagogy assumes evenly distributed power within such peer groups. This second assumption is directly related to the first, for it, too, is founded on the belief that students can leave their ideologies (including prejudices, biases, and preconceptions) outside the classroom, shedding them like coats or hats. Beliefs cannot be removed or replaced at will. Power rules in these peer groups as much as it rules on the football field, in the chemistry lab, or at the local dance club. Only the hierarchies are different. That members of a peer group come together with differing ideological preconceptions is unavoidable. The way others dress and talk, the color of their skin, the way they wear their hair, the activities in which they are involved, the intelligence and persuasiveness with which they speak—all of these are elements weighed and measured by students as they begin to work with one another.[11] Race, class, and gender, are among the most distinguishing characteristics in the classroom, but a peer writing group steered by any prejudice will remain hampered by the biases of its members. Prejudice is unavoidable, but it is also made manifest when ignored and not factored into the workings of peer writing groups. Recognizing that differences exist—rather than minimizing them by emphasizing consensus—and making them an explicit part of the writing class offers an alternative to Bruffee's community-driven pedagogy.

Bruffee's final assumption about collaboration and student writing groups is closely allied to the issue of power in the academy, for he assumes that the collaborative processes at work in these peer groups resemble closely the processes by which knowledge is generated within academic discourse communities. This association is partly a result of his taking the metaphors of community and conversation too literally. Rarely do members of a discourse community meet with the expressed purpose of hammering out consensual policy, standards, or conventions. And when they do, an unstated or even explicit agenda and hierarchy are already in place. The peer group, as it is characterized by Bruffee, does not model the academic discourse community, for, in fact, neither the academy nor the writing classroom can be described as a "community of status equals" ("Collaborative" 642). The peer group is an ideologically driven, hierarchically structured entity, and in this it models communities in the academy. In both cases, the underlying structure and hierarchy remain unstated, but each member recognizes her implied place in that group. Unlike members of academic communities, however, students whose commonalities do not extend past their membership in a single required writing course do not constitute a community of like-minded peers.

## THE STUDENT WRITER AS INITIATE

Recently, a number of influential and widely read rhetoricians, generally perceived as social constructivists, have come to describe the writer as defined by her inclusion in or exclusion from a particular discourse community—usually an academic one.[12] One of these scholars, David Bartholomae, suggests a view of the writer as she lives and uses language within an established cultural context, unlike Elbow, who emphasizes internal exploration, or Bruffee, who employs peer response and critique. In "Inventing the University," Bartholomae describes the process whereby basic writers struggle to "appropriate" the discourse of the university. He characterizes these underprepared students by their relationships to (1) their inherited culture, its language, and common-places; (2) the academy; and (3) the texts that they read and produce. Patricia Bizzell's work, which is decidedly more politicized than Bartholomae's, suggests that students entering college, and basic writers in particular, must adjust their dialects, discourses, and therefore their world views and knowledge paradigms in order to succeed in college. For some students, the adjustment is only a matter of fine tuning; others must change channels altogether. Those students who resist change are viewed most often as underprepared.[13]

"Inventing the University" examines student texts as intentional texts. Students attempt, Bartholomae writes, to "invent the university by assembling and mimicking its language" (135). They produce texts that approximate the language they are reading and hearing (or expect to read and expect to hear) in the course of their college careers. They write what they assume college professors reading their writing expect to see.[14] However flawed, these attempts, Bartholomae argues, are a necessary step for a student as she negotiates the transition to academic discourse. She must, as it turns out, use academic discourse before she knows what it is, before she has had the chance to discover its requirements, standards, and conventions. She recognizes it when she reads it, and she may have a sense of its argumentative or persuasive form, but she can only marginally replicate it in her own discourse. As a result, her text may include oddly phrased conclusions, summations, or proofs along with or instead of more conventional errors in spelling, grammar, or mechanics.

Not surprisingly, many students are uneasy with or unsure about the complex academic pursuits of research, analysis, and evaluation that college writing requires of them. Many falter as they attempt to respond to such placement essay prompts as the one Bartholomae mentions: "Describe a time when you did something you felt to be creative. Then, on the basis of the incident you have described, go on to draw some general conclusions about creativity" ("Inventing" 136). Students, and particularly basic writers, are (understandably) uncomfortable with the roles of researcher, scholar, and expert that this sort of question asks them to take on. Not only do they recognize their own subordinate position within the knowledge community they are joining, but they also have had little if any contact with people and texts that undertake research of the sort they are asked to produce in this placement essay. Finally, and not incidentally, students are also very much aware of the role of placement essays in their own educations. Failure to pass and be categorized as basic writers remain demeaning and even debilitating prospects.

Although many students may have difficulty addressing the question of creativity posed by the placement prompt above, Bartholomae notes that basic writers have the greatest difficulty adopting the persona of researcher. In response, I am compelled to ask, "Are basic writers unable to answer this question adequately, or are students considered basic writers because they cannot speak effectively or persuasively as 'authorities'?" That is, do basic writers fail at this exercise or are students categorized as basic writers because they are unable to mimic or replicate some academic form in their responses? If the latter is the case, as I believe it is, then Bartholomae has initiated a new set of criteria in determining student placement in writing courses. While he ostensibly defines basic writers as those students "traditionally placed in remedial composition courses," or as those "students who are refused unrestrained access to the academic community," Bartholomae also redefines the locus of evaluating these writers:

> Basic writers . . . [are those who find it difficult] to take on the role—the voice, the persona—of an authority whose authority is rooted in scholarship, analysis, or research. They slip, then, into a more immediately available and realizable voice of authority, the voice of a teacher giving a lesson or the voice of a parent lecturing at the dinner table. They offer advice or homilies rather than "academic" conclusions. ("Inventing" 136–37)

Put differently, basic writers cannot mimic well the argumentative forms of academia and instead rely on more familiar and comfortable methods of problem solving. One presumes, as well, that these writers might have similar difficulty mimicking other forms: business genres, bureaucratic prose, or screenwriting.

Any one utterance—a student essay, for example—is an accumulation of various discourses, voices, and colorations. In many instances, as with the students Bartholomae cites, writers rely most heavily on the discourse strata most familiar to them—in this case, parental and instructional discourses, the discourses of home and school. What Bartholomae and other compositionists want instead is for students to develop a heavier and more extensive reliance on academic and scholarly responses. I do not want to suggest that such students be exempted from a basic writing course. What I am intimating is that teachers of writing must resist perceiving the voices of the elder, teacher, or parent as "breaks" in student writing. Instead, we must realize the validity of these voices and their power in our students' lives as a point from which to begin discussing alternative authoritative voices privileged by the academy. The cultural commonplaces—among them the voices of parents and teachers—used so freely by students also indicate for Bartholomae a less sophisticated writing style. A "commonplace," he suggests,

> is a culturally or institutionally authorized concept or statement that carries with it its own necessary elaboration. We all use commonplaces to orient ourselves in the world; they provide points of reference and a set of "prearticulated" explanations that are readily available to organize and interpret experience. ("Inventing" 137–38)

Commonplaces are not universal although some do have a broader cultural recognition. They are as much a product of discourse communities as are other linguistic elements.

What I infer from Bartholomae's text (and here I am reading quite a bit into it, going well beyond any particular statement) is that young writers, novices, or basic writers must graduate from generalized cultural commonplaces to more specific academic commonplaces. Among other things, the commonplaces that a writer invokes reveal the discourse community from which she writes.[15] I suggest, however, that a writer's use of her culture's most accessible commonplaces may be interpreted instead as an attempt to identify with an audience with whom, as an eighteen-year-old college student, she has little in common beyond a certain general understanding of shared culture. It is as if, not knowing how to communicate with her audience on its (academic and scholarly) level or on her own (punkish, avant garde, or street-wise) level, she resorts to the lowest cultural common denominator, the language and structures that she assumes her rather unknown, strange, and even faceless reader understands. As she becomes more familiar with the scholarly discourse of those with whom she is conversing, commonplaces will not disappear; instead they will be replaced by a more distinctive set.

Let me next set forth this postulate: Any student who has not considered self-consciously her position in her culture will be a less successful writer than the student who has begun to question the validity of commonplaces, common opinion, and objectivity. This is, I think, implied in both Bartholomae's and Bizzell's work. Moreover, it is supported and perhaps explained by the Bakhtinian notions of authoritative and internally persuasive discourses. Examples may clarify what I mean here when I write of students who have or have not placed themselves self-consciously within their cultures. By this I suggest that the social and/or educational environments from which these students emerge do not or have not taught them to value writing. Mike Rose puts it more completely and perhaps more compassionately when he writes that

> The literacy backgrounds of people who end up in remedial, developmental, or adult education classes are more complex than that [a dichotomy between orality and literacy]: they represent varying degrees of distance from or involvement with printed material, various attitudes toward it and skill with it, various degrees of embracement of or complicated rejection of traditions connected with their speech. ("Narrowing" 293)

In the end, Bartholomae misses the same point as Bruffee. By stating that "[o]ur students . . . [must] appropriate (or be appropriated by) a specialized discourse," and do so "as though they were easily or comfortably one with their audience" ("Inventing" 139), Bartholomae disregards the reasons—cultural, social, or intellectual—why students do not or cannot meet the academy's expectations. To suggest that there are only two alternatives—appropriating or being appropriated by the hegemonic discourse—is misleading, for a student has more than just these two choices. She may choose to do something other than "speak to us in our terms—in the privileged language of university discourse—or . . . as though we were children, offering us the wisdom of experience" (138). She may choose to speak on other terms, elsewhere (outside the academy), or not to speak at all.

Bartholomae discounts those strata of a basic writer's discourse that fail to approximate successfully academic discourse. Student writers who rely on the discourses and commonplaces of the street, high school classroom, or even of society in general are writers who remain deficient in their attempts at imitation. The fault lies not wholly with the student but also with the university. The university errs in not recognizing the validity and power of these alternative and subversive discourses. We must not only "examine the essays written by basic writers—their approximations of academic discourse—to determine more clearly where the problems lie" but also begin to examine the "points of discord that arise when students try to write their way into the university" as the points at which academic discourse fails *them*. I agree with Bartholomae that "[t]he challenge to researchers . . . is to turn their attention again to products, to student writing" ("Inventing" 162). My purpose, however, differs from Bartholomae's. A basic writer's essay may indeed reveal "struggles with and against the languages of our contemporary life," but surveying and studying those texts to search out and eradicate difference will do little good. Basic writers, and many college students not segregated into basic writing classes, live precarious educational existences on the border between the competing worlds of their home cultures and the foreign discourses of academia. Such a multicultural frontier provides every teacher of first-year writing a rich and unique landscape to survey. The student's essay is a subversive, centripetal text—a text of dissonance *and* harmony, of rebellion *and* accommodation, of rejection *and* acceptance. The voices that infuse that essay cannot be extracted from it or from its writer without severing the elemental characteristics of linguistic and ideological identity.

Bartholomae and Bizzell, despite their insightful commentaries on the basic writer and her plight in attaining any academic status in the university, generally overlook the obvious hegemonic quality of academic discourse itself. Bizzell points out the obvious: the languages of U.S. culture are significantly different from those of the academy. She then concludes that as academicians and rhetoricians, we must continue to "elucidate our assumption that our rhetorical methods can develop 'the justification of the possibility of a human community in the sphere of action,' to 'give meaning to human freedom, a state in which a reasonable choice can be exercised'" ("Thomas Kuhn" 771). It seems to me a problematic leap from claiming difference between academic and cultural discourses to valorizing academic discourse on the basis of its ability to achieve "human freedom" or allow for more "reasonable choice." On different terms, Bizzell makes a plea for establishing the discourse of the academy as a predominant discourse. Even if I were to agree that the academy offers a more "reasonable" (and implicitly valorized) world view, I find it difficult to justify it as the preferred knowledge paradigm, for that entails replacing one centripetal discourse, one hegemonic discourse, for another.

VOICES, THE STUDENT WRITER,
AND WRITING INSTRUCTION

Bakhtinian concepts do not so much contradict as alter and enhance the work of Elbow, Bruffee, Bartholomae, and other compositionists. Bakhtinian notions of author could be said to range from internal dialogue through the collaborative to the social collective. Bakhtinian inner speech is dialogic and recognizes that language and knowledge are created and revised as members of language spheres interact. But these methods of generating knowledge always take place within the undeniable power of social collectives recognized by Bartholomae. As a whole, the Bakhtinian corpus is most concerned with declaring the inevitability that all verbal behavior is determined by the social setting in which that behavior takes place. Reading current versions of the author in composition studies through a Bakhtinian lens allows us to inspect the ways that the discipline defines and describes "writerly-ness" to our students.

Elbow's doubting and believing games, as much as they resemble Bakhtin's centripetal and centrifugal discourse, are not "dialogic." Doubting and believing do not serve Elbow (as they do Bakhtin) as a paradigm of linguistic or ideological formation. Bruffee, despite his explicit statements about the social nature of writing and thinking, relies on dominant metaphors of community and consensus, which hinder the heteroglossic understanding of discourse offered us by Bakhtin. Bartholomae, who visualizes the writing classroom as the arena in which students struggle to gain admission to the academic discourse community, adopts a theory most nearly Bakhtinian; nevertheless, students' writing as a convergence of social and cultural voices does not yet achieve a standing of centrifugal force.

Just what *is* the "Bakhtinian Writer"? Put plainly, the Bakhtinian writer is utterly social. No thought lies beyond the reach of the social, so to refer to a writer as a single creator of a discourse is misleading. A writer physically creates an utterance by generating it, but an utterance is created only on interindividual territory. "The word is a two-sided act"; it is a "bridge," Volosinov writes, "thrown between myself and another" (*Marxism* 86). I may initiate building the bridge of communication, but the distance between my audience and me can only be spanned with help from the audience. The construction is influenced and determined by the readers (users of the bridge) and the environment in which the bridge is placed. As representatives of a language sphere, readers have a creative power over the utterance, as do the immediate and remote social contexts in and from which the author composes. Just as a structure of a bridge conforms to rules of gravity, calculations of civil engineering, demands of climate, and expected use and function, so will the utterance be informed by context, audience, and purpose. Immediate context—the physical surroundings or the purpose of the discourse—and audience determine the form and style of an utterance, while the "deeper layers of its structure are determined by more sustained and more basic social connections with which the speaker is in contact" (87). More elementally, the extended sociocultural context and the language spheres to which a writer belongs affect discourse from its inception.

A Bakhtinian polyphony of voices and the ideologically bound psyche, taken together, provide a new set of metaphors for composition studies as it answers the call for a philosophy and pedagogy informed by postmodernism. In many respects, the discipline has already answered the call with respect to voice, as Wertsch's "voices" and Bialostosky's "dialogic self" suggest. Volosinov's commentary on language as heteroglossic and the psyche as thoroughly ideological demands that we reimagine our discussions of voice. Scholars of composition studies, among them Berlin, Faigley, and Knoblauch, critique expressivists for promoting a romantic and individualistic notion of voice. Comments such as Donald Stewart's that writers working from "borrowed ideas and borrowed words" are writers who do not work from an "authentic voice" (225) are lambasted as naive, idealistic, or purely subjective.

To achieve a more productive understanding of voice, scholars reimagine the term, noting the plural rather than singular nature of voice, its polyphony, and its ideological nature.[16] Although many compositionists now acknowledge the myriad voices that make up a given individual's writing selves, they do not recognize the complex, long-term, and even violent project entailed in understanding how these voices interact. The person writing must face not only the conflict inherent in the words themselves but also the conflict inherent in the project of ideological becoming so central to the educational process. "The notion of heterogeneity," Wertsch writes,

> calls on us to consider why certain forms of speaking and thinking (voices) rather than others are invoked on particular occasions. It also forces us to recognize that we cannot answer this question simply on the basis of the metaphor of possession, which focuses on what humans "have" in the way of concepts and skills. Instead, we must consider how and why a particular voice occupies center stage, that is, why it is "privileged" . . . in a particular setting. (14)

Compositionists have been particularly remiss in recognizing that our own practice of privileging the voice of "writer" in our composition classrooms undermines students' heterogeneity of voice.

> Just because I write, can I call myself a writer? Do my meager efforts afford me a place in the same category as Woolf and Hurston and Atwood? Can my five paragraph essay on *To the Lighthouse* stand beside *A Room of One's Own* in the annals of literary history?
>
> —Caroline Hudak[17]

> Writing is learned by writing, by reading, and by perceiving oneself as a writer.
>
> —Frank Smith[18]

OK, here's the situation. . . . There are six people sitting at the front of the room, Charles Baxter is one and to give the other names would be completely pointless. . . . The main question to the whole panel of six: how do you see yourself as a writer? . . . We started out with the five people . . . [and] ended with Charles Baxter giving his opinion and summing things up. . . . The general opi[ni]ons of the five were important though. Most writer[s] don't see themselves as writers. . . . Writers are people that live in Paris and where [*sic*] berets and smoke unfiltered lucky strikes and drink J.D[.] whisk[e]y. Well, Charles Baxter is a writer and he wasn't smoking or sportin' a beret or even tweed. He came from Michigan and not Paris, almost shocking. . . . He told stories about how his first paper failed and his teacher threw it on the floor[.] I thoug[h]t "THERE IS HOPE!"

—undergraduate expository writing student[19]

Most of us would probably agree that it is unlikely that an essay penned by a college student like Caroline Hudak, a junior English major at Ohio State University, would "stand beside" Virginia Woolf's work in the "annals of literary history." Caroline, an exceptional student—bright, sensitive, articulate—nevertheless raises an important issue with regard to students and authorship. In this quotation, which is taken from a journal entry in a tutoring log she kept for English 467, "Writing and Learning," Caroline inquires into the nature of "writerly-ness" and its meaning for her as a student who writes but does not consider herself a "writer." She asks what I see as a fundamental question: "Just because I write, can I call myself a writer?"

I have struggled—both as a person who writes and as a teacher of writing—to come to terms with the almost universally accepted and unquestioned assumption among composition teachers and scholars that the students in expository writing classrooms are "writers," that these classrooms constitute "communities of writers," and that coming to voice in those communities means coming to voice as a writer. Smith's quotation speaks directly to this issue from a perspective far different from Caroline's. For him, as for nearly all writing teachers, students must image themselves as writers to construct good writing. Smith certainly seeks to empower students by claiming for them a privileged position from which to speak and write, but such an assumption can also be problematic, even debilitating, for students enrolled in first-year writing classes. In foregrounding (and therefore privileging) "writer" in the classroom, expository writing teachers assume an identity for their students that the students themselves are often unwilling or unable to imagine (or choose) for themselves. Furthermore, claiming the persona of writer as a means of defining our students marginalizes and renders subordinate students' other subjectivities and self-representations. Students cultivate their voices not as writers, but as people engaged in the act of writing about their lives and their beliefs—as mothers, chicanas, historians—as people immersed in and struggling to make sense out of the tensions between and among the worlds they inhabit as they come to our writing classrooms.

The notion of "writer" also carries with it so many cultural, social, moral, and political assumptions that students often find it difficult to define themselves as writers even secondarily. Many undergraduates do not have the opportunity to see and hear writers discuss their work, and as a result they often formulate unrealistic expectations about writers, their processes of writing, and the special nature of the writer and her world. Attempting to dispel our students' misunderstandings about the nature of writing by presenting draft pages from a Joyce short story or a Waugh novel may well show students that even skilled and recognized writers draft and revise their prose, but it does little to convince them that they themselves might be named a writer. Our students' notions of writing and real writers are informed by images from television and film. To them, writers are people who write creative texts such as plays, poetry, or other types of fiction. Writers write for a living and without external motivation. Their books line the shelves of bookstores. Their writing is not compulsory. Writers have a willing audience.

We gain additional insight into the pervasiveness of the struggle to come to voice as a writer from the undergraduate who sent the e-mail message in response to a roundtable discussion conducted at Ohio State University in 1995.[20] Her comments illustrate that students who write to fulfill undergraduate requirements more readily rally around writers' frustrations and failures than their successes or positive self-images in forging a sense of community: "Most writer[s] don't see themselves as writers. . . . Writers are people that live in Paris and where [*sic*] berets and smoke unfiltered lucky strikes and drink J.D[.] whisk[e]y." The focus of the roundtable—to examine the notion of writer and the communities to which writers "belong"—was not lost on this student, however. Despite her initial representation of "writer," one informed by visions of Ernest Hemingway, Gertrude Stein, or Dorothy Parker, she realizes that "Charles Baxter is a writer and he wasn't smoking or sportin' a beret or even tweed. He came from Michigan and not Paris, almost shocking." Her comments suggest that only by imaging writers—in this case, Charles Baxter—as *not* writers or as once unsuccessful writers can she begin to have faith that her own writing might also succeed: "He told stories about how his first paper failed and his teacher threw it on the floor, I thoug[h]t, 'THERE IS HOPE!'"

In addition to having their construct of author formed largely by the popular media, our students sometimes read, admire, and then face the exhortations of such writers as James Michener, who is reported to have advised aspiring writers, "Unless you think you can do better than Tolstoy, we don't need you."[21] Although I am offended by Michener's exclusionary, "we don't need you" rhetoric and his self-promotion in situating himself as a member of an elite literary club that includes Tolstoy, his message is ingrained in the lore of, and repeated every day in, writing classrooms across the country. Nearly all of our textbooks, in fact, are founded on the assumption that students, to write successfully and confidently, must consider themselves writers.

Consider the following passages from just two composition textbooks, the first intended for a basic writing classroom and the second for a more general student audience:

> How can we help our students develop their writing abilities? We can create an environment that *enables them to see themselves as writers*, and we can provide opportunities for them to be writers—to be *writers at work*.
>
> Students who use this book are *treated as writers*. Instead of being victims of their writing backgrounds, they play an active role in their own development by first locating themselves historically as writers. (Gay xvii; emphases added)

> *You may not think of yourself as a writer, but we do.* We are going to treat you like a writer. A writer isn't some peculiar absent-minded genius who goes into a trance and magically produces good writing. A writer is someone who writes a lot and who cares a lot about it. The best writers struggle. You may well already *be* a writer. If not, we can help you become one in this non-magical sense of the word—someone who enjoys writing, cares about writing, and struggles but gets satisfaction from the struggle. (Elbow and Belanoff 5; emphasis in original)

In both of these cases, the authors of these writing textbooks—like Frank Smith—seek to empower students by naming them as writers.[22] Still, I want to question the assumption by looking to the colonizing, hegemonic nature of this move: Gay, Elbow, and Belanoff do not question, perhaps do not even recognize, the colonizing gesture they make when they claim the right to name for students the role they will assume in a writing classroom, or that their gesture necessarily subordinates students' wishes, self-representations, and other voices to the teacher's expectations and demands. I do not want to make this point too emphatically with these two texts alone, however. The practice of naming students as writers in our classrooms is systemic and logical. It makes sense on some level to refer to the students in writing classes as writers because they are writing. (Interestingly, though, we do not refer to students "doing" history in a first year history course "historians" or in first-year math classes "mathematicians.") For example, in the preface of her text, Gay introduces a series of scaffolded projects in which students work from personal knowledge toward a more "dialogic" understanding of a given topic until they are ready to " 'go public' with the explorations and tentative conclusions they have expressed in writing" (xi). Gay's program is similar in its construction and philosophy to that developed by David Bartholomae and Anthony Petrosky in *Facts, Artifacts, and Counterfacts* and enacted in *Ways of Reading*. Elbow and Belanoff, as well, inform their text with carefully sequenced assignments designed to usher the student into the world of university writing with a strong sense of the value of their own writing selves and experiences.

Both texts strive to democratize the notion of writer through self-assessments that ask students to examine themselves as writers. In an early exercise in the opening chapter, "Developing Your Writing Ability," Gay directs the students using her text to assess themselves as writers, asking them to "look at your story or past as a writer, and to set some goals" by composing a short "response to this question: How do you see yourself as a writer" (4). Again, Gay works under the assumption that students are willing and able to see themselves as writers without asking what I believe to be a much more crucial question: Do you see yourself as a writer? Some of the excerpts from student responses included by Gay in the text illustrate students' uneasiness with the notion of themselves as writers and with writing generally: "I'm not sure if I'm a good writer or a bad writer." "I'm a confused writer." and the very telling "I've never really thought of myself as a writer" (4).

Gay also includes an unedited response from a student, Patti Fervan, that nicely articulates the tensions inherent in asking students to think of themselves as writers. Fervan writes, "Edgar Allan Poe, Emily Dickinson, Mark Twain, and Patti Fervan. Somehow that doesn't quite fit. When one thinks of a writer one thinks of the great minds of an era although in fact all of us are writers" (5). Like Caroline Hudak, Patti sees the incongruity in placing herself as "writer" beside Poe, Dickinson, and Twain. To ease the incongruity, Patti takes the democratic route, claiming that "in fact all of us are writers." Yet, this latter notion of writer is qualitatively different from "Writer." Here, with "writer," Patti finds a link between all people through the physical act of writing. This "writer" as the lowest common denominator does very little in the way of developing productive connections between Patti and Caroline and Poe, Twain, and Woolf, or in assisting students as they position themselves in a writing classroom in a way that encourages them to write productively.

Elbow and Belanoff offer students a similar exercise, what they call a "case study," in which they urge students to attend to their own writing processes. Unlike Gay, who introduces the self-assessment at the beginning of the writing course, Elbow and Belanoff present the case study as perhaps the last assignment, requiring students to examine their writing before and after enrolling in the course. The exercise, although more detailed than Gay's, includes similar prompts: students are asked to examine salient moments from their writing history, the kinds of writing produced, the contexts for writing, audiences chosen, the physical surroundings preferred when writing, the myths encountered and/or dispelled. And like Gay, Elbow and Belanoff ask students to consider "writerly-ness": "Who do you think of as a writer? What are the characteristics of a writer? Can you think of yourself as a writer? If not, why not" (317). Elbow and Belanoff include in this unit several examples from undergraduate and graduate students, as well as published authors writing about their composing processes and senses of themselves as writers. The first of these, a case study written by Barbara Smith, a graduate student, again echoes my concerns about naming students as writers:

It is only recently that I have come to think of myself as a writer. As a student, of course, I have done a lot of writing, but I would think of this only as a method of communication, that is, to make the teacher aware of my grasp of the material. . . . Even then, though, I didn't see myself in terms of a "writer" any more than I considered myself a "phone caller" or a recording secretary. Writing was one of the many activities which I employed as a tool in my role as a student and in my life as a functioning human being. (324)

Barbara Smith's narrative raises at least two critical points. First, only "recently," she writes, has she come to view herself as a writer, and only after a series of rather dramatic events over several years, all of which led to her returning to pursue graduate study. Second, writing for her functioned as an "activity," a "tool" as she lived and worked. Gay, Elbow, and Belanoff work to democratize their students' understanding of writers and writing by asking them to imagine themselves as writers; their request merely privileges writing and the writer and, by extension, teachers of writing and departments that administer writing courses. Asking students to see themselves as writers requires them to undertake a risky and difficult shift, one that they are generally not asked to undertake in history or math classes. As Barbara Smith's case study suggests, even when students begin to define themselves as writers, the process is protracted and influenced by far more than an instructor asking students to imagine themselves as such.

Gay's and Elbow and Belanoff's intentions are good. By encouraging students to name themselves as writers, Gay, Elbow, and Belanoff seek to empower them, to work with them to counteract, as Gay puts it, their past "victimizations" at the hands of writing and writing instruction. The method for ending the victimization is suspect, however, for Gay, and by extension any writing instructor who asks students to think of themselves as writers, claims and reclaims her own position of privilege when she argues that it is only through naming themselves as writers (e.g., naming themselves as part of *our* venture, *our* world view) that students can escape their ongoing victimization. Naming our students as writers in the classroom protects our own self-interest, our own privileged position in the academy and the privileged position accorded the writer in academe.

A much more productive assessment for first-year writing students might ask them not to imagine themselves as writers but to examine the voices that populate their speaking, writing, and thinking. Take the Elbow and Belanoff exercise cited above and imagine this shift in emphasis away from the voice of "writer" to the polyphony of voices: "In what different ways (or roles) do you think of yourself? What are the characteristics of each of these roles and how do they impinge upon your writing? Can you think of your writing as made up of the voices of others that have influenced you?" By asking students to explore and valorize their various speaking subjectivities, composition teachers will have begun the task of introducing students to the tensions and complexities of coming to voice(s). As composition teachers, we must call into question our practice of asking students to image themselves as writers and our assumption that the expository writing classroom is a community of writers. As a writing instructor and as a person who writes, I find that I must turn to other more complex ways of defining who we are as we write in the academy, regardless of our disciplinary affiliations.

As Suellynn Duffey, then director of the First-Year Writing Program at Ohio State, introduced the speakers at the 1995 Roundtable, she noted that we were "named in other ways: by country of origin, by motherhood, by current academic rank, and so on." And as Paul Hanstedt noted in his comments that same afternoon, "Every good writer is . . . a member of a million different communities." Understanding and acknowledging that our students often do not recognize in themselves the qualities of writer is a first step in questioning the prevailing assumptions about writing classrooms as communities of writers. The second step is complicating "our efforts to liberate student voices" by constructing a "carefully theorized understanding of the ways [that] . . . power is reproduced in the classroom as a function of class, race, and gender" (Harkin and Schilb 8). By then foregrounding the various communities to which students (un)consciously and (c)overtly pledge allegiance, composition teachers may invite students to use writing as a way of celebrating, investigating, and perhaps ultimately questioning those images and communities. Composition teachers must thoroughly examine cultural assumptions about writers and writing and the way in which these assumptions influence how, why, and even whether we write.

# TWO

# Audience, Addressivity, and Answerability

A very commonly held opinion has it that the listener is to be regarded as
equal to the author, excepting the latter's technical performance, and that
the position of a competent listener is supposed to be a simple reproduction
of the author's position. In actual fact this is not so. Indeed, the opposite
may sooner be said to be true. The listener never equals the author.

—V. N. Volosinov

Once a stable referent, *audience* has become fractured into *audiences*, into
a not-always-peaceable and too-often-fragmented kingdom of terms, complete with colorful relatives, feuding rivals, strange bedfellows, and new arrivals turning up each month.

—Jack Selzer

These quotations, the first taken from Volosinov's "Discourse in Life and Discourse in Art" and the second from Selzer's "More Meanings of *Audience*,"
demonstrate two pivotal elements in understanding audience (listener, reader)
in a postmodern age. Volosinov points to the generative capabilities of the listener in his role as co-creator of discourse while Selzer articulates the explosion
in theorizing about those audiences. The two together form a compelling backdrop for a discussion of audience in composition studies, for the discipline has
come to realize the powerful agency of audience and its effect on discourse. At
the same time, perhaps because of its realization of the active role of audience
in the construction of discourse, the field of composition studies has been pre-
occupied with defining just what or who audience is for students writing in
composition classrooms. Along with these two central concerns, compositionists have found themselves struggling with several other complex questions regarding audience, namely, (1) how do the confines of the composition classroom headed by an instructor as evaluator complicate the notion of writing
for an audience, (2) how can students best analyze audience, and (3) how can
a teacher most successfully represent to students his own understanding(s) of
audience?

In an effort to address these and other related issues regarding audience, I begin this chapter by outlining some of the work on audience in composition studies: Ede and Lunsford, Ong, Park, Selzer, Thomas, and others provide a view of the conflicted understanding(s) of audience in the field, some of the "colorful relatives, feuding rivals, strange bedfellows, and new arrivals" that Selzer mentions. Some of these articulations of audience are echoed in the work of both Volosinov and Bakhtin. Their metaphors of addressivity, creative understanding, immanent listener, superaddressee, and intertextuality come together to construct an interactive and dialogic relationship between writer and reader and reader and text. The Bakhtinian audience functions neither as an "equal to the author" nor a receiver of the discourse but as a coauthor of discourse.

After outlining the Bakhtinian understanding of listener (audience) and emphasizing the ways that intertextuality creates a more diachronic notion of audience, I turn to more detailed discussions and analyses of the work of Elbow, Bruffee, and Bartholomae, focusing on their explicit and implicit definitions as I demonstrate that several notions of audience inform their pedagogies. As one might expect, Elbow assumes an internalized audience through which an author acts as his own reader in order to anticipate an immediate reader's response. Bruffee, like Bakhtin, focuses on the metaphor of conversation when discussing audience. For Bruffee, however, the metaphor functions as a means of critical testing and improving discourse while for Bakhtin it remains a metaphor of the process of cooperative meaning-making in which, on a theoretical level, at least, consensus is not only discouraged but also dangerous, for when discussion and conversation end in either agreement or annihilation, the process of discovering meaning also ends. Bartholomae takes another approach to characterizing audience. By limiting audience to a particular "discourse" community, and in the case of writing students, that community is the academy, he names the classroom teacher as the community's representative. In both closing and continuing the discussion about audience, the chapter looks to the ways that current thought might be productively revised to (1) define audiences in terms of their relationships with the writer and subjects of discourse and (2) make explicit the role of the teacher as an evaluative audience and the implications of that role.

## THE AUDIENCE IN COMPOSITION STUDIES

"What exactly are the differences and relationships between 'evoked' and 'invoked' audiences?" Jack Selzer asks,

> [o]r between "narratees" and "implied readers"? Or between "demographic" and "fictionalized" audiences? Or between "fictionalized," "intended," "ideal," "inscribed," and "universal" audiences? What is the difference between "audience" and "discourse community"? What do technical writing textbooks mean by "multiple audiences"? Is it useful to conceive of audiences and readers as distinct

entities? How do texts signal the differences among all of these characters? And how does one devise a pedagogy for "audience" that would improve reading and writing? (161)

As Selzer's series of questions suggests, to define audience for students in composition classrooms or imagine a pedagogy that addresses the various audiences that impinge upon their writing in the university is a difficult task. Even what appears to be fairly simple—distinguishing between audience and discourse community—can prove formidable. As Selzer notes, a "discourse community is something broader than audience" (172), yet as Martin Nystrand demonstrates, the differences between the two constructs are also informed by historical, disciplinary, and contextual differences. Disciplinary lines between linguistics and rhetoric, however, do not in themselves resolve the conflicts within composition studies regarding audience, for while Nystrand articulates distinctions between audience and discourse community, he does not examine differences of opinion regarding audience in composition studies. Within the field, interpretations of audience differ, as Selzer's questions suggest, ranging from an "audience invoked" or "intended" to an "audience addressed."

The definitions, summaries, and commentary that follow are not intended as an exhaustive survey of current research on audience. Instead, this survey is intended to provide a glimpse into the ongoing attempts in composition studies to come to terms with audience.

## Defining Audience

Lisa Ede and Andrea Lunsford's 1984 "Audience Addressed/Audience Invoked: The Role of Audience in Composition Theory and Pedagogy" still serves as a benchmark in scholarship on audience in composition studies, in part because the authors draw a clearly defined distinction between two types of audience that continue to serve as the foundation for discussions in many composition textbooks. Ede and Lunsford discuss audience by outlining the debate over its definition in practice. Is the audience of a writer's discourse the actual audience (addressed) or the fictional audience (invoked)? Scholars in the debate articulate competing definitions that Ede and Lunsford claim must be integrated to provide a writer with a complete concept of audience that will assist him in creating an effective discourse. According to Ede and Lunsford, the audience addressed is perceived by many scholars as a "concrete reality," as an actual reader of a text.

In addition, these scholars "share the assumption that knowledge of this audience's attitudes, beliefs, and expectations is not only possible (via observation and analysis) but essential" (156). That is, by determining an audience's vital statistics (age, gender, race, religion, political partisanship, and so on), a writer is better able to project that audience's expectations for and responses to a particular discourse strategy. Such an audience analysis, however, does little to assist the writer vis-a-vis "invoked" audience. Invoked audience, like the "fictional" audience of Ong, is constructed and created in the discourse itself. That is, the "role or roles the writer wishes the reader to adopt in responding to the text" are written in, encoded in the discourse (Ede and Lunsford 160). The invoked audience, then, informs the text and may be determined through the text. Ede and Lunsford end by arguing for synthesizing both addressed and invoked audiences, which provides, they argue, a more complex understanding of the term.[1]

Although these two categories may oversimplify the distinctions and hide the variations among varieties of audience, they nevertheless provide a starting point for the discussion that follows. Questions form immediately: What happens if the audience addressed is not homogeneous? Who is the "real" reader of a college essay—the addressed (intended) audience (e.g., the ACLU, Young Republicans), the invoked audience, or the teacher? Is a teacher an invoked or an addressed audience? Can an audience be both addressed and invoked? How can a teacher show a student the audience that is invoked in his discourse?

### Analyzing Audience

Douglas Park, in "Analyzing Audiences," provides not only a survey of rhetorical analysis of audience, but also an understanding of audience and audience analysis necessarily set within social context. Park argues against biological and social determinants as adequate means for what he calls "traditional audience analysis" (478) in favor of a situational analysis of audience. Traditional methods of audience analysis, he argues, are intended for persuasive discourse aimed at relatively homogeneous audiences and do not provide information relevant to the possible responses of heterogeneous audiences. The most troublesome problem with traditional analyses, however, is that even if a writer knows his audience (its age, gender, social standing, and educational background), this knowledge will not provide him with an understanding of how the audience will receive and act upon a discourse. A more useful approach to analyzing audience, Park suggests, is one that determines not the static characteristics of an audience but an understanding of where an audience stands in "relation to the particular aim and issue at hand" (479). To put Park's point in more Bakhtinian terms, a writer would do well to analyze audience in relation to the speaker and his aim and to the subject being considered.

What becomes problematic, Park concludes, is not that students cannot visualize "hypothetical real people," but that they have trouble "grasping a situation in which real readers could constitute an 'audience'" (487). If no audience naturally exists, then how can teachers assist students in discovering an audience? Park responds by suggesting that students in composition courses write to real people in real contexts, such as letters to newspapers or reports to administrators. This seems a common sense alternative, and Park's rationale for it is amenable to Bakhtin's understanding of immediate and broader social contexts. A "social setting" must exist, Park argues, in which writer, audience, and discourse will interact with particular goals and functions; the audience must exist as part of the broader social context of an "institution or social relationship," and the discourse produced must "perform [an understood function] within that social relationship" (482). This understanding, in turn, provides a role for discourse.

Park does not overlook immediate context, however, for the audience must "assemble" in a particular "physical setting" (483). This setting then makes new demands on discourse, as both Park and Bakhtin claim: tone, style, structure, genre, word choice, and so on, are all affected. In yet another Bakhtinian turn, Park emphasizes the necessity of an author understanding an audience's relationship with the subject of discourse, a point I take up in greater detail in chapter 3.

## The Role of the Audience in Discourse Production

For all of these compositionists, as well as for Bakhtin, audience carries with it social, political, and theoretical meanings. In short, the audience is to one degree or another a "co-participant" in generating and composing discourse. Robert Roth and Umberto Eco characterize the audience as a creative force in a discourse as well. "The reader," Eco argues, "as an active principal of interpretation is part of the picture of the generative process of the text" (4). Eco, like Park, argues for emphasizing the "sociocultural circumstances in which a message is emitted" (5). Roth, in "The Evolving Audience: Alternatives to Audience Accommodation," suggests a contextual understanding of audience, but in turn suggests that as composing progresses, the "invoked" audience of that discourse also changes. Roth proposes that the willingness to "project oneself onto one's audience . . . may be just the capacity needed to successfully reread one's own emerging text in what George Herbert Mead calls 'the role of the other'" (50–51). In suggesting this, Roth constructs something similar to Bakhtin's notion of "creative understanding" in which a reader (or, in this case, an author taking the place of the reader) attempts sincerely to take on an "other's" perspective on a discourse. To do so, however, both Roth and Bakhtin argue, requires full and dynamic interaction of language, author, audience, and subject.

Similarly, the author, Eco argues, must "foresee a model of the possible reader . . . supposedly able to deal interpretively with the expressions in the same way the author deals generatively with them" (7). A reader's competence may be discerned in and invoked by the discourse itself. Audience is presupposed by discourse, but at the same time, the audience's competence is constructed within the text. The reader, as well as the author, is a "textual strategy" made manifest in the discourse. Note the similarity between Bakhtin's definition of author and Eco's, which follows: "The author is textually manifested only . . . as a recognizable *style* or *ideolect*—this ideolect frequently distinguishing not an individual but a genre, a social group, a historical period" (10). The writer, like the reader, is constructed, represented as a fiction in the discourse, and that representation shifts throughout the writing process. Eco's definition of reader is comparable to Bakhtin's as well: "[T]he Model Reader is a textually established set of felicity conditions . . . to be met in order to have a macro-speech act (such as a text is) fully actualized" (11). The reader exists, in other words, as he is invoked in the text. The audience of discourse is audience implied, informed, constructed, and constitutive.

### BAKHTINIAN CONCEPTIONS OF AUDIENCE

Ede and Lunsford divide audience between addressed and invoked because they perceive that the division best suits the issue of audience as it stands in composition studies. Bakhtin's concepts, while they fit these same categories fairly well, are not constructed in an attempt to find "the best way to help students recognize the significance of this critical element in any rhetorical situation" (Ede and Lunsford 155). Volosinov and Bakhtin have no such pedagogical concerns; rather they are experimenting with theoretical concepts in much the same way as Eco. Consider this quotation from Bakhtin, in which he names the varieties of audiences available to an author:

> This addressee can be an immediate participant-interlocutor ["real" reader or listener] in an everyday dialogue, a differentiated collective of specialists . . . a more or less differentiated public, ethnic group, contemporaries, like-minded people, opponents and enemies, a subordinate, a superior, someone who is lower, higher, familiar, foreign, and so forth [intended audience]. And it can also be an indefinite, unconcretized *other* [immanent audience]. ("Problem of Speech" 95)

Although Volosinov definitively states that by "listener" he does not mean "the reading public," the question of just what the audience and its function are (rather than who or what they are not) remains ambiguous. Although Volosinov refuses to acknowledge the entire "reading public" as "listener," both he and Bakhtin show a fair deal of concern for a "real" audience, for the "real" listener, as this quotation suggests.[2]

### *The Allied Audience*

Both Bakhtin and Volosinov include in their writings an understanding of the listener that assumes a set of alliances among speaker, listener, and "hero," noting in particular that no discourse can exist without its own "special conception of the listener, of his apperceptive background and the degree of his responsiveness" (Bakhtin, "Discourse" 346): "the listener normally stands *side by side* with the author as his ally, but this classical positioning of the listener is by no means always the case" (Volosinov, "Discourse in Life" 112). Every discourse, Bakhtin adds, "presupposes a specific distance [between speaker and listener]" ("Discourse" 346).[3] A speaker, in constructing a *meaningful* discourse must discern the level of background knowledge of the listener in addition to "his views and convictions, his prejudices . . . , his sympathies and antipathies" (Bakhtin, "Problem of Speech" 95–96). To what extent is the listener familiar with the subject and context of the utterance, and what is his position on it? Also of import are the relative social standing of the speaker and listener and the degree of their personal or professional relationship.[4]

The question of a listener's "apperceptive background" is repeated in "Discourse in Life and Discourse in Art." In this essay, Volosinov summarizes the relationship between speaker and listener and the common elements that must exist between them for the communicative act to be completed. Implied in his explanation is the understanding that communication cannot effectively take place outside of a shared social purview. The shared background, beliefs, experiences, and opinions help form the assumed premises of the utterance.[5] An utterance is enthymemic, Volosinov declares, and the elements of shared assumptions include both the physical surroundings of immediate context (in the case of direct conversation between speakers or of readers reading particular journals) and the

> *community of value judgements* [*sic*]—the speakers' belonging to the same family, profession, class, or other social group, and their belonging to the same time period (the speakers are, after all, contemporaries). Assumed value judgements [*sic*] are, therefore, not individual emotions but regular and essential social acts. ("Discourse in Life" 100)

The shared assumptions implied here by Volosinov may be compared to Gordon Thomas's concept of "Mutual Understanding," which is also an enthymemic construct of knowledge shared among members of a particular community. Thomas includes as a type of "Mutual Knowledge" a person's realized understanding of conventions, language, and cooperation (586–87). These shared assumptions are not limited to face-to-face conversations between speakers for either Volosinov or Thomas. Such assumptions, when expanded in time and space, form the basis of a "language sphere." Volosinov, by emphasizing shared assumptions as necessary to discourse, constructs a discourse theory whose end emphasizes the joining and strengthening of communities, of language spheres and social purviews. Because Bakhtin focuses on the listener's role of "choral support," he implicitly calls into question the purpose of discourse.[6] Are its goals those delineated by Cicero—to prove, charm, or sway? Or are they those of Augustine—to teach, delight, or move—or others not yet systematized or theoretically articulated?

In Bakhtin's work, Ciceronian and Augustinian rhetorical ends are secondary to the use of language as a means of establishing and maintaining (social, political, professional, and so on) communities. Volosinov's work on the relationship between author and audience, particularly in "Discourse in Life and Discourse in Art," reminds us that the goals of discourse are not solely those advanced by traditional agonistic rhetorics. Discourses take a ceremonial or epideictic form, calling for political, social, or cultural affirmations that transcend traditional notions of persuasion, proof, instruction, or pleasure.

In terms of allied audience, then, Bakhtin seems to have done little to forward the discussion about audience in composition studies. The Bakhtinian understanding of the allied audience takes into account, for example, neither the always already contrived nature of institutionally sponsored writing in a context (the classroom) that does not fit the typical rhetorical situation of self-sponsored writing nor the intrusive role of the teacher as audience within that specialized instructional context. Volosinov does recognize, however, that the relationship(s) among interlocutors impinge upon discourse. He concludes that because interlocutors share a "*common spatial purview,*" "*common knowledge and understanding of the situation,*" and a "*common evaluation*" of that situation, the "*situation enters into the utterance as an essential constitutive part of the structure of its import*" ("Discourse in Life" 99–100; emphasis in original). Volosinov's conclusion here interests me most with regard to the composition classroom and the problematic position of the teacher as audience-behind-the-audience. If we understand the classroom and the teacher's place in it as a part of the "situation [that] enters into the utterance as an essential constitutive part of the structure" of discourse, we begin to understand that we cannot look at the discourses students construct in first-year writing courses as *other* than constructed within and informed by that immediate context and, concurrently, that we cannot ignore the problematic nature of the teacher's role in discourse production.[7] We can no longer argue that students have written with their authentic voices untouched by the collaborative or collective influences of the classroom context or without the imprint of teachers, classmates, and institutions.

### The Immanent Audience

Bakhtinian comments on the audience of discourse might easily be misconstrued as referring to an "addressed" audience of a particular discourse if we consider only comments on allied audience. But early passages in the "Discourse in Life" make clear that the audience about which Volosinov speaks is not limited to the actual reader or interlocutor, but closely approximates Ede and Lunsford's "invoked" audience or, perhaps even more closely, Eco's "Model Reader." The immanent listener, Volosinov writes, is "an immanent participant in the artistic event who has determinative effect on the form of the work from within" ("Discourse in Life" 113). The immanent listener is no less than a socially grounded construction, an embodiment of the influences, constraints, value judgments, and cultural and conceptual horizons available to the author:

> The listener . . . is taken here as the listener whom the author himself takes into account, the one toward whom the work is oriented and who, consequently, intrinsi-

cally determines the work's structure. Therefore, we do not at all mean the actual people who in fact made up the reading public of the author in question. (110)

The immanent listener's knowledge and relative position to the speaker and to the subject are implied in the resulting discourse—in the choice of genre, devices, language, tone, and style. Audience is implied in the form and material of the discourse. Because the author may not have considered the actual readers of his discourse (those who happen to take up the text but are not intended by the author), these readers do not have a formative effect on that discourse.

Ede and Lunsford critique Ong, who, in claiming the audience is a fiction, overlooks the generative role of audience that Volosinov claims: "Ong fails adequately to recognize the constraints placed on the writer, in certain situations, by the audience. He fails, in other words, to acknowledge that readers' own experiences, expectations, and beliefs do play a central role in their reading of a text" (165). Volosinov, in contrast, recognizes audience as a determiner of discourse from before its conception. Reiterating his concept of an immanent audience (listener), Volosinov writes that, in contrast to the actual reader-listener,

> [t]his [immanent] listener . . . is an essential, intrinsic factor of the work and does not at all coincide with the so-called reading public, located outside the work, whose artistic tastes and demands can be consciously taken into account. Such a conscious account is incapable of direct and profound effect on artistic form in the process of its living creation. ("Discourse in Life" 113–14)

Again, the reading public is neither a constitutive part of the discourse nor an integral part of the dynamic relationship of author, audience, subject, and sociocultural context.

The immanent listener is, according to Volosinov, an "authorized representative" of the author's social group. Although he does not ignore the possibility of disagreement between the speaker and listener with respect to the subject of the discourse, Volosinov writes that the listener will often take on the role of ally. To conceive of audience only as actual *readers* limits the function of audience to evaluation. In addition, to imply to students that writing an essay to a particular addressed audience is to encourage them (inappropriately) to alter the discourse, its content, and/or its style merely to accommodate the audience. The loss of the immanent listener that one encounters when considering only the reading public as audience deprives the writer of the necessary force of social intercourse as well as "all sources of sustenance" and results in a discourse "devoid of any artistic productiveness" ("Discourse in Life" 114). In this, students learn to write not successful and rhetorically powerful prose but compromised discourse that, as Ede and Lunsford suggest, "tends to undervalue the responsibility a writer has to a subject" (159). By altering discourse to suit an external audience, writers undermine the role of the subject in that discourse as well—possibly compromising it to mollify a reader. "Know your audience well" may be a useful rhetorical rule of thumb; compromising in order to ingratiate that audience or to win its approval oversteps good rhetorical sense. In fact, Bakhtin argues that taking into conscious consideration the responses of a reading public *diminishes* the effectiveness of the discourse, relegating it to a "lower social level." By this Bakhtin implies that the discourse becomes mere rhetoric, seeking to please, persuade, or pander.

### The Superaddressee

The final Bakhtinian formulation of audience is articulated in Bakhtin's "Toward a Methodology for the Human Sciences" as "neither an *empirical* listener nor a psychological idea" but as an "abstract ideological formulation" that is "essentially a mirror image of the author" (165; emphasis in original). This abstract formulation, the "superaddressee," is a construct that appears in "The Problem of the Text" as a "third party" "presupposed" by the author,

> whose absolutely just responsive understanding is presumed, either in some metaphysical distance or in distant historical time (the loophole addressee). In various ages and with various understandings of the world, this superaddressee and his ideally true responsive understanding assume various ideological expressions (God, absolute truth, the court of dispassionate human conscience, the people, the court of history, science, and so forth).[8] (126)

Bakhtin's articulation of the superaddressee as the "loophole" addressee is especially appropriate, for the superaddressee rescues the utterance from the horrendous possibility of a "*lack of response*" (127; emphasis in original). Marilyn Cooper interprets the superaddressee as "the available possibility that the utterance could be understood differently" (536), understood again beyond the more immediate and temporary meaning assigned to it in any given epoch.

The superaddressee works in terms of what Bakhtin terms "great time," those long stretches of "metaphysical" or historical time. The superaddressee is a linguistic necessity, given the dialogic nature of all language and the Bakhtinian insistence that the utterance "always . . . seeks responsive understanding, and does not stop at *immediate* understanding but presses on further and further (indefinitely)," beyond temporal and spatial horizons (Bakhtin, "Problem of the Text" 127; emphasis in original). For the purposes of writing pedagogy, the superaddressee is much less critical than either the allied or immanent audience. It stands as a theoretical safeguard for Bakhtinian dialogics against claims of either endless interpretation or no interpretation. With the superaddressee Bakhtin has constructed the possibility of full responsive understanding.

### Addressivity, Intonation, Active Response, and Intertextuality

The Bakhtinian utterance, in addition to being defined in terms of particular kinds of audience, may be defined in terms of six necessary qualities: addressivity, intonation, answerability, active response, creative understanding, and intertextuality.

*Addressivity.* An essential (constitutive) marker of the utterance is its quality of being directed to someone, its *"addressivity.* . . . When constructing my utterance, I try actively to determine this [addressee's] response. Moreover, I try to act in accordance with the response I anticipate, so this anticipated response, in turn, exerts an active influence on my utterance" (Bakhtin, "Problem of Speech" 95). All discourses are characterized by addressivity, a "quality of turning to someone," and because there is "no such thing as an abstract addressee," no addressee, no audience is devoid of ideological grounding; even the most general images of an audience are determined by the author's social surroundings (99; Volosinov, "Discourse in Life" 99). That is, even an immanent audience is contextualized and ideologically driven.

The Bakhtinian concept does not neglect the self as audience, for a writer may serve as his own audience or as an "other" audience. In either case, the utterance carries with it an addressee, and the utterance can only be completed through the creative understanding and active response of that addressee. The addressee cannot passively receive the utterance but must respond to it actively. As the following quotation suggests, the Bakhtinian addressee plays an essential role in a developing discourse:

> Nothing is more perilous for aesthetics than to ignore the autonomous role of the listener. A very commonly held opinion has it that the listener is to be regarded as equal to the author, excepting the latter's technical performance, and that the position of a competent listener is supposed to be a simple reproduction of the author's position. In actual fact this is not so. Indeed, the opposite may sooner be said to be true. The listener never equals the author. The listener has *his own independent place* in the event of artistic creation; he must occupy a special, and what is more, a *two-sided* position in it—with respect to the author and with respect to the hero— and it is this position that has determinative effect on the style of an utterance. (Volosinov, "Discourse in Life" 112; emphasis in original)

The audience, because of its relationship with the author and with the subject of discourse, determines style, genre, intonation—the entire construction and structure of a discourse. Style embodies the author, his ideology, and his social orientation, and an audience's ideology influences the style of the discourse and its author. By virtue of the dialogic relationship between author and audience, the psyches and ideologies of both are affected. Compositionists write quite frequently of the ways that an author constructs or depicts an audience, but Bakhtin turns the influence around, commenting on the ways that, through the discourse, the audience constructs the author. Author and audience are depicted in the discourse; author and audience are constructed by the discourse and become "textual strategies," as Eco argues.[9] The intrapersonal dialogue, when shifted and translated onto interpersonal grounds, takes on not only the colorations of the author but also of the audience. In accommodating an audience by altering the style of discourse, an author alters himself. In creating an audience, an author also recreates a persona, an ideological ethos through which he speaks. To some extent, then, both the author and the audience are fictions established for a particular dynamic discourse within a particular context.

*Intonation.* Other Bakhtinian comments on audience also provide an interesting insight into its constitutive power, which carries with it significant influence over an utterance. The intonation of an utterance, for example, is directed in great part toward the listener. Within the context of an utterance, the listener may play one of two roles within the special set of alliances: ally of the speaker or ally of the hero. In the first of these instances, the listener provides the speaker with a "choral support" that establishes a sympathetic context and enlists the support of the listener.

On the other hand, if "no such firmly dependable 'choral support'" exists, the tone of the utterance will be quite different (Volosinov, "Discourse in Life" 102). If, for example, a person writes a letter to the local consumer protection agency telling how his home was burglarized and the robbery had gone undetected because his in-home security system failed, the letter would most likely be received by a sympathetic audience, one allied with the writer. The consumer agency would look into the complaint on the consumer's behalf, as his ally. In this case, the writer's intonation toward the subject of the utterance, the faulty system, would express anger and reproach while his intonation toward the reader would be one of trust. A second letter to the makers of the system would carry a much different intonation. In both letters, the consumer's opinion of the system is the same, but because the audience has changed, so will the intonation. Here, the makers of the alarm will most likely ally with their system, the subject of the utterance, and the consumer's relationship with them, as the audience of his correspondence, will most likely be adversarial or confrontational. In either case, however, the listener holds a pivotal position in the formation of the utterance and its tone.

The utterance, then, is defined in Bakhtinian terms by the interrelationships between and among speaker and subject, speaker and audience, and the audience and the subject. The audience's role is not, therefore, defined solely, or even primarily, by its position relative to the author, as current rhetorical analyses most often suggest, but also by its perspective on the subject of the discourse. The consumer protection agency and the makers of the home security system, for example, have a relationship with one another, one that will directly influence the reception of both letters. So not only are the writer's alliances (or dearth of alliances) with the two audiences and the subject (the faulty security system) constitutive of a discourse, so, too, is the relationship between the audiences and the subject. Again Park's comments prove relevant: Audience analysis must not concentrate on a contextualized demographic information but on the relationship between the audience and the issue under discussion.[10]

*Active Response and Creative Understanding.* Just as the author has a responsibility to create an "answerable" discourse, the audience has a responsibility to understand creatively, to respond actively. To make an utterance complete and actively intertextual, the audience is obliged to respond. The listener must creatively understand and actively respond to an utterance for dialogue to occur: "[r]esponsive understanding is a fundamental force" of all utterances, Bakhtin writes, "one that participates in the formulation of discourse, and it is moreover an *active* understanding, one that discourse senses as resistance or support enriching the discourse" ("Discourse" 280–81).[11] In actively responding, the audience necessarily contributes to the utterance.

Let me reiterate that active response does not imply acceptance, for responsive understanding does not entail agreement. The speaker delivers his utterance and receives active response in return. And the speaker himself is, in constructing a discourse, actively responding to a previous utterance, contributing to a complex hypertext of utterances. Still, this is not as simple an exchange as it may seem at first, for the speaker and his utterance face a number of obstacles. In preparing his discourse, the speaker anticipates the response of the listener; his style, composition, tone, and so on are informed by that expected active, creative response. Then, as an audience receives the utterance within its metalinguistic context, it brings with it various opinions, intonations, and alien words and meanings, many of which may not have been anticipated by the speaker. From this interaction, the audience composes a response that is framed in terms of its own beliefs. Bakhtin describes the interchange this way:

> The speaker strives to get a reading on his own word, and on his own conceptual [belief] system that determines this word, within the alien conceptual system of the understanding receiver; he enters into dialogical relationships with certain aspects of this system. The speaker breaks through the alien conceptual horizon of the listener, constructs his own utterance on alien territory, against his, the listener's, apperceptive background. ("Discourse" 282)

So just as the listener interprets the speaker's utterance in terms of his own belief system, the speaker, in actively responding to the listener's eventual response, constructs his discourse with a greater knowledge of his listener's beliefs and the sociocultural context in which the interchange takes place. Communication defined in terms of creative understanding consists of a series of dialogic utterances that form a picture puzzle of interlocking pieces of discourse.

*Intertextuality.* In her introduction to *Frankenstein*, Mary Shelley reminds us that

> [e]verything must have a beginning, to speak in Sanchean phrase; and that beginning must be linked to something that went before. The Hindus give the world an elephant to support it, but they make the elephant stand upon a tortoise. Invention, it must be humbly admitted, does not consist in creating out of void, but out of

chaos; the materials must, in the first place, be afforded: it can give form to dark, shapeless substances but cannot bring into being the substance itself. (x)

The "invention" of discourse is not a creation from nothing (a point upon which classical rhetoricians and Bakhtin alike would agree) but from chaos, the heteroglot wor(l)d. The utterance, like Frankenstein's creation, is a mosaic, a bringing together. The implication for both Frankenstein and the speaker is the same—the creation is not brought into being from nothing but from a "moulding and fashioning" of the materials present.[12] Shelley's quotation points, as well, to the intertextual nature of *all* discourse, of the forward and backward glance of any utterance, a notion that at once complicates and problematizes the notion of audience in composition studies.

Bakhtin refers to this forward and backward glance, the linking of one utterance to another as "intertextuality." A significant contribution to the notion of audience, intertextuality establishes the diachronic context of statement and response characterized by addressivity and active responsive understanding. Intertextuality might most easily be defined as a discourse's heteroglossic nature, what Julia Kristeva refers to as a "mosaic of quotations, . . . the absorption and transformation of another" (37). An utterance, then, not only looks forward to the receiving audience, but also looks backward toward inceptive one(s). Intertextuality, like heteroglossia and dialogue, is the natural condition of language interaction and interanimation. All discourse is intertextual in that it speaks *to* other utterances as well as *from* them. Every utterance is created in response to and in anticipation of other utterances, past and future.

So, to speak of audience only as those individuals to whom a spoken or written utterance is directed—as do most writers in literary and composition studies—severely limits, and in fact distorts, a rich and influential number of people and texts to which an utterance responds and from which it expects response. Bakhtin extends the notion of audience by including previous commentators or speakers who have discussed the same topic in the same language sphere. Any utterance is not only influenced in form and content by previous utterances but also directed to them in its statement. Intertextuality, in its forward and backward glance, demands that we reconstruct our understanding of audience as more than synchronic. Audience expands across time, becomes diachronic, determined and contextualized by sociocultural situations and the inherent intertextuality of the utterance.

A now familiar metaphor, "conversation," defines most accurately for Bakhtin the life of the utterance. In using a metaphor of conversation, Bakhtin addresses reception and response, the metaphoric give-and-take of dialogue. The utterance in its intertextuality is described by Bakhtin as the latest contribution to an extended conversation that has a life and memory longer than its own cultural epoch. The variety of utterances (texts) that have influenced the writing of this text, for example, may be considered as a conversation that is neither spatially nor temporally confined. I am conversing with Bakhtin, Bartholomae, Berlin, Bialostosky, Bizzell, de Man, Kinneavy, Kristeva, and others. As in a dinner conversation or an intellectual discussion, I argue with some, agree with others, and anticipate responses from still others. These responses are not necessarily direct responses to me but are instead the next round of comments on Bakhtin and composition studies. Also part of this conversation, of course, are the sophists, Aristotle, Socrates, and a host of other rhetoricians who have written on ethos and the influence of the social on discourse. The success of my utterance may then be judged by the extent to which later writers respond to it. As Bakhtin notes, an influential utterance is not so much judged by the extent to which it is accepted in its own time but by the extent to which it lives past its own epoch.

## METAPHORS OF AUDIENCE IN COMPOSITION STUDIES

Despite the work of scholars like Ede, Lunsford, Park, and Selzer, compositionists have not worked out a successful means of discussing or presenting audience in the writing classroom. As the following portraits of audience demonstrate, composition pedagogies do not sufficiently enact a postmodernist notion of audience.

### Ignoring Audience, Ignoring Authorship

Among the variety of audiences demanding the attention of student writers, Peter Elbow mentions several: those who will read the text, the writer's preconceptions about audience, an audience implied in the text, the discourse community, and "ghost or phantom 'readers in the head' that the writer may unconsciously address or try to please. . . . Classically, this is a powerful former teacher" ("Closing My Eyes" 50n). In other words, Elbow considers both addressed and invoked audiences as well as an "immanent" audience. Of the audiences listed by Elbow, the language community of the author is perhaps the closest to Bakhtin's notion of the immanent listener. But it is interesting to note that even ghost or phantom readers are unsettled representatives of a language community that is informed by ideological assumptions about a given topic. The most receptive audiences available to a writer are most often classmates. This audience, Elbow implies, does not cause much difficulty for a novice writer.

Other manifestations, however, do. In "Closing My Eyes As I Speak: An Argument for Ignoring Audience," Elbow takes a seemingly unpredictable turn in his more individualistic theoretical stance by invoking Vygotsky, Bakhtin, and Volosinov. But it soon becomes clear that Elbow cites them only to argue for "the value of learning to cultivate the private dimension: the value of writing in order to make meaning to oneself, not just to others" (60). He cites them, in other words, in order to argue that "the enormous power exerted by society and others" causes unusual difficulties for young writers (60). Certainly, institutional and social constraints do exert power over any writer's discourses, and yes, these impinge upon a student's writing. But they may also inform his writing in advantageous ways. By focusing only on the constraining elements of the languages that students must negotiate when writing (the "obscuring mist," as Bakhtin writes), Elbow ignores the generative power of those same languages. His philosophy of authorship still firmly entrenched in an individual notion of the author, Elbow remains largely suspicious of the influence of others' words on an author's discourse.

In making his case for the importance of personal writing that is initially unconcerned with audience, Elbow argues that students benefit from writing for themselves before considering audiences, particularly inhibiting audiences. Students write better, Elbow argues, when freewriting or composing journal entries unconstrained by course or instructor requirements. Elbow argues that students who produce much better freewriting than completed essays do so because they are not constrained by a topic and are not overly (or obsessively) concerned with audience ("Closing My Eyes" 53). I don't deny that many students are frustrated and hindered by the thought of an audience, but I am less inclined to agree with Elbow that the fear comes from the implied audience. I argue, in contrast, that while novice writers sometimes have difficulty writing because they are all too aware of their relative position with regard to their audiences, they are more often constrained by the ambiguity of audience rather than its formidable nature. They are also constrained, even paralyzed, by public writing because they are unfamiliar with the contexts and conventions of the genres in which their teachers ask them to write.

A student writing an informative essay that is intended to direct a hypothetical incoming first-year student through the intricacies of registration at a major university is less likely to be intimidated by a real student reading his essay than by the audience-behind-the-audience, his instructor. Inside the classroom, this essay has no real rhetorical purpose; it is an exercise, not a discourse.[13] If the student were writing an informative article for the campus newspaper or a university student handbook, however, his work might then create some anxiety for him; but I submit that anxiety has less to do with finding and addressing a particular audience than with publication. A student writing in any course whose goal does not reach outside the classroom must always consider the teacher his most immediate (and sometimes most intimidating) audience. A peer response group may also evoke such concern if a course is structured in such a way as to involve peer editing, reading drafts aloud, and peer evaluation of student work. My point remains the same, however; the invoked and addressed audiences will not in and of themselves constrain a student writer. Behind the frustration always rests the paradox of writing for a fictional audience when the immediate audience is one's peers or an instructor.

Although students clearly struggle with understanding audience, it is not audience alone but the combination of unknown or foreign, immediate, and broader social contexts that cause most difficulties. I would argue, as Bartholomae does, for an alternative understanding of students' inability to write successful "public" prose. Students produce ineffective public prose (analyses, explanations, or critiques) not because they are freed from a constraining topic or audience but because they are unfamiliar with the discourse of the classroom, the demands of academic prose, and the codes of the dominant social collective, the university. Certainly, audience and subject play a role in the way that any student goes about writing, but to argue that these are the primary culprits in students' inability to produce *public* prose is specious.

Most damaging to Elbow's essay on audience is his conflation of audience and social context. Elbow implies that peer responders and immediate context are synonymous when he writes that Vygotskians view students as "just congeries of voices that derive from their discourse community. Ergo, let's intensify the social context—use peer groups and publication: make them think about audience when they write!" ("Closing My Eyes" 57). Certainly, the students who critique one another's essays are part of the immediate audience, but they do not make up the entire social context in which a student writes. The "congeries of voices" that make up a writer's voice, first of all, do not come from a single language community. Rather, the voices of any one individual come from numerous language spheres, from many communities. Second, the classroom in which peer groups are set is not a complete social context. It is, rather, only a part of the larger social context of the university and of other social contexts. Elbow accepts a premise that appears consistent with one forwarded by Bakhtin. Elbow writes that John Trimbur clarifies for him Bakhtin's and Vygotsky's understanding of audience when Trimbur notes that,

> audience is not really out there at all but is in fact 'always already' . . . inside, interiorized in the conflicting languages of others—parents, former teachers, peers, prospective readers, whomever—that writers have to negotiate to write, and that we do negotiate when we write whether we're aware of it or not. The audience we've got to satisfy . . . is as much in the past as in the present or future. (61)

What Elbow's interpretation of Trimbur overlooks is that these previous voices—whether they are past teachers, parents, or others who have spoken or written about the subject at hand (a potential and vital audience omitted by both Trimbur and Elbow)—are more than censors; they are coauthors of the discourse whose roles are generative, not merely evaluative.

### Audience as Commentator

One of the guiding metaphors of Kenneth Bruffee's work is the construct of collaborative learning as "conversation." Bruffee borrows the term from Michael Oakeshott who argues that not only discourse, but also education is best defined in terms of conversation.[14] In this conversation, however, it is the educator's *mandate* to initiate the conversation and initiate students into the "skill and partnership of this conversation" ("Collaborative" 638). Bruffee's concerns and goals for writing instruction are similar to Bartholomae's: An instructor must assist students in achieving the level and type of discourse worthy of the conversation they are entering. They must learn to construct what Rorty has called "normal" discourse. Yet, despite their common goals, Bruffee and Bartholomae differ in the ways that they attain the desired results. Certainly, Bartholomae supports collaborative learning as a useful and perhaps irreplaceable classroom strategy, but Bruffee proposes it as a "particular kind of social context" through which students most successfully attain an understanding of and facility with a community's conversation.

Bruffee's pedagogy is informed by a number of Bakhtinian notions of audience and the relationship between writer and reader as co-participants in the construction of discourse. The collaborative classroom, in fact, externalizes and makes explicit the author-reader relationship implied in the Bakhtinian notion of the utterance as constructed on interindividual territory. At every turn of the page, Bruffee's text insists on a dialogue between writer and reader. In fact, the general construction of his writing text, *A Short Course in Writing*, revolves around a series of drafts, peer responses, writer's responses to peers, and a second round of peer responses. "Conversation" takes place in the form of responses to writing. When articulating to students their roles in the collaborative classroom, Bruffee writes that they should "focus primarily on what each other has to say" and "examine the ways other students and they themselves make judgments and arrive at decisions" (*Short Course* 6). The collaborative classroom urges students to interact by providing an environment that allows them to observe the writing and thinking processes of others. This second function is for Bruffee the key to successful collaborative learning. Students, through observing others thinking and writing, will learn more about their own processes and perhaps adapt those processes by adopting other, more useful strategies modeled by other students. "Learning," Bruffee concludes, "is largely the result of changes in the kinds of relationships that occur among the students involved" (6). In other words, as relationships between readers and writers—and, specifically, among peers in a writing class—grow and change, knowledge is generated and writing improves.

Bruffee clearly understands the power of the reader-writer relationship to affect knowledge. Yet, his implied claim that this is best achieved in a collaborative classroom assumes too much. Gregory Clark's characterizations of Bakhtin's comments on dialogue and response serve to contextualize my criticism of Bruffee:

> Bakhtin rejects . . . discourse that "pretends to be the last word". . . . Instead, he celebrates discourse that acknowledges itself as incomplete, as the partial perception of one, as a statement that joins other incomplete statements expressing diverging ideologies in a dialogue where each is held answerable for itself in the interaction of assertion and response. In this dialogue all statements are exposed

to the collaborative process of judgment, revision, and redefinition that enables people to construct beliefs and values they can genuinely share. (10)

I do not wish to suggest that Bruffee is attempting to apply Bakhtinian principles in his work. He does not make such a claim. Bruffee is, however, aware of Bakhtin's work; he cites Bakhtin as a theorist influential in the formulation of social constructivist thought.[15] In his pedagogy, Bruffee enacts the "collaborative process of judgment, revision, and redefinition" about which Clark writes. Because the community of a writing classroom is not one based on shared beliefs, the collaboration that results does not redefine judgments, world views, or values so much as it refines sentence-level writing strategies. The transient and ephemeral nature of the community of the writing classroom, coupled with students' inexperience with peer response and other strategies of the collaborative classroom, presents obstacles difficult for many instructors to surmount. In addition, the students themselves are ignorant and suspicious of the rationale for collaboration. The concerns of some students may be alleviated by an instructor willing to discuss the complexities of conversation and community, but still many will remain unconvinced of the value of collaboration, arguing that they are not knowledgeable enough to assist themselves, much less others.

Toby Fulwiler addresses these very issues of authority, community, and educational responsibility when writing about the students he encountered during his early experiences teaching first-year writing. Students were not, he recalls, prepared to write to one another as an audience: "[t]hey came to my class after being schooled for 12 years, yet they had never learned to write for one another; to read their own writing to others; to listen seriously to what their classmates wrote; to give and receive positive criticism." His experience—one very common to college composition teachers—underscores the difficulty students have with even the most basic strategies of collaborative learning. At the same time, Fulwiler pinpoints the most critical shortcomings of the traditional teacher-centered classroom; it does not prepare students to address one another effectively as an audience. Collaborative learning pedagogies like Bruffee's may help students overcome these difficulties, but again we must ask, is it the goal of college level writing to prepare students to write for one another or for some other audience—an academic one, for instance? Bruffee argues that the goal of writing education is a part of the entire mission of the university to "induct people into the mores and values of the 'state'" ("Kenneth" 77). In achieving this end, Bruffee turns to collaborative learning, which requires of the student a social responsibility within the class that is comparable to the responsibility he must bear in society. A student is first and foremost an active member of a community. He and his peers are authors and critics, writers and readers. Unfortunately, in Bruffee's work, collaboration—as the *means* to more effective writing—overshadows the desired end—improved student writing.

Let me rearticulate several of my concerns. First, although the writing classroom is certainly a "particular kind of social context," it does not resemble a social context outside the academy, or even outside first-year writing courses in English departments. Second, Bruffee, like Elbow, suggests that the classroom community is made up of "status equals." Such is not the case. Students bring with them all sorts of prejudices and preconceived hierarchies, and these are not mysteriously absent from the writing classroom. Third, the "community" that is developed there in no way "approximates the one most students must eventually write for in everyday life, in business, government, and the professions" (Bruffee, "Collaborative" 642). These language spheres are indeed constructed around conversations essential to their institutional vitality, but they are not the models of community reflected in the collaborative writing classroom.

Because students actively participate more in a collaborative classroom than in a traditional lecture-based course, the success of the collaborative class depends upon the students. In the collaborative classroom, daily activities focus on the writing produced and critiqued by the students, not on the process of writing or on the teacher's evaluation of that writing. As the audience shifts from the teacher to the editorial groups, the students are undeniably empowered; they begin to understand the power of language, personal commentary, and their own responses to others' writing. But the teacher still exists as an audience and evaluator; so long as grading remains part of his role, a teacher cannot be merely a facilitator.

In the collaborative classroom, collaborative learning proponents might argue, students now actively participate in their own writing education: students discuss their work with others; explain their subject and audience selection; defend word choices, personal opinions, organization; discuss changes in format, alterations in means of support; and come to consensus with their peers. They see immediately the reactions of an audience to their words; they field questions, clarify ambiguities, and discuss the alternatives accepted and rejected in drafting their papers. Simply put, their levels of writing consciousness are raised. This scenario of a collaborative writing classroom does *not* depict meaning-making; it illustrates peer editing. These students are not finding new ways of seeing; they are finding answers to immediate questions. Certainly, such improvements are important. For students to discuss writing and learn to foresee problems in their work as a result of peer response is invaluable. Still, what is happening here is not analogous to what happens when members of an academic discipline or business people come together as a community to discuss their concerns.

### The Academy as Audience

Bartholomae writes in "Inventing the University" that "every time a student sits down to write for us, he has to invent the university for the occasion— invent the university, that is, or a branch of it, like history or anthropology or economics or English" (134). Volosinov makes a similar claim that "an utterance is something like a 'password' known only to those who belong to the same social purview" ("Discourse in Life" 101). In this description, we begin to see the near absolute power the academic audience has on student writing. The university functions as an overarching academic discourse community within which exist individual discourse communities defined by academic pursuits, departments, areas, or emphases. In the cases of student writers—and basic writers in particular—gaining admission into a discourse community within academia is the first and most crucial step toward acceptance into the white collar worlds of business or graduate and professional schools.

Bartholomae goes much further than either Elbow or Bruffee in setting out the political and social implications of students writing in the university. For Elbow, the social is embodied in the restrictive mandates murmured in the recesses of a writer's unconscious. For Bruffee, the peer group functions as a microcosm of social interaction, group dynamics, and intellectual problem solving. And although in the end I argue that Bartholomae does not go far enough in setting out the political agenda of the university and the writing classroom, he, along with Patricia Bizzell, introduces to composition studies the influence of the social collective, the university as a social institution, and the need to study the university's effects on student writing. In Bartholomae's work, the audience for student writing is the teacher who reads as a member of the academic discourse community generally and as a member of a discipline specifically. The teacher as audience, then, reads as literary critic, historian, or anthropologist, embodying the codes, nuances, and demands of that academic community's discourse(s). This may call up the old "teacher as gatekeeper" metaphor, but Bartholomae's intent is quite different. Instead of restricting students' entrance into the academy, the teacher takes on the role of one who initiates others into a new field or activity.[16]

### *Teacher as Initiator, Student as Pledge*

If we accept that Bartholomae's assumption is correct, that a student does in fact "invent the university" when he begins to write, we can also assume that, along with inventing the social construct, he invents an audience as well. The audience, it seems safe to say, is most often the instructor in that student's course, the evaluator of that student's writing or perhaps Elbow's past teachers. Bartholomae goes on to say that along with constructing the university, the student writer must learn elements that might be included as part of the "Mutual Knowledge" of which Thomas writes. In addition to inventing the university, the student must also "learn to speak our language, . . . to try on the peculiar ways of knowing, selecting, evaluating, reporting, concluding, and arguing that define the discourse of our community" ("Inventing" 134). In other words, the student must become schooled in those assumed premises or passwords that exist behind the assumptions and enthymemes that make up a great deal of language convention and presentation in academic settings.

A quotation from Volosinov bears repeating here: "Thus, every utterance in the business of life is an objective social enthymeme. It is something like a 'password' known only to those who belong to the same social purview" ("Discourse in Life" 101). The concept of an utterance as a social enthymeme does, of course, work two ways. On the one hand, students engage one another in discourse within a language sphere that excludes the professor, for which he has no password. On the other, these students do not know the password that will open the door to the language of the academy for them, and it is the teacher who stands at that door. The teacher as initiator seems to describe accurately one of the functions of a college writing instructor, for we are most often those upon whom the fates of many of our students rest. Not only must they pass our classes to gain official status within the university community, but they must also, as Bartholomae points out, understand the life and workings of university language communities.

Mike Rose characterizes the type of student of whom Bartholomae writes in "Inventing the University" as one who has not achieved control over academic discourse. In describing his own experiences with language, Rose recalls that

> I continually misused words and wrote fragments and run-on sentences and had trouble making my pronouns agree with whatever it was that preceded them. . . . I was struggling to express increasingly complex ideas, and I couldn't get the language straight: Words . . . piled up like cars in a serial wreck. I was encountering a new language—the language of the academy—and was trying to find my way around in it. (*Lives* 53–54)

To achieve a sense of power within the alien language sphere is, as Rose's experiences indicate, much more complex and difficult than simply pointing out the differences between the languages students bring to the classroom and those that they must master before leaving it. The problem of power, however, exists in a number of different relationships. The student writer must gain authority over the text *and* within the academy. The latter, I propose, is contingent upon the first. As a reader's relationship with a text changes, Bartholomae writes, so, too, do his relationships with others. A student gains a position within the academy and in relation to his instructors only as he gains authority—as a reader and writer—over texts. To do this, Bartholomae argues, the student must make the texts his own, altering them and at the same time rejecting their implied or assumed authority. In doing this, the student redefines himself, texts, and his audience through his reading and a growing understanding of a community's discourses. The hierarchical relationship between student and instructor will not dissolve as a student gains more and more facility with the discourses of academia. That is not to say that the relationship does not shift; it does. As students gain a greater sense of control over texts, they feel more free to respond to them, other students' comments, and even their instructors.[17] As students' understanding of texts improves, so does their understanding of what it means to become part of the academy. They redefine themselves, then, *in terms of* their audiences, in terms of the academy. When this occurs, the role of the audience shifts as well.

### AUDIENCE IN THE CLASSROOM:
### LAYING BARE THE PLAY OF POWER

The problems surrounding audience—what it is, which audience is most appropriate for student writers to consider as they write, how to present audience(s) in the writing classroom—are not easily resolved. Nor, perhaps, should we attempt to resolve them, for if audience is as diverse and dynamic a construct as Bakhtin would have us believe, we may do well not to overly systematize or quantify it. Whether immanent, addressed, invoked, or fictional, audience is vexing and elusive. A few things remain clear, however. Audience cannot successfully be determined by a simple listing of such static characteristics as age, gender, class, or race, as Ede and Lunsford imply and as both Park and Bakhtin explicitly argue. Nor can audience be successfully or usefully analyzed apart from its relationship to the writer, the subject, and the immediate and broader social situations in which an utterance takes place. Audience extends beyond the individual psyche and into a sociocultural context. To restrict that context to the immediate situation in a writing class as do both Elbow and Bruffee is to minimize the dynamics of the larger social context and its influence on students as they come together to discuss their ideas. Such a restriction makes synchronous a phenomenon that is inherently diachronic and utterly intertextual.

The writer stands at the threshold between past and future discourses. To imply—as I do here by discussing intertextuality as a function of audience— that Bakhtin necessitates a redefinition of audience is to argue that the writer, as he writes, is both author and audience. Moreover, previous discourses determine a discourse and may be said to "coauthor" a text. Such a diachronic understanding of audience emphasizes the intertextual nature of discourse as well as the answerability and responsibility of the author as he enters the conversation of a given social group. Even a teacher who, as an audience, acts as a guide to students seeking admission to more specialized language spheres must realize and articulate the intertextual nature of all utterances, as well as a particular discipline's discursive conventions and constraints, if he is to usher his charges successfully into the academy.

Selzer's question bears repeating here: "Where does all of this leave the teacher in search of the meanings of *audience*?" Selzer suggests that "it might be best to end by smoothing over the distinctions a bit" (172). With regard to the debates underway regarding distinctions between invoked, addressed, and fictional audiences, and so on, I'm inclined to agree with Selzer. The terms are so obtuse and indistinct that students would surely become confused. Selzer makes this statement with pedagogy clearly in mind. What would students gain, he might also have asked, by becoming informed about these various conceptions of audience? My answer to that question is, very simply, not much. Selzer's own three constructs—intended reader, "reader in the text," and "real" reader—are relatively discrete entities that define readership quite productively. But they still do not get to that central issue of the teacher as audience-behind-the-audience in the classroom, which remains for me the central issue with regard to audience in composition studies. In every case, when a student writes a classroom essay, teachers, peers, or academic communities remain as possible audiences. The question of finding an audience for an expository college essay proves problematic for students' writing. Ideally, in defining audience, instructors intend to clarify to whom their students are writing, but the complexities of the academic and classroom contexts make that definition especially difficult, and the current scholarship on audience does not take us very far in addressing this issue. Neither does it address the intertextual nature of audience nor the effects of previous readers on students' discourses.

By way of responding concretely to Selzer's question about where all of the theorizing on audience leaves us, let me articulate a somewhat defined plan for instructing students about the various *uses* of audience available to them as they compose. I refer to these constructs as uses of audience because I imagine that each of the constructs functions as a heuristic for students as they compose. I do not intend these as categories describing kinds of audiences so much as I intend them as a means by which students might articulate various readerships and engage those audiences as they write. I have defined for my own instruction the following six audiences—projected, previous, immediate, textual, public, and evaluative—which I describe to students in much the way I outline them here.[18]

### Projected Audience

Although all of the audiences serve heuristic ends, the first two—projected and previous—serve students best when considered as a means of initiating and sustaining the composing process. The first of these uses, the projected audience, functions initially, like Selzer's intended reader, as a heuristic, a means of defining how to go about devising a text. A student writing an essay can benefit from making more explicit to himself a projected audience, one that assists him as he develops a text. As composing progresses, the student might use the projected audience as a way of testing the efficacy of particular lines of argument or methods of organization.[19] Such a projected audience then conditions the developing text.

As I wrote *A Pedagogy of Possibility*, I worked with a variety of projected audiences, each with its own demands and expectations for a theoretical text on composition studies, and some were more successful in assisting me as I wrote. When I imagined postmodern theorists of composition as an audience, for example, I struggled to construct a text I believed would be persuasive, so I reconfigured my projected audience and redefined who I held in my mind as readers. As I refined my goals and my understanding of my projected audience, I found a more comfortable audience in classroom teachers—those readers who are interested in composition theory but only insofar as it has direct bearing on their pedagogy. By projecting this audience for myself, I was able to foreground one of my central concerns in the book: bringing theory to bear on the classroom and, perhaps more importantly, making theory answerable to pedagogy. By projecting classroom teachers as my audience, I simultaneously reinserted myself into the text as author and audience. I am not a postmodern theorist, and when writing with this group as a projected audience, I found little room to define my own authority, as there is very little I feel I can say to postmodern theorists about theory. Shifting the projected audience to classroom teachers put me on more comfortable ground, in part because I define myself professionally as a teacher as opposed to a theorist. By instructing students to project an audience for their writing, composition teachers arrange for students a strategy for imagining an audience that is at once forgiving and demanding—an audience that enables them to write a successful draft.

*Previous Audience*

Analogous to the previous voices that have spoken on a given topic, the *previous audience* is always already a coauthor of the text. A text is addressed not only to projected, immediate, public, and evaluative audiences, it is also addressed to those voices who are a part of a conversational history. *A Pedagogy of Possibility* is a response to Bakhtin, Bartholomae, Berlin, Bruffee, Ede and Lunsford, Elbow, Selzer, Volosinov, et al. In many ways, I write to this previous audience as much as I write to my projected or public audience (and, in fact, some members of this previous audience will very likely become part of my public audience). The *previous audience*, like the projected audience, serves a heuristic function. These scholars provide me ways of thinking about and actively engaging their ideas, and their work informs my own utterances about writing instruction. By urging students to imagine and articulate previous audiences for their writing, a composition teacher offers his students the opportunity to become part of a larger collective of thinkers and writers concerned about a particular topic. Previous audiences are also powerful reminders of the complexity of subjects and, as such, serve as useful heuristics for determining the variety of sources for and stances on a given subject.

Patricia Bizzell and Bruce Herzberg's *Negotiating Difference: Cultural Case Studies for Composition* enacts this intertextuality of previous voice and establishes in its very approach to history, historiography, and composition the intertextual nature of all writing.[20] The text includes what Bizzell and Herzberg (after Mary Louise Pratt) refer to as case studies of "contact zones," those volatile points in American history that set citizens against one another in political, moral, and racial clashes. In each of the case studies (e.g., the women's sphere of the nineteenth-century, the Japanese internment, Vietnam), Bizzell and

Herzberg present contemporary primary sources that speak to the issues at hand. The case study on the Japanese internment, for example, includes Franklin Roosevelt's 1942 executive order that "provide[d] the legal basis for internment," a 1942 public notice of evacuation, a 1943 Department of War report on the immanent threat of Japanese living on the West Coast, a 1940s legal challenge to the internment, selections from over half a dozen testimonials from interned citizens ranging in date of publication from 1953 to 1987, and a 1982 report from the U.S. Commission on Wartime Relocation and Internment of Civilians that "concludes that the internment was both unnecessary and unjust" (xxii–xxiv). As students work from these readings into assignment sequences on "What is 'assimilation'?" "What is 'race'?" and "How could this happen in the United States?" they have already encountered previous voices on the subject that become previous audiences for them as they write about assimilation, race, and American domestic policy.

In addition to the published voices of the primary documents, Bizzell and Herzberg encourage students to seek out other previous voices and audiences through the JACL, internment museums, and historical societies as they initiate research projects that examine such suggested subjects as white racism, the Sansei, the treatment of German Americans during the Second World War, and the relationships between the internment and government policy toward American Indians.

### Immediate Audience

Because students might choose to write about a subject about which they have already formed an opinion or, conversely, about which they are relatively uninformed, the *immediate audience* of a student's essay is particularly important to a student who is attempting to construct previous audiences and compose a draft that both responds to those voices and accounts for the responsive understanding of the projected audience. For students writing in a classroom that utilizes collaborative peer groups, the immediate audience might best be described as that group of living readers in classrooms who work with one another on composing, revising, and editing their texts.[21] The immediate audience serves three general functions, the first of which is generative: assisting the author in exploring and engaging previous audiences. The second function of the immediate audience is more evaluative: it serves (insofar as it can) as a mock public and/or evaluative audience. In this second function, the immediate audience responds to a text *as if it were* the public or evaluative audience in an effort to determine whether the text will be successful when brought before the public and/or evaluative audiences.

The immediate audience as I imagine it is not a microcosm of a discourse community, nor does it constitute a community in its own right as Bruffee and others suggest. What is more, this immediate audience—like any projected, public, or evaluative audience—can only be defined productively in terms of its relationship to the author and the subject of the discourse. An immediate audience, in all its various responses to a given essay, reminds the author that demographics alone tell him very little about audience response. That is, even as readers in an immediate audience work with an author to construct an essay that will be effective when brought before a public or evaluative audience, their responses, too, are informed by their social purviews and their ideological assumptions and biases. The student must recognize, then, that the nexus of power relations among his classmates affect the readings that they offer. He must respond to those readings with an understanding of each one as informed by a particular way of seeing him and interpreting the subject of his discourse. Because members of the immediate audience might also be part of the projected audience or even the public audience, their responses are important, even telling.

### Textual Audience

The third function of the immediate audience is *analytical*. In addition to working with the author to determine the conversational history of his subject as a mock public or evaluative audience, the immediate audience also serves to analyze the features of the discourse, to determine the *textual audience* of the piece. In contrast to the intended reader, Selzer describes the "reader in the text" (what I here am using as a basis for textual audience) as an amalgam of "inscribed" or "ideal" readers, those readers who, through their influence on a text via conventions, determine the shape of a text, its generic, rhetorical, and stylistic forms. That is, the form an essay takes, while determined and informed in part by the projected and previous audiences, is also determined and informed by the conventions and demands of the textual audience. By articulating a textual audience, students, with the assistance of an immediate audience, begin to unearth the ways that the social collective, the textual audience, impinges upon the discourse through the conventions it follows—its generic, stylistic, and rhetorical features.

In these three roles, the immediate audience takes on a particular significance, for it functions in generative, evaluative, and analytical roles that are pivotal for the author as he strives to construct a successful discourse. Because of these roles, I use peer response groups in the composition classroom. The success of the groups, moreover, is determined largely by the clarity and effectiveness with which I articulate their functions. That is, when a peer group understands that its goal during a peer response session is to function in a generative, evaluative, or analytical capacity, that group is more likely to give productive feedback. The teacher, when responding to an early draft of an essay (or any piece of writing that he does not grade), may also serve as an immediate audience. To define himself as an immediate audience as he responds to drafts of essays is, in fact, a useful way of demonstrating the difference between that role and his second role as an evaluative audience, but it does not dissolve the problematic evaluative relationship altogether. The teacher as immediate audience is fraught with complications. Any teacher who uses peer response knows that students very often consider a teacher's comments on a draft more closely than the responses of peers. Students are clearly aware of the possible implications of not heeding the advice of an instructor who responds as an immediate audience. Selectively heeding the advice of peers carries with it comparatively minor consequences for a student.

## Public Audience

More and more frequently compositionists, such as Douglas Park and Irene Ward, are calling for students to write for audiences outside the classroom, for *public* audiences to whom students will forward completed copies of their work. These compositionists base their argument on a reasonable rhetorical principle: Students who compose discourses that have a real and defined purpose compose more meaningful, productive discourses. Classroom discourses, they argue, which do not reach a public audience, which do not move toward Freirean action are, by contrast, mere exercises in proficiency. Even some of the most accomplished compositionists do not escape Ward's critique on this account. Ira Shor's work, she argues, in fact "reveals how Freirean theory can be misused and how a true dialogic approach can be undermined even in the name of dialogic pedagogy" (104). Ward's complaints about Shor's Freireanism revolve around the "Monday Morning: Critical Literacy and the Theme of 'Work'" chapter in Shor's *Critical Teaching and Everyday Life*. Ward argues that Shor's "dialogic" pedagogy (a term that Ward, not Shor, uses) as it is represented in "Monday Morning" fails to construct teacher and students as equals or direct students' writing toward Freirean action. Instead, Ward writes, "Shor has moved away from his students' 'everyday lives' and on to his own academic interests" (109) and in doing so has not allowed them the opportunity to define for themselves the public audiences for their writing.

Ward presents a public audience success story in her review of an essay by Kyle Fiore and Nan Elsasser that recounts one of Elsasser's college writing classes at the College of the Bahamas. In this class, Elsasser constructed a classroom informed by many of the dialogic principles Ward demands, among which is articulating a "clear rhetorical purpose" (124) as the "students intervene in their social environment by writing an open letter to the men of the Bahamas that was eventually carried in both daily newspapers" (126). Elsasser encouraged the students to compose a discourse intended for a public audience, one that had a productive effect. In considering a public audience as she writes, a student must take into account and explicitly explore the relationship between the public audience and author and between the public audience and the subject of the discourse.

*Audience, Addressivity, and Answerability*

*Evaluative Audience*

The *evaluative audience*, what I have referred to until now as the audience-be-hind-the-audience, is a function of the writing classroom but not unique to it. Professional writers, researchers, business people, and others who compose documents that must pass the approval of colleagues or supervisors before reaching their public audiences face an evaluative audience. The stakes, although not the same for all of these writers, are similarly problematic. A student who writes an essay judged to be inferior, like an employee who composes a inferior report, might be said to have failed at his task and faces negative consequences. The relationship between teacher and student might be productively compared to the therapist/client relationship articulated by Volosinov, for in both relationships the power dynamic is determined by the subordination of one party (student/client) to another (teacher/therapist) in which the superordinate has a sanctioned and unquestioned right to authority over the subordinate. Just as a doctor affects his client's discourse, so does an instructor affect his student's. The differences that Volosinov notes exist between doctor and client (age, gender, class, and profession) also exist between teacher and student. The power relations between client and doctor determine the discourse created, Volosinov argues, and from this, one may conclude that the utterances of the client are

> scenarios . . . first and foremost of the immediate, small social event in which they were engendered—the *psychoanalytical session*. Therein that complex struggle between doctor and patient . . . finds expression. What is reflected in these utterances is not the dynamics of the individual psyche but the social dynamics of the interrelations between doctor and patient. (*Freudianism* 79; emphases in original)

The translation to the classroom context is almost eerie: "scenarios . . . of the immediate, small social event in which they were engendered"—the *writing classroom*. "Therein that complex struggle between" *teacher and student* . . . "finds expression. What is reflected in these utterances is not the dynamics of the individual psyche but the social dynamics of the interrelations between" *teacher and student*. The writings completed by students in our composition classes are most certainly scenarios constructed within the confines of the social situation of the writing class and a result of the dynamics of the teacher/student relationship, not the individual student's "self." This superordinate/subordinate relationship exists even in the most nonauthoritarian relationships between teachers and students, as well as therapists and clients, for in each case the work of the subordinate party is informed by the superordinate. The teacher as evaluator possesses—simply by virtue of his position as the representative of the institution—an inherently superior position relative to the student. (The same may be said of the therapist relative to the client.) As much as composition teachers try to divest themselves of power, the evaluative nature of their role remains. Like the therapist, the teacher has an authorial role in students' discourses.

In *A Community of Writers*, Elbow and Belanoff write about the "'double-audience' situation" that teachers face, which is a result of their dual pedagogical goals of encouraging and evaluating. What is most interesting about this section of their textbook is not so much their comments on the "trick role" of the teacher as audience but an inset "Process Box" that includes the following excerpt from Eunsook Koo (presumably a student or former student):

> I used to have a teacher in elementary school who asked his students to keep a diary and who read his students' diaries in order to check whether they were keeping enough entries. Since I knew that he was going to read my diary, I used to make up events and people to fill up the pages instead of writing honestly about my everyday life. I was outraged by the fact that the teacher had the authority to read all of his students' diaries. . . . Whenever I had to write a diary at the end of the day just before going to bed, the face of my teacher used to appear in the back of my mind and hover over me as I wrote. (423)

Koo's comments demonstrate rather graphically Volosinov's comment that "what is reflected in these utterances is not the dynamics of the individual psyche but the social dynamics of the interrelations between" superordinate and subordinate parties. Koo's commentary on her elementary school teacher's surveillance suggests the degree to which the dynamics of the classroom— informed as they are by the relative positions of teachers and students in the institution—affect (and serve to coauthor) students' writing, yet Elbow and Belanoff decline to comment on the political nature of the relationship as suggested in Koo's reflection.[22] Students write under the influences of many social constraints and demands, but by far the most immediate is that of the teacher-student relationship.

Our students sense these constraints intuitively. When they ask, "What do you want?" or "What are you looking for?" they are searching for clues that will assist them in defining parts of this social relationship in terms of expectations about the texts. They are attempting to establish commonalities between their (mis)perceptions about the form and content of their texts and the instructor's expectations for those texts. In striving to find a common extraverbal context, students are, in effect, attempting to establish a common perspective, a "common . . . understanding of the situation." More importantly, they are attempting to establish a "common . . . evaluation" of it (Bakhtin, "Discourse in Life" 99). These commonalities are, of course, the sorts of assumptions that members of a language community take for granted. For example, a composition instructor internalizes certain structures and conventions for writing an essay that describes and evaluates the methods of characterization used in a novel by Jane Austen. A student searching for "what the teacher wants" is asking for an articulation of those assumptions. (I realize, of course, that some students are asking for much more than this; they themselves have hidden agendas, the most pressing of which is making the grade.) After he achieves a common understanding of the "extraverbal context" of a writing situation, a student may then actively construct a discourse that attempts to meet the requirements of a particular language sphere. That is, once he attains an element of mutual knowledge and realizes the assumed premises of the social enthymeme of the classroom context, he may engage in discourse as a co-participant with the instructor. Until that time, he remains "ignorant of the immediate pragmatic context [and] will not understand" the utterances and conventions of the community (Volosinov, "Discourse in Life" 101).

The unnamed difficulties in all of this are, of course, the student's ability to find the assumed premises and the instructor's ability (or willingness) to articulate those premises. This is made even more problematic when, as Volosinov notes, a value judgment—a tacit value or an assumption—within a community or language sphere "becomes a matter of dogmatic belief, something taken for granted and not subject to discussion" ("Discourse in Life" 101). Such a situation exists in academia. Instructors who insist that students find the passwords, search for the keys, or embark on the journey without directions are instructors who refuse to discuss the assumptions behind their beliefs and knowledge. Others are themselves simply unaware of their discipline's assumptions. In either case, educators must unveil and disclose as well as they are able the dictates and assumptions of their disciplines.

Education is no secret society—or at least it shouldn't be. As Bakhtin notes, only by opening up our assumptions to discussion and to scrutiny—to dialogue—will those assumptions remain powerful yet flexible. Laying bare the play of power, as a Bakhtinian approach to the role of audience in the classroom suggests, is not an easy or comfortable task, for it entails questioning the assumptions that have guided composition teaching for decades. In "Literacies and Deficits Revisited," Jerrie Cobb Scott recognizes the inherently seductive power of control that teachers have as evaluators of students' writing. Not until they critically examine their own assumptions about the nature of discourse, pedagogy, and power, Scott argues, will teachers truly begin to understand the interestedness of their own positions in the academy at the expense of their students' subordination. As a teacher of first-year writing, Scott, together with Volosinov, encourages me to acknowledge (rather than to deny through vague and empty references to decentering authority and student-centered or dialogic pedagogies), question, and lay bare the play of power inherent in my role as an evaluative audience. By defining myself both as an immediate audience whose role is to respond generatively, evaluatively, and analytically to students' writing *and* as an evaluative audience—one who evaluates a text on a defined set of terms that emanates from this complex set of audiences—I acknowledge that, because of my position between students and the institution, my roles in the classroom as audience are complex, even contrary to one another.

# THREE

# The Subject as "Hero," Genre, and Authority in Written Discourse

As a discipline, composition studies has over the past twenty years increasingly embraced the notion of rhetoric as epistemic and writing as a transactional, meaning-making activity. The wave of epistemic rhetoric in the 1970s, Jim Berlin suggests, is best described by Michael Leff, who distinguishes epistemic rhetoric from the communicative orientation of earlier rhetorics. An epistemic rhetoric, Leff argues, conceives of knowledge as a rhetorical, historical, social, and linguistic construct. Epistemic rhetoric is also characterized by its understanding of language as heteroglossic and meaning as a set of interrelationships among various conceptions of the external world, all of which "simultaneously act on each other during the process of communicating" (Berlin, *Rhetoric and Reality* 167). Despite the increasingly important role of epistemic rhetoric in composition pedagogy, and despite the extended, heteroglossic nature of an active, interactive subject of discourse that emanates from that material world in its relationship to author and audience, the Bakhtinian "hero" has not yet had a significant effect on composition pedagogy. Helen Ewald notes the scarcity of commentary on the "hero," the Bakhtinian term that appears in several texts to define the "*topic* (the who or what) *of speech*" (Volosinov, "Discourse in Life" 105), the "anthropomorphized 'subject'" of an utterance (Ewald 339).[1]

Although the notion of subject as hero might be timely in composition studies, the lack of commentary on the hero in the discipline is understandable for at least two reasons. First, the term appears most frequently and in the greatest detail in Bakhtin's texts on literature—*Problems of Dostoevsky's Poetics*, *The Dialogic Imagination*, and *Art and Answerability*, which includes the lengthy essay, "Author and Hero in Aesthetic Activity." In these texts, as opposed to "The Problem of Speech Genres" and "Discourse in Life and Discourse in Art", the hero is defined solely in terms of artistic genres, most notably the novel. It becomes difficult to reconcile the Bakhtinian notion of the "hero" as a character in the polyphonic novel with the more general subject of an utterance in a non-artistic or other speech genre, to reconcile, in other words, an aesthetic notion ("hero") with a broader discursive notion of "subject." The distinction between the two is not, however, overly problematic, except to the degree that it is problematic for compositionists who resist the literary-ness of Bakhtinian descriptions and examples.

The lack of commentary on the hero in composition studies is also related to a second consideration. More than either author or audience—who are speaking, writing, listening, and responding human beings—the subject of discourse relies on its relation to others, human others as well as textual others, to define and inform it. The hero is embedded in the utterances of speaking subjects and as such only comes to interlocutors in the form of (or through) others' utterances. A text, for example, can neither "speak" on its own the way an author can nor "respond" to another text the way a listener debates a speaker. The subject of discourse relies on the author and the extended discursive context from which that author writes for its inception, and relies, as well, on an audience for its reception and interpretation. To explore the possibilities of reconstructing the subject of discourse along Bakhtinian lines, I begin by surveying the present state of the discussion in composition studies.

## THE "SUBJECT" AS OBJECT IN COMPOSITION

When composition instructors introduce writing assignments to students, we generally present the subject as an object, a static body of knowledge, a list of sources, or possible pro and con positions. We go little further in noting a subject's dialogism than to ask students to look at the various perspectives on an issue when writing, implying a false separation of perspectives on a subject (held by people) and the subject itself (as an object, somehow removed from those perspectives). A quick, selective glance at only a few composition textbooks demonstrates the two most prominent orientations toward the subject of discourse in composition pedagogy—what I refer to as communicative and rhetorical orientations.[2]

*The Technique of Composition* by Kendall B. Taft, John Francis McDermott, and Dana O. Jensen is a fairly typical book for its time in that it devotes the first two-thirds of its contents to issues of mechanics: grammar, punctuation, diction, style, manuscript considerations, paragraphing, and organization.[3] Part 2 addresses the modes (exposition, narration, description—but not argumentation) and presents formulae for the précis, research paper, and letters. Although they warn the writer against ignoring the demands of audience, the authors claim that "simplicity and clearness" are matters of selecting an appropriate vocabulary suited to the lay reader. Effective communication, the goal of written composition, relies upon a writer's ability to bring a unique "style" to the prose.[4] In their discussion of exposition, the authors define communication as the aim of composition, and in doing so construct a paradigm that entails only two constituents, writer and reader: "Reduced to its simplest terms, then, composition is an activity that requires two (or more) participants—a speaker and a hearer, or a writer and a reader" (473). There is no mention of the role of subject matter in the development, composition, or arrangement of discourse.

James M. McCrimmon's *Writing with a Purpose*, while it varies significantly from Taft et al. in its pedagogy, continues to emphasize the communicative nature of written composition. In *Writing with a Purpose*, the "Larger View" of composition (e.g., the form of the essay—invention, development, paragraphs and sentences) appears first, followed by diction, grammar and mechanics, and "special assignments" (e.g., synopses, research papers, critical reviews, letters). As the title of the book suggests, McCrimmon's overriding communicative concern is with the ways that the purpose of the discourse determines the composition: "A clear grasp of his intention [purpose]," McCrimmon writes, "becomes the only criterion by which a writer can wisely choose between alternatives—between one form of organization and another, between different patterns of development, between formal and informal styles, between alternative usages in diction, grammar, and mechanics" (vii). The writer's intentions, in other words, are the sole determining factor in the development, arrangement, and delivery of discourse.

McCrimmon's book was groundbreaking for its time, for he argues for a much less prescriptive approach to composition, suggesting to students that their purposes in writing should be the primary factor in determining their choices in writing. As he discusses "Choosing a Topic," McCrimmon depicts the task of students as looking carefully at personal experience as a rich source of topics, reassuring them that "good writing is not confined to subjects dealing with unusual experiences, that the everyday events of ordinary living can be recorded freshly and effectively by a student who *knows how to exploit them* for writing purposes" (11; emphasis added). McCrimmon's views on the subject here are decidedly colonial: like natural resources or the American West, the wealth of topics available to an author are hers for the taking. She merely determines what she wants and then gets it. And in the end, the "choice of subject is . . . less important than what you *do* with that subject" (29; emphasis added). Although McCrimmon does not ignore the role of the subject in a discourse as Taft et al. do, his gesture here—dismissing the importance of the subject through exploitation—is much more damaging, for the subject is relegated to such a subordinate position (the exploited) in the construction of the discourse that it becomes an afterthought, tertiary to the author's purpose.[5]

The second orientation toward the subject of discourse, the rhetorical, gains prominence in composition textbooks after the publication in 1965 of Edward P. J. Corbett's *Classical Rhetoric for the Modern Student*, a text that reinvigorated the study of classical rhetoric in the practice of composition.[6] The rhetorical orientation continues to emphasize the author and audience of the communicative orientation but also addresses argumentation, the writing process, and logic as central elements in the development of writing skills. Maxine Hairston's *A Contemporary Rhetoric*, for example, assumes a decidedly Aristotelian approach to composition. Hairston invokes Aristotle's *Rhetoric* and focuses on such topics as induction and deduction, logical fallacies, persuasive appeals, and audience analyses. This classical tradition allows Hairston to articulate the development of written composition in a much more complex manner than either Taft et al. or McCrimmon insofar as she addresses the particular roles of audience, purpose, and persona. Her discussion of the subject, however, is couched in terms of methods of developing and incorporating arguments into written discourse, and her extended discussions on argumentation do not consider the ways that the subject of discourse might itself *suggest* particular lines of development, arrangement, or argumentative form. Hairston examines argumentation, in other words, as a mode of discourse apart from any subject matter.

As these descriptions demonstrate, both communicative and rhetorical orientations toward the subject of discourse encourage students to treat their topics in a comprehensive fashion. The metaphor of treatment suggests a problematic relationship of the domination of a topic by an author. The author, from her superior position, assumes an inherent right and ability to review, dissect, and interpret the subject without any necessary infusion from or engagement with the subject or any need for self-examination in relation to the subject. Like a medical doctor, the author "treats" the patient but is not affected/infected by the patient. No reciprocity exists between doctor and patient, between author and subject.[7] Perhaps the most insidious metaphor is the colonizing metaphor of mastery, which, like the metaphor of treatment, denies the dialogic relationship between author and subject and the ability of the subject to affect/infect the author. The implied goal in each of these representations—examination, treatment, and domination—of the author's relationship with the subject of her discourse is *control*.[8] To write competently about a subject, these textbook writers suggest through their descriptions that students must exhibit control over the topic—control over the style in which the subject is presented, the form of the discourse, the argumentative approach, and the scope of the subject. To write effectively, the author must examine, colonize, domesticate, and master the subject.

## Engaging the Subject of Discourse in Composition Studies

Rather than rely on communicative or rhetorical orientations toward discourse that relegate the subject to, at best, a tertiary importance and promulgate metaphors of domination and domestication, compositionists might turn to an *epistemic orientation* toward discourse and the subject, and with it invoke a *metaphor of participation* to characterize the relationship of author to subject as one of participating in the "continuous process of becoming" in the life of a subject (Volosinov, *Marxism* 81).[9]

Only a few compositionists have begun to invite students to look for heteroglossia *within* a topic. Rise B. Axelrod and Charles R. Cooper suggest, for example, that students "research the topic further to see what others have written about it" as they work to develop their ideas (*St. Martin's* 12), a statement that passingly acknowledges that others' utterances have a generative effect upon a student's developing discourse. Their characterization of the role of the subject, however, does not meet the criteria that Nancy Welch establishes: "[A] Bakhtinian reading [of a text or discourse] enables students and teachers to recognize the multiple perspectives and multiple messages a single text communicates through its moldable, reverberating collections of personal and public voices" (501). In one of the most recent comments regarding the relationship between author and subject, Pamela Gay informs students that "[m]eaning is not something you find; you create meaning through your own interactions or dialogue with the text you are reading" (9). Her advice entails a participative orientation toward the subject:

> Looking (really looking) goes beyond simply taking in or receiving what you see. Critical reflection requires you to *participate* in the viewing by *engaging* in an inner dialogue or conversation that we call thinking—to think and think again, reviewing until you can position yourself, holding firm your vision (or version) at least for the moment (10; emphasis added).

The epistemic and participative orientation toward the subject of discourse (or, more generally the material world and its relation to authors and audiences from which discourses are constructed) suggested in Gay's text appear in a much earlier text, one that Berlin, in *Rhetoric and Reality*, cites as a significant moment in the development of an epistemic rhetoric for composition.

Richard E. Young, Alton L. Becker, and Kenneth L. Pike's *Rhetoric: Discovery and Change*—despite its problematic emphasis on rationalism, empiricism, problem-solving, and ocular metaphors—articulates some important elements of an epistemic rhetoric and participative orientation toward the subject of discourse. These elements, presented by Young, Becker, and Pike in a series of six "maxims," illustrate methods of discovering and interpreting the material world that itself is uniquely "mirrored" in the mind of each person:

> Constantly changing, bafflingly complex, the external world is not a neat, well-ordered place replete with meaning, but an enigma requiring interpretation. This interpretation is the result of a *transaction* between events in the external world and the mind of the individual—between the world "out there" and the individual's previous experience, knowledge, values, attitudes, and desires. Thus the mirrored world is not just the sum total of eardrum rattles, retinal excitations, and so on; it is a creation that *reflects* the peculiarities of the perceiver as well as the peculiarities of what is perceived.[10] (25; emphasis added)

Notice the description of the external world as dynamic, enigmatic, baffling, and "replete with meaning." This is not the neatly ordered world of McCrimmon, waiting to be mined for any given purpose. This is a world that resists order and description and defies interpretation. As people encounter this puzzling world, the authors continue, they face problematic inconsistencies in their relationship with it that might have a

> number of causes: a paradoxical "fact" that doesn't make sense, a situation that is incompatible with a person's values, an apparent opposition of two respected authorities on an important issue, the seeming inadequacy of a strongly held theory, a clash of two sets of values to which a person is deeply committed. (72)

To assist students as they work to address (but not necessarily reconcile) those inconsistencies through their writing, Young, Becker, and Pike set out six maxims, among which are the following:

Maxim: *Units of experience are hierarchically structured systems* (29; emphasis in original).

Maxim: *A unit of experience can be viewed as a particle, or as a wave, or as a field.* That is, the writer can choose to view any element of his experience *as if it were static, or as if it were dynamic, or as if it were a network of relationships or a part of a larger network* (122; emphasis in original).

The authors make a rather commonsensical observation with the first of these maxims. People attend to the details of their experiences by focusing on different sets of phenomena. The authors illustrate this maxim by describing the various "events" to which a person might attend while watching a baseball game at a stadium. The vantage point from which a person views the phenomena and the phenomena themselves *together* determine the reality of the person's experiences. Young, Becker, and Pike note, as well, that the person may shift her focus, increase or decrease the "magnification" of that focus, and focus on "two different parts of the whole . . . simultaneously, one in central or *nuclear* focus and the other in subsidiary or *marginal* focus" (29; emphasis in original).

The second maxim—which introduces particle, wave, and field—extends the first maxim by describing the ways that a person might interpret her observations: The event or behavior can be viewed as static, dynamic, or relational. These two maxims are noteworthy because through them the authors assume an active and interactive external world, one that engages the observer/author in an epistemic, generative, and participative relationship. These maxims echo Volosinov who writes that

> [t]he form of a poetic work is determined . . . by *how the author perceives his hero*— the hero who serves as the organizing center of the utterance. The form of *objective narration*, the form of *address or apostrophe* . . . , are determined precisely by the *degree of proximity between author and hero* (Volosinov, "Discourse in Life" 111; emphasis in original)

When I reread this passage, I am reminded of the essay, "The Loss of Creature," anthologized in *Ways of Reading*, in which Walker Percy argues, among other things, that a person's observations of the material world are always already distorted by "the symbolic complex which has already been formed" in the knower's mind (395). This "symbolic complex" takes many forms—all of which might be described in Bakhtinian terms as "previous utterances." The sightseer at the Grand Canyon, to use Percy's example, does not meet the Canyon head on. Her encounter with it is informed/preformed by both public and private images: television specials, movies, postcards, Park Service marketing, and so on, all of which impinge upon the seer's greater or lesser "degree of proximity" to the hero, and therefore her manner of representing it in a given sphere through a given generic form.

Percy himself is a case in point. In introducing Percy as an author, Bartholomae and Petrosky characterize him as an author for whom the academic essay "published in obscure academic journals" proved to be an inadequate vehicle for his writing, as he moved in his later writings "away from academic forms of argument and to depend more and more on stories or anecdotes from daily life—to write, in fact, as a storyteller and to be wary of abstraction and explanation. "Robert Coles," they continue, "has said that it was *Percy's failure to find a form that would reach a larger audience that led him to try his hand at a novel*" (393–94; emphasis added). In other words, Percy's relationship with his audience and subject matter—his proximity to his subject—compelled him to change the forms in which he wrote. And, I would add, Percy's essays (along with other professional and academic essays anthologized in college textbooks) have had an impact on the changing face of the forms of academic essays published in those "obscure academic journals" about which Bartholomae and Petrosky write. Bell hooks writes in *talking back* about the events surrounding the publication of *Ain't I a Woman*, which illustrates for hooks a book not intended to inform "white women about black women but rather as an expression of my longing to know more and think deeply about our experience" (16). This relationship to her subject, one that moves away from representation and explanation to engagement and exploration, necessarily determines the forms in which she writes.

THE "HERO" IN THE BAKHTINIAN SCHEME

> Invention consists in the capacity of seizing on the capabilities of a subject and in the power of moulding and fashioning ideas suggested to it.
> —Mary Shelley, *Frankenstein*

The role of the subject as "hero" in an utterance is among Bakhtin's more novel notions, particularly with regard to composition studies, yet the attention of theorists has focused very little on the subject—a point Titunik cites as understandable but unfortunate. The Bakhtinian author, in writing about a given subject, does much more than (re)present the subject; she enters into a relationship with it in which both subject (hero) and author are affected by one another. Like other twentieth-century philosophers, scientists, anthropologists, historians, and literary theorists—among them Polanyi, Rosenblatt, Sontag, and White—Bakhtin proceeds on the assumption that knowledge is contextual, constructed, and reciprocal; that a person's views of reality are "personal" (Polanyi); that the material of discourse from which the "hero" or subject emanates might best be seen as an "event in time" (Rosenblatt); that as a person's assumptions and beliefs change, so does reality (Sontag); and that history and historiography are, like Susan Sontag's images, conditioned by the historian's theories and philosophies of history (White).[11] Mary Shelley's introduction to *Frankenstein* demonstrates the power of the reciprocal relationship between knower and known, author and subject: An author does not invent out of nothing but instead works from the "capabilities" inherent in a subject, designing from the ideas that the subject suggests. Shelley's comments themselves suggest the power of the subject in determining the constructed utterance. To articulate the notion of hero and its generative power as an ideological formulation, I begin with Bakhtin's comments in the *Problems of Dostoevsky's Poetics* and *Art and Answerability*.

### The Novelistic "Hero"

The term "hero" is no doubt a foreign one when applied to the topic of discourse, but Bakhtin's reasons for selecting it over "object" make a linguistic and philosophic statement. The hero of discourse has indeed been treated as an object, Bakhtin argues, with no active, generative, or epistemic role assigned to it. In many other discourse theories, Schuster suggests, the "hero" has less control over the construction of an utterance than either the speaker or the listener because the subject is seen as a static object. In contrast to this, Bakhtin characterizes the subject of an utterance as a "third person." Schuster describes "hero" by contrasting it to a more traditional and familiar term, the "object" of discourse. "According to Bakhtin," Schuster writes,

> a speaker does not communicate to a listener about a "subject" instead, "speaker"; and "listener" engage in an act of communication which includes the "hero" as a genuine rhetorical force. The difference here is significant. In our conventional analyses of discourse, we talk of the way writers "treat" subjects, the way they research, describe, develop, analyze, and attack them. Subjects are actually conceived as objects. They are passive, inert, powerless to shape the discourse. In Bakhtin's terms, the hero is as potent a determinant in the rhetorical paradigm as speaker or listener. The hero interacts with the speaker to shape the language and determine the form. At times, the hero becomes the dominant influence in verbal and written discourse. ("Mikhail Bakhtin" 595)

As "object," the hero is denied the power to shape meaning or take an active part in constructing an utterance. Like many who chastise their lovers for treating them as objects, the hero of a discourse generally has been overlooked as an active *subject*—in the sense of a dynamic entity—in discussions of discourse situations.[12]

The "hero" of *Art and Answerability* and *Problems of Dostoevsky's Poetics* refers, for the most part, to character. As Schuster indicates, Bakhtin perceives of the character as "hero" in the polyphonic novel, but that hero is not merely "the subject of a rhetorically performed or conventionally literary [mode of address]" but also a co-participant that actively engages in a conversation, as it were, with the author and audience (Bakhtin, *Problems* 63). Throughout the Dostoevsky text, Bakhtin creates an image of character as ideologue, and as much more than an extension of the author writing a novel or persona narrating the story. In his discussions of it in the novel, Bakhtin emphasizes the "hero" as a self-conscious and independent ideological being. He goes so far as to describe the hero not as "he" but as an autonomous "thou" (in much the same spirit as Martin Buber's I-Thou relationship), one deserving of a "deeply serious, *real* dialogic mode of address" (63).

By granting such autonomy to the hero, Bakhtin allows for a dialogic relationship in which the hero engages the author in an exchange, a conversation. Like the listener, the hero is never identical to the author. Moreover, the author's process of coming to understand the hero entails an unmasking of both the hero and herself in relation to the hero, a peeling away of the "layers . . . sedimented upon his [the hero's] face by our [the author's and culture's] own fortuitous reactions and attitudes and by fortuitous life situations" ("Author and Hero" 6). Coming to an understanding of a hero is itself a dialogic activity, one that requires the author to engage the hero not as a static entity (character, object, body of knowledge) but as a dynamic, changing, living force with which she has a defined, yet shifting relationship. Coming to understand the hero, then, means the author comes to understand the hero in terms of herself; their relationship is contextualized in terms of their relative positions to one another and to the audience.

These selective "heroic" characteristics, as well as those detailed by Schuster, are helpful in establishing the subject of discourse as an active participant, a third person in the creation of an utterance with whom the author has a dynamic relationship. But it is not enough to base such a construct for more pragmatic genres solely on a Bakhtinian *aesthetic* theory of artistic genres. Additional essays written later in Bakhtin's career discuss more extensively the subject of discourse, its characteristics, and its relationship to author and audience. The notion of hero, when supplemented by these later essays, proves valuable in characterizing the subject as a co-participant in non-artistic discursive utterances.

## "Hero" as Subject in the Later Bakhtinian Scheme

In his discussion of Bakhtin as a rhetorician, Schuster depends solely on the *Problems of Dostoevsky's Poetics*, *The Dialogic Imagination*, and Volosinov's *Marxism and the Philosophy of Language* (*Speech Genres* had not yet been published). As a result he was unable to extend the definitions of hero to non-artistic, rhetorical genres or demonstrate the powerful influence of previous utterances on the configuration of a subject. Nor was he able to show the extent to which such utterances inform the subject and dictate its reception by both author and audience. By perceiving the subject of discourse only as the hero of the novelistic form, as a character constructed in and through the discourse, Schuster could not address a number of elements critical to establishing a theory of the subject in non-artistic prose. Unavailable to him were the heteroglossic nature of the subject and the effects that previous utterances have on the reception and interpretation of the subject by readers and writers. Schuster's characterization of the hero is extended, rather than denied or contradicted, by Bakhtin's later comment that the "relationship to others' utterances cannot be separated from the relationship to the object . . . nor can it be separated from the relationship to the speaker himself. This is a living tripartite unity. But the third element is still not usually taken into account" ("Problem of the Text" 122–23).

The subject of discourse, the "hero," "becomes," Bakhtin writes, the "arena where his [author's] opinions meet those of his partners [audience] (in a conversation or dispute about some everyday event) or other viewpoints, world views, trends, theories, and so forth" ("Problem of Speech" 94). The hero serves as an "arena," a milieu of previous utterances dialogically arranged, of shared and idiosyncratic knowledge, in, through, and against which authors and audiences formulate their own utterances and responses. No communication and no responsive understanding exist without the subject. We cannot speak about or out of nothing.

As an arena where opinions meet, converge, and collide, the subject of a discourse is best described not as a set of discernible data, or even solely as the speaker's conscious and recollected experiences, but as a collective of others' utterances about the subject. These utterances themselves become part of the subject and indistinguishable from it, for they are themselves part of the subject. Our perspectives on environmental policy, for example, are formed only partly through our understanding of scientific descriptions that are themselves the constructed utterances of others interpreted as scientific fact or belief. Our understanding of such topics as ozone destruction, the greenhouse effect, global warming, or the slashing of Brazilian rain forests are also constructed from our own experiences, as well as the utterances of others who have spoken and written about them, from Henry David Thoreau and Barry Commoner to Edward Abbey, James Watt, and Greenpeace. The environment as a subject of discourse is no longer the sole property of scientists. To those concerned about it in 1999, the environment as the hero of discourse cannot be separated from the voices and authority of the non-scientists who have championed it and sung its praises, from Bob Dylan to Sting.

My point is not to argue that opinion must be based on more than science (although I would be willing to make that claim), but that a subject cannot be separated from those that have spoken and written about it. In fact, the words of the others *are* the subject itself, and the ways that an author or audience views those others determines the ways that ensuing utterances are created or received. The very ways that these previous voices are represented in a new utterance reveals the author's relation to and interaction with them. Schuster suggests that the hero, just as the speaker or listener in discourse, carries "its own accumulation of values and terms. It too carries with it a set of associations, an ideological and stylistic profile" ("Mikhail Bakhtin" 596), but he never states explicitly that these values and terms become associated with a subject through others' articulations. Bakhtin, on the other hand, insists that the topic of a discourse is replete with the discourses of others:

> The topic of the speaker's speech, regardless of what this topic may be, does not become the object of speech for the first time in any given utterance; a given speaker is not the first to speak about it. The object, as it were, has already been articulated, disputed, elucidated, and evaluated in various ways. Various viewpoints, world views, and trends cross, converge, and diverge in it. The speaker is not the biblical Adam, dealing only with virgin and still unnamed objects, giving them names for the first time. ("Problem of Speech" 93)

In creating, or even hearing or reading, a discourse, a person comes into contact, and very often in conflict, with the ideological positions within the subject—as represented by Barry Commoner and James Watt, for example. Just as the author has to contend with the alien discourses of the audience, so too must she encounter and contend with the alien discourses that are always already present in the hero of her discourse. Ultimately, she must position herself among these alien discourses in order to present her own.

### The Subject and Its Relationship to Genre

> The author's relation to what he depicts always enters into the image. The author's relationship is a constitutive aspect of the image.
> —Bakhtin, "The Problem of the Text"

> The genre represents the utterance's social baggage in the sense that the utterance must take on a determinate and public form that communicants can identify. Consequently, the genre constitutes the public form that an utterance must assume in order to be comprehensible.
> —Thomas Kent, "Hermeneutics and Genre"

It is a small and logical step for Bakhtin to move from the premises that the author and subject of discourse have an active, generative relationship and that meaning is not made from or out of a subject but along with it to the conclusion that this relationship is made manifest in the form of the utterance—its genre. The genre of any utterance is, of course, also determined by audience and the language sphere in which the utterance is situated. Genres are, according to Bakhtin, *"relatively stable types"* of language use developed within a given language sphere ("Problem of Speech" 60); they are comprehensible, public forms, according to Kent. The social construction of genre does not, however, preclude the possibility of individual variation in the construction, arrangement, or style of an utterance. Imagine the complex and sometimes contentious nature of the task before an author. Already immersed in various previous discourses about a given subject, but required (by circumstance, desire, or need) to construct an utterance, an author battles, negotiates, and compromises on several different fronts. On one front, the author engages the audience and its relationship to her and the subject. On another, she contends with the demands of the subject, its heteroglossic tensions, and previous utterances. And on yet another front, she works within a particular language sphere that dictates to greater and lesser degrees the expectations and conventions of her discourse. The negotiated text—its content, form, and style—together reflect and are informed by the context through and out of which the author writes.

An example helps to characterize the complexity of the author's situation. In constructing her summation, a defense attorney representing a young woman accused of assaulting an abusive former boyfriend must consider several issues, and as she does so, she works within the generic judicial framework (genre) of summation. Yet, despite its relative stability (rules exist regarding what lawyers may or may not do in summations), the genre is also plastic. The attorney may consider not only her available means of persuasion but also the relationships among the generative constituents of the discursive context in the courtroom. She may, in turn, evaluate her relationship to the audience (the jury and judge—even the media and general public) as she settles on an *ethos* in her summation. She may also consider her *allied* relationship to the hero of her utterance—the accused. The nature of her relationship with her former boyfriend and the circumstances of her crime will both affect the jury's relationship to the accused. The attorney may also review and evaluate the previous utterances in related cases about which the jury might have knowledge. These might include, but are not limited to, cultural sensibilities regarding battery, spousal abuse, battered wives' syndrome, and a host of other discourses that might inform a jury's decision in similar cases. Although a court proceeding clearly defines the generative nature of the subject of the utterance as well as the dynamic relationship among the constituents of the discourse, it also demonstrates the unparalleled significance of "other utterances within the limits of a given sphere of communication" on the utterance (Bakhtin, "Problem of the Text" 122). The relationship between the utterance, the previous utterances, previous voices, and the "hero" or subject in "great time"—are paramount.

Addressivity and answerability cannot, however, be easily characterized. In any speech genre, which exists for Bakhtin within a given sphere of communication, addressivity and answerability are complicated by the relative social positions of the constituents and the nexus of relationships I have already discussed: the author to immediate, evaluative, and public audiences; the author to the larger social collective; the author to the subject; and the audience to subject. In each of these relationships, the authority of the writer is mitigated by her relationship to multiple others. How the defense attorney goes about her summation will most likely include the information I outlined above, but her actions will also be guided by her relative position in the courtroom and legal profession. Her discourse is both *constrained and enabled* by who she is as she speaks relative to audience, subject, and social collective. Like the attorney planning her summation, the student enrolled in a first-year writing course writes from within a complex web of relationships that together frame and form the discourses she produces. The question then becomes whether compositionists recognize and engage this web of relationships—particularly the relationship between author and subject—as they construct writing assignments and what the implications are of the generic forms of these assignments.

### FORM AS IDEOLOGY IN COLLEGE ESSAYS

Given that discussions in composition studies of the subject of discourse have remained essentially unchanged in recent years, it is perhaps not surprising that college essay forms, along with their objectified notions of the subject of discourse, have remained relatively static as well. If we are to believe Volosinov, who argues that cultural and social changes are reflected in the discourse forms of a given community, then it follows that the changes in writing pedagogy and education in the past twenty years ought to be discernible in the discourse forms within the discipline.[13] Still, a surprising standardization of form among college essay genres remains. Even some of the more progressive composition theorists promote prescriptive organizational formats. Why is it the case that college essay forms have not seen significant revision? Perhaps the changes in writing pedagogy are not as dramatic as we are led to believe, or perhaps the academy insulates pedagogy from some of the conditions that may affect changes in generic forms.

Volosinov's work provides grounds for a plausible explanation for the seemingly static nature of college essays, one that examines the relationships between the individuals within the academy as a mitigating force in the engagement of subjects and construction of essay genres. In the case of student writing within the university setting, the primary relationships are those between student and teacher, student and institution, and student and subject. These relationships together regulate the form of the college essay, yet they have not changed it significantly in the past twenty years. The forms of utterances, Volosinov writes, are *"conditioned above all by the social organization of the participants involved and also by the immediate conditions of their interaction"* (*Marxism* 21). So, the form of the essay, we might argue from a Bakhtinian perspective, is determined by the nexus of relationships the student encounters and in particular by the relationship of student and teacher, which itself has undergone little change in recent years. The form of the essay, its genre, is also determined by the subject of the discourse, by whom and how the subject has been engaged previously.

Compositionists have heard calls for liberatory (Freire), critical (Giroux), feminist (hooks), and transgressive (hooks) pedagogies, and these calls have effected change in composition pedagogy as college essay forms and conventional discourses have come under intense scrutiny by compositionists who have come to associate ideology and form as ideology *in* form.[14] Yet, composition textbooks continue to present college essay forms in problematic terms. In the analyses that follow, I seek to demonstrate that three forms of the college essay—what I refer to as "Essay as Organic Whole," "Form Without Function," and "Form as Approximation"—reveal particular and definable ideological positions with regard to the relationship between (1) author and evaluative audience, (2) author and social collective, and (3) author and subject. All three forms, each of which retains a strong following in composition studies, denies to greater and lesser degrees the epistemic role of the subject of discourse.

### The Essay as Organic Whole

It is probably unfair and certainly misleading to characterize as naive the writing pedagogy that has come to be called "expressivism." While often disregarded as idiosyncratic, apolitical, or "romantic," expressivism nonetheless gained great popularity and notoriety among teachers of writing during the 1960s and 1970s. The current workshop method of teaching writing as a process, and an emphasis on heuristics and pre-writing, may be traced in some form or degree to the expressive movement of this and earlier eras. Expressivist theorists—Murray, Rohman and Wlecke, Stewart, and others—have contributed significantly to current thought in composition studies. Along with the romantics' focus on self came a sense of the essay as an "organic whole," as an expression of an author's perspective on a topic "through study of the ways in which language is involved in expressing one's perceptions of a private, intuitive version of reality" (Berlin, *Rhetoric and Reality* 152). The metaphor of organicism, also characteristic of new criticism, suggests that an essay evolves from within the mind of the writer, growing and developing organically, as a seed into a flower. All of the parts exist in a sort of embryonic form in the mind of the writer, waiting only to be put to paper and allowed to progress through the stage by stage organic development of the text.

Through all of this, Berlin notes, the goal of writing instruction remains cultivating an "authentic identity and voice" (153). Elbow, for example, in presenting the metaphor of "growing as a developmental process" in *Writing Without Teachers*, recognizes that individual writers have different processes, but in every case growth comes from within, not from without. "It is the characteristic of living organisms," Elbow writes, of "cell creatures, to unfold according to a set of stages that must come in order. The paradigm is the fetus going through its stages" (43). An essay, then, like a fetus, is conceived within the author, develops and grows within the author, and only upon completion is presented to others.

As a self-contained entity, the essay as organic whole is not only sheltered within the individual psyche but also removed from dialogism. The individual psyche serves as a sanctuary for the essay. Safely cradled at the bosom of the psyche, individual expression remains unsullied by the outside world. Theoretically, students remain "true" to themselves and their own ideas by retaining full responsibility for and autonomy over their writing. One can retain autonomy only over that which one has complete control. It is no accident, then, that, like many other expressivists, Elbow believes that writing is an art that can be learned but not taught, for if it can be taught, then the author must relinquish control over her writing to a teacher. The notion of autonomy over a text also denies the generative power of both audience and subject in the construction of the essay, for it assumes that the author constructs first from deep within the psychic sanctuary away from the demands of audiences and/or subjects. It is this perspective—that which valorizes an individual's right to autonomy over her text—that caused many compositionists to encourage their students to break with the confining restrictions of the college essay.[15] The rallying cry was for individual autonomy.

Although the notion of an essay as an organic whole does not work directly against a Bakhtinian metaphor of the utterance as conversation, it emphasizes different attributes of writing. The element of organicism most incompatible with the metaphor of conversation is the implication that all elements of the text are latent in the author's mind and simply wait for articulation. Conversely, to characterize an utterance as part of a conversation is to understand it as addressed, as responding to previous utterances as well as anticipating other utterances that may respond to it. The utterance—a student essay, for example—is not a unique articulation of one individual's opinion on an issue, for that individual's opinion is shaped by previous contributions to the topic. To suggest to student writers that their essays are their own organic creations implies that these are individual and isolated works. "Organicism," as Elbow defines it, implies an entity whose parts work together as elements of a single enterprise in an individual articulation of an idea. Like the organic unity of the human body, the essay with its constituent parts—introduction, body, and conclusion—exists independently from all other texts, or "bodies," as an isolated being.

Contrary to the notion of the essay as an organic whole, Holquist writes that Bakhtin posits "wholeness" as a "relative term," a "fiction." "[W]holes," Holquist continues, are "never *given*, but always *achieved*"; "the struggle to effect a whole out of the potential chaos of parts" is the work of genre ("Introduction" x, xxiii). A text does not have an inherent wholeness simply because it emanates from an individual psyche. An author achieves a sense of wholeness in the process of constructing a text within a certain generic form and as a coauthor with audience and subject. Genre as a conventional form provides the author with a rough approximation of wholeness with which and against which he works.

Consider the case of Walker Percy, who moved from writing essays in those obscure academic journals to writing novels. To what degree might the academic essay genre itself have been implicated in the shift? Was the relative wholeness of the academic essay insufficient for Percy's utterances? Perhaps Percy, given his shifting relationship to his subject and its demands for a certain kind of wholeness, was compelled by his subject and the inadequacy of the essay form to seek, in addition to a different audience, the new kind of wholeness available through fiction.

As a theory of the essay, the notion of the organic whole limits itself by its isolationist philosophy of form. As late-twentieth-century life sciences have shown us, even discrete organisms exist in relation to other organisms and within defined biospheres that determine the health of each discrete organism. Any changes in the life of the biosphere, any damage to its cohabitants, affect the lives of all organisms despite their seeming autonomy. The situation is analogous for students writing college essays. Their utterances are intimately related to the other utterances surrounding them and are constructed within a given sphere, which, like a biosphere, affects and conditions the discourses within it. Students who are writing are better served if they understand their essays not as organic wholes emanating from themselves as unique and unadulterated voices, but as utterances emanating from the complex network of relationships in which they find themselves in the university.

## Form Without Function

The notion of a prescriptive college essay form—generically conceived as the five paragraph theme—is a construct much criticized throughout college level composition circles. Yet, it remains a dominant form among college students, university professors in other disciplines, and even with such compositionists as Bruffee. That he does not acknowledge the disjunction between a dynamic, socially constructed, unique formulation of an utterance and the static, formulaic, and imposed structure of a standard essay form suggests Bruffee's inattention to the subject as interactive and dynamic. Unlike compositionists who characterize the essay as an organic whole, Bruffee ignores altogether the ideological issue of an essay's form. In fact, Bruffee relies throughout his text, *A Short Course in Writing*, on a preformed and rigid essay structure. And unlike compositionists who promote the organic whole metaphor of form that eschews traditional essay forms because of their infringement on the autonomy of the individual, compositionists who require prescriptive forms separate form from function entirely.

Granted, many compositionists, Bruffee included, do this out of a pedagogical concern; they believe students have enough to worry about in constructing the argument, developing support, and so on, without having to worry about how they'll put an essay together. Bruffee's work, like all utterances, is conditioned and informed by the voices of others, and in this case, Bruffee revises the dominant objectivist five paragraph theme format, using it as the basis for all of the essays presented in *A Short Course*:

> To help you learn one basic form for developing your ideas, exercises 5 through 9 ask you to write all your essays in the same basic form. Then they show you how to vary the way you defend or explain your position *within that form*.
>
> The form required in these essays is not the only form to write an essay in, but it is a good one. When you can write easily in this form, you will be able to write essays (including examination essays, term papers, and reports) with confidence. Eventually you will be able to make up your own variations of the basic form, explore other common forms, and *even* invent forms that are entirely new.
>
> But for now, please stick to this one form.
>
> Each of the five essays [required in exercises 5 through 9] should be about five hundred words. You don't have to count words. Make an estimate.
>
> Make each five-hundred-word paper three paragraphs: one paragraph to introduce the proposition, and two paragraphs to defend it.[16] (53–54; emphasis added)

This description supports so many of the myths about writing that college writing teachers try to dispel that it is difficult to understand why Bruffee would present it as a set structure from which good writing emanates. To use the standard five-hundred-word essay as the basis for a pedagogy that claims to promote critical thinking and collaboration undermines the notion of negotiated meaning. Rather than concede that various types of writing may demand different sorts of patterns of exposition, organization, or development, Bruffee does the opposite; he implies that one form is sufficient despite the differences in purpose, audience, and subject. Bakhtin argues that such standard generic forms allow for very little generic individuality. By restricting a writer's decisions about form, Bruffee restricts one of the most elemental decisions made by writers as they produce an utterance.

Whatever his pedagogical motivation, Bruffee's gesture separates the form of an essay and the subject of the discourse from their functions as generative constituents in the construction of the discourse. The above quotation from Bruffee demonstrates the paternalistic, even repressive, nature of a pedagogy that only allows students one way of writing; students are directed to "stick to this one form." They will, of course, be allowed to construct "*variations* of the basic form" and "even invent forms that are entirely new," but only after they have mastered the standard form. On the face of it, this makes pedagogical sense: Students work to perfect one way of writing before moving on to more challenging or complex forms. However, a closer look uncovers the troubling premise that the skills acquired in learning this one form are transferable. By arguing that mastering the prescribed form enables students to write "examination essays, term papers, and reports" with "confidence," Bruffee implies that the prescriptive form is an all-purpose approach to writing the kinds of college essays students often face. This premise not only ignores the generative nature of form but also disregards the intimate relationships among audience, social context, subject, and author in the development of conventional discourses within particular language spheres.

Bruffee's approach to the form of the essay carries with it objectivist ideological assumptions about form, and in this the theory behind his pedagogy lags behind those compositionists who demand an individual's right to determine her own form. Bruffee is not alone in his requirement that students use a particular form in writing college essays, however. Textbooks are crammed with models of essay forms, report genres, and research outlines, all of which suggest or require students to follow particular forms. Despite comments to the contrary (e.g., "Eventually you will be able to make up your own variations of the basic form, explore other common forms, and even invent forms that are entirely new"), students, who occupy a subordinate position in the classroom, are politely yet powerfully discouraged from working outside the established form—if not by explicit wording in a textbook, then by their position relative to the teacher and the institution. Textbook authors, as teachers and representatives of the institution, sometimes consciously (but more often unconsciously) use their authoritative positions to close off any negotiation of form. Students have no choice in the matter, and as a result the network of relationships that forms an utterance is severed, for no longer is the form of an utterance or its subject an active constituent in that construction.

### Form as Approximation

In investigating students' texts in "Inventing the University," David Bartholomae explores the relationship between a novice writer and the conventions and demands of college writing by working to discover what it takes for a student's placement essay to be deemed sufficient or successful. Bartholomae's conclusions are both insightful and controversial: A writer must first come to terms with and question the cultural commonplaces and cultural assumptions of the dominant culture, and then self-consciously place herself within that culture, before she can function effectively within the discourses of that culture's institutions. And more specifically with regard to the institution, only as she manages to imitate recognized model(s) of argumentation can she then manipulate the academy's discourses. This, the third characterization of the college essay form, suggests that a student's essay is an approximation of another form of discourse, a more or less successful attempt to imitate and achieve some standard form.

More than either the essay as organic whole or prescriptive formulations of the college essay, the essay as an approximation foregrounds the effect of the larger social collective on a student's construction of discourse. Here, Bartholomae recognizes that the social collective—through its genres, conventions, and argumentative approach—determines what discourses students write, and he demonstrates that their attempts can be evaluated according to how well they mimic the standards of academic argumentation. By articulating form as approximation, Bartholomae also assumes, as Deborah Mutnick has pointed out, that "insider status" is "more 'a matter of imitation or parody than a matter of invention and discovery'" (39).

As stimulating as it is, however, Bartholomae's discussion, which explores the relationship between a student's home discourse and academic discourse, pays little attention to the generative nature of the subject under discussion in the utterance itself. Bartholomae asked students to write on "creativity" by both defining it and offering examples from their own experiences that depicted them in a creative moment. Students wrote placement essays on a variety of subjects, among them football and jazz. By focusing on the method of argumentation and not on the subjects of these students essays, Bartholomae misses the opportunity to examine the relationship between the subjects of discourse and the final arrangement and argumentative form of the essay. That is, he does not ask three provocative questions into the very processes of conducting placement examinations that ask students to write on a single question: "How does the subject of these essays impinge upon a student's ability (or willingness) to engage in a productive discourse informed by academic approaches to argumentation?" "What are various students' relationships to 'creativity?'" and "How do those relationships impinge upon the writing that they do?"

Rather than investigating the relationship between author and subject and how this relationship might either negatively or positively affect the ways students write, Bartholomae examines instead the degree to which the form of a student essay approximates another type of discourse. Jane E. Hindman suggests that Bartholomae, like many compositionists, in working to enable his students, unconsciously redoubles his students' marginalization by assuming that the models for imitation should be those of the academy. This "enabling of the status quo within our discipline (professing English)," Hindman argues, "fails to give real power or place or freedom to them [students] because it does not elucidate the source of English professors' authority within the discipline; our pedagogy does not contextualize our own writing within the academy" (59).[17] In effect, Bartholomae makes a crucial first step in "Inventing the University" by examining the problematic position of the student in the university, but he does not, as Hindman suggests, question the nature and motives of the institution and its discursive forms and expectations.

Bartholomae and Petrosky demonstrate in *Ways of Reading* a composition pedagogy tailored to initiate students into the ways of reading, writing, and thinking in the academy that, like Bartholomae's commentary in "Inventing the University," does not problematize the nature of academic discourse and a pedagogy based on achieving facility with that discourse. The selections in *Ways of Reading* are those that "we talk about when we talk with our colleagues" (iv). In a democratizing gesture, they acknowledge that they have learned that they can also talk about these same texts with their students. This gesture is based on a decidedly undemocratic assumption, however, for the selections about which students should read and write are those privileged in the academy, as are the *forms* of the selections: those of Emerson, Fish, Freire, Oates, and Ruskin. Not only are the argumentative forms of the academy privileged, so are the subjects: Education, Entitlements, Expertise, Taboo, Composing. We don't see in *Ways of Reading* the complex and difficult texts from students' language spheres—the spheres of popular culture or political activism, for example. Students are reading and engaging our world, not theirs.

## AUTHORITY AND FORM IN THE ACADEMIC ESSAY

Each of these forms of the essay overlooks the generative and epistemic nature of the subject of discourse. Moreover, the first two constructions also overlook another notable feature of discourse: the impact of the relationship between the author and social collective. These forms of the essay do not allow for what hooks refers to as a "liberatory voice," one that "will necessarily confront, disturb, demand that listeners even alter ways of hearing and being" (hooks, *talking back* 16). None of these three essay forms demands any sort of disruption or alteration of the listeners' "ways of hearing or being." On the contrary, the forms are designed to allow the listeners (instructors, the institution) to maintain their present ideologies.

The position of the student, particularly in Bruffee's and Bartholomae's work, is defined in terms of her ability to construct a discourse pleasing to the academic social collective (usually in the person of her writing instructor or a panel of placement evaluators), not a disruptive or liberatory discourse that challenges the social collective. The ideology of these forms becomes clearer. They are a means of initiation, yet they lead to only a provisional membership, for once a form is mastered, students are set a higher mark, which, if met, leads to yet another level of provisional membership. That is, the form that Bartholomae advocates implies, at best, an apprenticed position for the student as author.

In their retrospective on "Audience Addressed/Audience Invoked," Ede and Lunsford note that in this article they did not address adequately how audiences and larger institutional and cultural demands impinge upon a writer's discourses. In addition, the authors reflect that they also did not "consider the powerful effects of ideology working through genres, such as those inscribed in academic essayist literacy, to call forth and thus control and constrain writers and audiences" (171). As I demonstrate here, college essay genres indeed place powerful constraints on students' writing. The constraining qualities of genre and of the social collective that enforces them are not, however, limited to just the three forms I outline above. Students in the process of writing—like business people, academicians, or consumers—implicitly, and sometimes explicitly, define themselves through their writing and in terms of their relationships with audience, subject, and social collective. The more recognized an author is, the more easily she and her discourse claim authority. What this means, of course, is that the student in a first-year writing course is, relative to the other residents in the academy, the least authorized to speak, and as a result her discourses must demonstrate rather than claim or assume their authority if they are to convince the evaluative audience of their value. This places the student in a position very different from Walker Percy or bell hooks.

Genre is relative, flexible, and fluctuating, but more so for established academicians and professional writers like hooks and Percy than for students. The degree to which a person can engage playfully with(in) a genre and conventions has much to do with her relationship to the social collective and the subject of the discourse. The position of the author relative to the subject matter and larger social collective necessarily determines and constrains the generic options available to that author. If we assume—as Bakhtin suggests and as Young, Becker and Pike imply—that the form of an utterance is determined and informed by the relationships among its participants, then we can discern in the form of an essay (or in a theory of the essay form) the nature of those relationships.

Examining the nature of the relationship between students and the social collective through a contrastive analysis of the relationship between the professional academician and the social collective sets in relief the difficulty students face as they construct discourses and "play" with forms. Just as evaluative audience, social collective, and the subject of discourse inform student writing in the academy and compositionists' theorizing about essay forms, so, too, do they inform the writing of professional academics. Linda Brodkey's *Academic Writing as Social Practice* offers a series of pointed statements regarding authority and authorship in the academy, statements that recognize the implications of the position of the author relative to the social collective. Like the student who writes to become authorized in and through the institution, academicians are authorized in and through publication. The route to publication and authorization, Brodkey writes, is part of a "long history of reciprocal social arrangements of mutual benefit. Just as an academic culture creates the material conditions for academic discourse (sabbaticals, reduced teaching loads, travel allowances for conferences), a community of publishing scholars justifies an Academy" (8). Academic culture also "creates the material conditions" for student discourse (honors classes, tutorial assistance, student professional and academic organizations) and provides a mechanism for evaluating student performance. Professional authorization (and with it tenure) is not immune to changing fiscal policy, as Brodkey also notes, for colleges and universities reserve the right to terminate untenured faculty if financial exigency deems it necessary.

All of this is to illustrate that academicians, like students, write within and are authorized through a powerful credentialing system—a social collective with its own goals, motivations, demands, and expectations. For students and untenured faculty alike, authorization comes a term, a course, a paper at a time, yet authorization is granted on an accumulation of authorizing events (grades, requirements, publications, teaching, and service). More specifically, students and untenured faculty work from an implied relationship to their subject matter. That is, the institution expects the author to use discourse as a way of demonstrating knowledge. Because they have not been authorized through the granting of tenure, untenured faculty sit in a position analogous to first-year students. Both have been provisionally admitted into the university, and the quality of their performances (in both cases judged at least partly in terms of their writing) after admission determine their continued affiliations. As a result, students in first-year writing courses, like untenured faculty, are constrained by a lack of academic freedom, for neither group may write without the possibility of censure.[18]

The freedom to write *as one wishes*—which is, of course, a fiction—comes only with authorization. Tenured academicians, for example, have a very different position in the institution vis-a-vis their writing; that is, they have much more freedom to compose nontraditional essays. As I imagined whose work I might write about in this section on authority and discourse, a number of possibilities came to mind—bell hooks, Jane Tompkins, even Robert Connors and Andrea Lunsford—but the name that stood out was Victor Vitanza. Vitanza is, perhaps more than any other contemporary rhetorician, known for his transgressive discourses. A tenured professor at the University of Texas at Arlington, Vitanza has for many years constructed discourses that embody poststructuralist principles, both in their form on the page and in their content. Two passages from "Octalog: The Politics of Historiography," itself a nontraditional essay, illustrate Vitanza's prose:

> My political/rhetorical/hysteriographical positions cannot be paraphrased; they can be only performed. Therefore, forced to write a paraphrase, I lie . . . and therefore at best give contra/dictory stage directions: ("Octalog" 8)

> VICTOR VITANZA: i. . . . faraway voices are telling us: Of arms and the *mask*uline and its history of rhetorik, We do not sing; instead, of "the body hysteric" and its histeries of the antibody rhetorics, We do sing.
> ii. In the nineteenth century, Walt Whitman wrote, "I sing the body electric."
> iii. Is this singing transcendentally above/beyond us? No! (To repeat, ever again) it is the body hysteric; . . . its locus is the body-*politic*-hysteric. . . . (15)

Vitanza engages subject and form in a radically constructive fashion, ignoring simple convention (capitalization, sentence boundaries, spelling) and simultaneously using these gestures to purposeful ends: *mask*uline, hysteries. His discourse is informed by his philosophical and theoretical relationship to the subject of his discourse—history and historiography. Although I cannot argue that these passages from Vitanza are free from academic genre, which is simply not the case, I will argue that Vitanza has taken a very playful, ludic, but nonetheless serious attitude toward academic discourse. These passages work against clarity and linearity and work with and from a hyperbolic abstractness.[19] What consequences must Vitanza shoulder for his playful and transgressive writing? Thomas Kent writes that a form that ignores or strays too far from the "determinate and public form that communicants can identify" risks be(com)ing incomprehensible. "[G]enre," Kent posits, "constitutes the public form that an utterance must assume in order to be comprehensible" (295), and forms that do not match with readers' generic expectations go misunderstood or unread. Vitanza, of course, realizes this.

I intend these few examples linking the relative positions of students and untenured faculty, and contrasting them with Vitanza's position, as illustrations of the ways discourses are constrained by and generated through institutional authorizing structures. Vitanza's decisions are determined in part by his relationship to and position in the ruling social collective, the institution. He is, despite his transgressive discourses, empowered by his authorization within and through the social collective and by his perceived "authority" over his subject. I use the colonizing metaphor purposefully here. Students ask, "Why can Hemingway write choppy sentences and I can't?" "Why can Faulkner go on for pages with a single sentence and I can't?" Or graduate students may well ask, "Why can Vitanza get away with this and I can't?" The bare and perhaps unsavory truth of the matter is indeed something akin to "You have to know the rules in order to break them." Or more precisely, "You have to prove (to "us") that you know the rules before we'll *let* you break them." Such is the response implied in writing pedagogies dominated by conventional, static, and hegemonic constructions of subject and genre. As people composing texts, students and faculty alike find themselves (consciously or unconsciously) facing a nexus of audience, subject, and purpose complicated by convention, expectation, and demands, but the consequences of breaking those conventions, of not meeting expectations or demands, varies significantly.

Genre (form) is determined by subject, audience, and author. For students, their relationship to the evaluative audience is the one that most impacts the generative power of the relationship between author, subject, and form. Students who face teachers as an evaluative audience are often constrained rather than empowered by that audience and as a result negotiate differently with the subject of discourse and form. That is, their constructive engagement with the subject is mitigated by their concern for and subordinate relationship to the teacher as evaluative audience. Similarly, untenured faculty who face external evaluators and senior colleagues as evaluative audiences are often more constrained than empowered by their audiences and therefore engage their subjects and construct their discourses partially in response to those audiences. Students search for clues to an instructor's biases, desires, and expectations. Untenured faculty are equally investigative and protective: Write what you need to write to get tenure (so the lore goes) then you can write what you want to write. This is not simply a commentary on the status of authorization in the academy;

these sorts of evaluations and demands are inevitable in *any* discursive situation, for all discourses are constructed within larger social collectives that determine what counts as knowledge. Nevertheless, this comparative analysis leads me to a rather problematic pedagogical question: Given the institutional context in which students are writing, and given the inevitable power of the evaluative audience on the construction of students' discourses, what does it mean to ask students to write in nontraditional essay forms?

### Situating the Subject in the Composition Classroom

If compositionists believe that the goal of writing instruction is not solely, or even primarily, to teach students to compose discourses that demonstrate knowledge but also to engage and explore their knowledge and their subjects as hooks suggests, then composition pedagogies and essay assignments must assume an epistemic and participative orientation toward the subject of discourse by encouraging students to "confront, disturb, demand that listeners . . . alter ways of hearing and being" (hooks, *talking back* 16). This is more easily said than done, of course. But it is not impossible. Initiating an epistemic and participative pedagogy with regard to subjects of discourses requires writing teachers to (1) emphasize the role of form in the construction and representation of knowledge, (2) articulate to their students a dynamic subject, and (3) lay bare the play of power within the classroom and institution in an effort to allow students to move away from pleasing discourses to discourses that work to encourage what Bakhtin refers to as "ideological becoming."

*Different functions, different forms.* If students are to engage genre as more than a template passively applied or slavishly followed, composition teachers must represent form as a constructive and active element in the development of discourse. Like Maxine Hairston who argues that people use different writing processes when composing different discursive products, I believe that different functions require and result in different forms. Just as processes vary according to the product, so, too, do forms vary according to subject, audience, and purpose. As the nexus of relationships among author, audience, and subject changes, so do the formal demands of the discourse. Conversely, as the form of discourse changes, so, too, do the relationships among, and proximity of, author, audience, and subject. Consider the difference between asking students to compose an essay as a city council person aimed at persuading corporate executives to invest in professional baseball in a midwestern city and asking students to compose letters as citizens to the local newspaper supporting the same venture. What composition teachers know, of course, and what we have always told students, is that these two discourses take on different forms because they entail different author-audience relationships, purposes, and contexts. What compositionists have not examined in any concentrated or programmatic fashion is the *generative effects* of having students "play" with subject and form as a means of exploring the specific ways that form changes, even constructs, meaning.

Like Volosinov, Walker Percy recognizes that a person's "sovereignty" over her right to see and know a subject (in Percy's essay, the Grand Canyon or a dogfish) without intrusion is a fiction. All subjects, images, and events are "preformulated." Percy argues, however, that a person can employ strategies to work against that preformulation. Percy discusses choosing to see without the benefit of "facilities for seeing" the subject (e.g., getting off of the beaten track, examining without the aid of dissecting tools) that, in conjunction with a later "dialectical movement" *back* to those same facilities, makes the familiar unfamiliar again, but "at a level above it" (396).

Although they do not explicitly present their assignment sequences as a means of examining the generative effects of discursive form, of working against the "preformulation" of subjects and genres, Patricia Bizzell and Bruce Herzberg provide students the means of initiating such an examination in *Negotiating Difference*. In an assignment sequence in their unit on "Wealth, Work, and Class Conflict in the Industrial Age," Bizzell and Herzberg present students with five assignments, each of which asks the students to engage from different authorial and generic perspectives the question of understanding class conflict in the United States. They ask students to compose a personal narrative relating their first conscious realization of social and economic class differences; a letter as a member of the Workingmen's Party of Illinois to Andrew Carnegie regarding his comments on inequality; a researched essay that describes how race compounds economic differences; an analytical essay that examines and evaluates divergent opinions on the Gospel of Wealth; and a final essay "in which you analyze the solutions to class conflict that are imagined in these selections [Alger, Carnegie, Conwell, Bellamy, Lloyd, a Senate Committee on labor relations]," interpret the various positions, and construct an answer to the question of class conflict (603–4). As the genre of the discourse changes, so, too, does the authorial relationship to the subject of class conflict. These shifting relationships and purposes generate new knowledge for the author. A student writing a personal narrative constructs one way of seeing class conflict. When she then writes analyses of others' opinions, she constructs another way of seeing that same subject. Each form presents its own generative capabilities.

*The subject's power of persuasion.* As Shelley's epigraph earlier in this chapter suggests, authors work from the capabilities inherent in a subject, designing from the ideas that the subject suggests. Yet, as I have demonstrated, most composition textbooks do not engage the subject of discourse as a generative constituent of an utterance. The essays students are asked to compose for college writing courses generally do not entail recognizing that the subject at hand is both persuasive and heteroglossic. Although the subject of a student essay does not speak in the same way the hero of a Dostoevsky novel can be said to speak, it can become an active participant in and coauthor of the discourse. Such a participative orientation toward the subject of discourse allows students and teachers to approach writing, reading, and research as epistemic activities.

Let me illustrate briefly what I mean by defining reading and research (in addition to writing) as epistemic. In classrooms structured around communicative and rhetorical orientations toward the subject of discourse, students undertake research as a means of demonstrating knowledge. Although their individual strategies for collecting and evaluating information differ, they all seek information from "outside" sources that support their position and serve them as they work to inform, move, or persuade their readers. By contrast, a classroom founded on a participative orientation toward the subject assumes that students do not formulate, defend, or demonstrate positions so much as they explore the various perspectives housed in their subjects and the ideological, rhetorical, and ethical implications of certain formulations as they work to construct their "own" perspectives. Through reading about, researching, and discussing their reading and research, students begin to understand their perspectives as engaged with, informed by, and dialogically related to their subjects and others' utterances about those subjects. This participative approach to research acknowledges the generative, epistemic power of subjects and sources in constructing the author's position.

Frank Farmer, in "'A Language of One's Own': A Stylistic Pedagogy for the Dialogic Classroom," describes a series of three exercise sequences and a final writing assignment that asks students to explore a subject (prosopagnosia, a type of neurological condition) and its various "voices" and ideological assumptions. Students begin the first sequence by locating, reading, and summarizing an article on prosopagnosia for a general reading audience. They then share their summaries with one another, revising their own definitions based on their classmates' summaries. In the second sequence, students read Oliver Sacks's "The Man Who Mistook His Wife for a Hat," and for the third sequence Antonio Damasio's scholarly article, "Review of Research on Prosopagnosia." Students summarize both Sacks and Damasio, as they did with the article in the first sequence, and then undertake a stylistic analysis of the two articles, looking for places where the two "sound like" one another and describing how the authors construct their voices. And in an important participative move, Farmer then has students "[r]eread closely the three summaries," looking for "changes or differences in the language you used to write your summaries" (21). How, Farmer asks students, does the type of writing affect *your* writing? By asking students to examine their own discursive practices and tendencies as they read and summarize others' discourses, Farmer asks them to reread themselves in terms of both their own discourses and the discourses of others.

As compositionists begin to imagine a participative and epistemic orientation toward the subjects about which their students write, the following series of questions serves as a starting point for engaging the persuasive power of the subjects of discourse.

- What are your initial positions on this subject? What sources inform your present positions? Why are these sources compelling for you? Why would they (not) be compelling for others?
- How (and why) did reading this cultural text confirm, alter, or question your positions?
- How does the position of this text relate to the information it presents or contrast with the positions of or information from other texts you've read? How can you reconcile or account for the differences/similarities?
- What sources inform this text? (Who is cited? referred to?) What effect do these sources have on your reading of the text?

A series of questions like this implies that "ideological analysis" need not "begin by assuming a common world of public language, but rather an already-divided, conflictual, and contested scene of social languages or 'discursive practices'" that compels a reader to search not for an ideological center but for the tensions and relationships among the ideologies present in the text (Klancher 83–84).[20]

By describing the subject as an active participant, an agent in the making of meaning, writing teachers demonstrate to students that the texts and subjects they study and write about can infuse them, engage them, and lead them to a productive self-examination at the same time they are examining their subject. Students can then begin to understand the generative nature of the subject.

*The subject of discourse and ideological becoming.* As students engage subjects and genres in the ways suggested by the work of Farmer, Percy, and Bizzell and Herzberg, they must also face the complexity and contradiction of voices within a subject and the daunting task of making up their minds about their own participative orientation(s) toward and relationship(s) with their subjects and others' utterances about those subjects. This making up of one's mind, this coming to know, is what Bakhtin refers to as "ideological becoming"—the "process of selectively assimilating the words of others," a "struggle within us for hegemony among various available verbal and ideological points of view, approaches, directions, and values" (Bakhtin, "Discourse" 341, 346). The process of ideological becoming, the struggle for finding and claiming an orientation toward and relationship to a subject, is punctuated by an eventual "liberation" of one's discourses from the "authority of the other's discourse" (348). To claim, as Bakhtin does, that one's discourse is "liberated" from the "authority" of another's discourse is not to say that the two discourses do not interact or inform one another, but rather that another's discourse no longer demands unconditional allegiance. One's discourse is "free" to question the authority of another's discourse, but one can do so only with its assistance. "Within the arena of almost every utterance," Bakhtin writes,

> an intense interaction and struggle between one's own and another's word is being waged, a process in which they oppose or dialogically interanimate each other. . . . [O]ne may speak of another's discourse only with the help of that alien discourse itself, although in the process, it is true, the speaker introduces into the other's words his own intentions and highlights the context of those words in his own way. (354–55)

The process of ideological becoming is a contested process with great consequences and great rewards. Students who actively engage their subjects, who seek to affect and be affected by others' discourses, emerge from the process with voices constructed out of and through the voices of others. Ideological becoming is not an easy or quick process, nor is it a process readily taught.

The extended, heteroglossic nature of an active, interactive hero and its role in students' ideological becoming suggests that compositionists might do well to revisit their understanding of the object of discourse. The hero—as it manifests itself in students' reading and writing—provides new directions for teaching students about the process of composing, particularly, perhaps, when that composing entails researched sources. As part 2 of *A Pedagogy of Possibility* demonstrates, compositionists are in a unique position within the academy to provide students the tools and strategies from which to pursue their own ideological becoming and work against the preformulations of their experiences. By understanding the subject of discourse as a hero, teachers of writing may begin to encourage among students a new understanding of their relationships with subjects and a deeper appreciation for the forms of their discourses and their engagement with others' discourses.

# PART TWO

## The Power and Politics of Pedagogy

During a pre-term orientation for new graduate students at the University of Texas at Austin in the late 1980s, John Ruszkiewicz, then director of Freshman English, spoke on the hazards of teaching writing on the basis of an accumulation of tips uninformed by a more comprehensive philosophy of composition. Ruszkiewicz was impressing upon the new students—most of whom would very shortly be teaching composition for the first time—the need for a pedagogy informed by a defined set of assumptions and beliefs about writing and writing instruction. Once a teacher has articulated a philosophy of writing instruction to himself, Ruszkiewicz suggested, he can then make decisions about how to conduct his classroom, develop writing assignments, and evaluate student writing. I recall Ruszkiewicz's comments at that orientation session each time I teach "Introduction to the Teaching of Writing" or mentor graduate students teaching writing courses. His comments are fundamental to the way I have come to define my own approach to teacher training. And in a way, *A Pedagogy of Possibility* is my own extended teaching philosophy, an elaborated statement of the beliefs and assumptions that inform my own pedagogy. Readers who have stayed with me this far will, I believe, appreciate the process that is reflected in this book. All of my comments are, in effect, preparatory to any actual instruction.

Middendorf finds such practical applications of Bakhtin wanting. I argue, somewhat contrary to her, that scholarly inquiry on Bakhtin and composition studies needs to establish an extended understanding of Bakhtinian principles and their implications for the teaching of writing before exploring possible applications of those principles. Nevertheless, I understand the desire of compositionists like Middendorf to see theory at work in pedagogy. As many of the scholars writing on Bakhtin and composition studies are aware, tensions exist between Bakhtinian theories and their application in the classroom. A passage from Jon Klancher speaks to this reluctance to implement Bakhtinian pedagogies:

I will not offer a simple classroom technique in which Bakhtin's method can be straightforwardly "applied." Composition pedagogy today is thick with techniques and technical solutions. Bakhtin's expansive cultural scope begs technical solutions to narrowly defined problems and invites us to redefine certain basic matters of writing and teaching themselves. (84)

Klancher articulates here a theme central to *A Pedagogy of Possibility*: Bakhtinian assumptions about language, culture, and ideology prompt us to "redefine certain basic matters of writing and teaching themselves." But that does not leave me without a desire to put Bakhtin to good use in redefining composition pedagogy. Bakhtin's work reveals much about the nature of language, reality, communication, beliefs, and knowledge, and these certainly inform how we teach writing, or any subject, for that matter. Like Klancher, however, I resist offering a simplified classroom technique in which Bakhtin's method can be straightforwardly 'applied.' Throughout this text I have strived to meet Klancher's challenge by suggesting a Bakhtinian reconfiguration of the discipline as well as redefinitions of the author, audience, and subject of discourse.

In this second part of *A Pedagogy of Possibility*, I continue to resist the move toward technique and solution by positing a series of issues to be addressed rather than problems to be solved. Those readers looking for sample assignments will be disappointed; I offer none. I provide something I believe to be more useful in the long run—new ways of thinking about critical reading, paragraphing, quotation, and paraphrase, four issues that writing teachers often take for granted and present unselfreflexively to their students. By examining these fundamental elements of writing instruction through a Bakhtinian lens, I undertake the process of "reknowing" proposed by Walker Percy in which I encounter the familiar, not "under approved circumstances" but on foreign ground, and then return through a "dialectical movement" to the "beaten track but one level above it" (396).

## TAKING A CUE FROM OHIO STATE

In 1994, Ohio State University Provost Richard Sisson and Vice President David Williams charged the University's newly formed Committee on the Undergraduate Experience (CUE) with conducting a review of the quality of the educational, social, and cultural lives of the undergraduate population at the university. That committee, which submitted its report to Sisson and Williams the following year, examined, among many other issues, the state of the relationship between university faculty and undergraduate students. Included in the final report is the following contract, entitled "Mutual Respect in the Classroom: Shared Expectations," with which faculty and students were urged to comply:

The *dynamic relationship between a college student and a teacher* is unique and can be profoundly rewarding. Successful higher education occurs when this relationship is effective and honored. Students, parents, the institution itself, and the public desire the best learning outcomes. When mutual respect is present in the classroom, the following expectations are fulfilled:

Teachers show respect for students and learning. Teachers:

- Are knowledgeable about the subject matter[.]
- Are prepared for class with materials and visuals designed with all students in mind, including those with disabilities.
- Approach each class with enthusiasm for the learning process and academic inquiry[.]
- *Foster an environment of collaborative learning, encouraging active participation rather than passive attendance.*
- Respect students as individuals, taking into account a student's learning style, background, and demands on time.
- Set high performance standards and communicate how to achieve them successfully.
- Clearly state the standards for evaluating student work when assignments are given.
- Return student work or respond to student inquiries in a timely fashion.
- Honor office hours and be reasonably available at other times.
- Refrain from using language, humor, or course examples that may be insulting or insensitive.

Students show respect for teachers and learning. Students:

- Prepare for each class and laboratory session[.]
- Approach each class with enthusiasm for the learning process and academic inquiry.
- *Are willing to be active learners in the classroom.*
- Value diversity in the classroom, refraining from using language that may be insulting or insensitive.
- Commit the necessary time and effort required in each course.
- Finish assignments in a timely fashion.
- Communicate with the teacher to prevent an issue from becoming an insurmountable problem.
- Respect the learning environment by minimizing distractions such as arriving late or reading other materials in class.
- Provide candid evaluations and recommendations for teachers. (12; emphasis added)

I include this section of the Ohio State CUE report to suggest that institutions, educators, and students alike are struggling to come to terms with the nature of their shared and interrelated responsibilities in the university. In its attempts, CUE characterized the conducive learning environment as a dynamic one in which students and instructors share responsibility for active learning. This same philosophy of learning informs *A Pedagogy of Possibility* and is further developed in this, the second part of the text.

## THE RUNDOWN ON PART TWO

Among the issues presented in part 2 are students' reading of texts, their methods of constructing discourse and reporting the words of others, and the discipline's recent debates regarding academic literacies. In all cases, Bakhtinian constructs—that is, authoritative and internally persuasive discourse, reported speech, and interanimation—redirect disciplinary discussions.

In chapter 5, "Active Engagement and Passive Reception: Critical Reading and Writing in Composition," I examine the first of these issues—students' reading of texts. I begin by introducing constructs from Bakhtin—as well as from Robert Scholes, William Perry, and Mary Belenky et al.—that I find useful in describing writers' processes of ideological becoming. After establishing this context and looking at the ways that Bakhtinian ideas enrich previous work on basic writing, particularly that of Mike Rose and David Bartholomae, I examine the assumptions behind my own uses of authoritative and internally persuasive discourse, concluding that the construct I initially developed simply reinforced deficit models. Partly narrative in form, the chapter moves through the process of change my own thinking has undergone with regard to these Bakhtinian terms. As such, the chapter develops through a series of discursive texts from undergraduate students, graduate students, and faculty until it reaches its conclusion in an elaborated understanding of critical reading and writing as essential in ideological development. Because of its stance on "no alibi learning," the chapter carries with it an inherent ethical imperative, one unmistakably present in the CUE Report and in Bakhtin's *Toward a Philosophy of the Act*, from which the phrase "no alibi living" comes.

Chapter 6, "The Politics of Reported Speech and the Ideology of Form," critiques current methods for teaching quotation and paragraphing. I select quotation and paragraphing because they demonstrate the degree to which composition pedagogy continues to rely upon current-traditional practices and because Volosinov speaks explicitly to these two elements and notes their ideological and rhetorical complexities. Redefining paragraphs as dialogic and reexamining quotation and paraphrase as ideologically bound activities are not the most critical issues facing composition studies, but suggesting that Bakhtinian theory reaches even to the most mundane elements of writing instruction attests to its power and appeal.

As I articulate throughout *A Pedagogy of Possibility*, one of the goals I propose is a writing course that shifts the focus away from improving student's individual performances on discrete writing assignments toward developing students' skills as people writing. In chapter 7, "Toward a Pedagogy of Possibility," I argue that the classroom must become an explicit site for introducing students to reading and writing as activities that demand both proficiency and productivity, emanate from both polemic and parodic contexts, and serve both polemic and parodic ends. The complexity of the dialogic and heteroglossic understanding of language that informs a pedagogy of possibility requires, as well, that teachers present and model for students strategies for orchestrating the various voices that inhabit their writing.

Changing teaching practices and philosophies will not be easy, as Marilyn Cooper reminds us: "[P]ractices that draw on the model of dialogic literacy are not easy to insert into current academic practices: they often do not feel traditional or comfortable; they may feel very threatening to some teachers and indeed to some students" (537). Many of the ideas and assumptions that inform a pedagogy of possibility are not entirely foreign to writing instructors, but their articulation as part of a comprehensive philosophy of composition probably is. A manifesto, of sorts, *A Pedagogy of Possibility* strives to reimagine the writing classroom as a dynamic site of education and intellectual challenge that recognizes both the constraints and possibilities of language in students' struggles to locate themselves in the university. A pedagogy of possibility, despite its foreign feel, offers compositionists a way of more fully implementing poststructuralist notions of authorship, language, and ideology without sacrificing the quality of writing instruction or ignoring the teacher's responsibility to prepare students for their work in the university and beyond.

# FOUR

# Active Engagement and Passive Reception
## Critical Reading and Writing in Composition

This chapter elaborates on the claim that successful critical reading and writing (defined as actively engaged reading and writing) are dependent upon a person's conscious efforts to represent others' words in terms of her own experiences, positions, and concerns. The argument is informed, in part, by a narrative thread that demonstrates the development of my own thought over the course of several years on the usefulness of authoritative and internally persuasive discourse in defining how people writing negotiate their own authority relative to their subjects. As the narrative demonstrates, I first examined authoritative and internally persuasive discourses solely in terms of basic writers' texts; only after several months of developing an argument that I later realized further marginalized them as deficient did I recognize that the process of actively engaging texts, and assimilating them as internally persuasive, was not a *problem* that basic writers alone faced, but a recursive *process* in any person's ongoing ideological becoming, her "growth and commitment" (Ronald and Roskelly's phrase).

As I looked beyond the confines of the basic writing classroom, and at students' writing, my own writing, and other academicians' representations of their own reading and writing, I reformulated my own understanding of the complexity of active reading and writing in the university and posited the two dispositions toward discourse, passive reception and active engagement, that inform this chapter. Authoritative and internally persuasive discourse hold great promise for composition studies as central features of passive reception and active engagement and of a pedagogy of possibility, which holds that only through productive (generative) reading and writing are students constructively engaged in education, in their own ideological becoming. As John Edlund points out, all of the difficulties students encounter with writing cannot be accounted for by invoking the inevitable tensions that they must negotiate as they test their beliefs, but defining critical reading and writing as means of ideological becoming provides an alternative way of constructing disciplinary discussions of the processes by which readers critically engage and then struggle to write about texts.

## CRITICAL LITERACY EDUCATION
## IN COMPOSITION STUDIES

Many of the recent clarion calls for educational reform in literacy education in American public schools and institutions of higher learning have centered around the need for improving the quality of students' critical reading and writing abilities. Just what is meant by critical thinking, reading, and writing, however, is less clear than the perceived need for such skills. Generally, within composition studies are two schools of thought on the definitions and goals of critical thinking and critical literacy. The first group, characterized by such scholars as Rise Axelrod, Charles Cooper, and Charles Bazerman, defines critical reading rather broadly, ascribing no *overt* political agenda to developing critical literacy skills. They posit critical thinking as a set of problem-solving strategies and as a means of inquiry. Critical reading entails, for example, that the reader "gather, analyze, select, and organize the information" (Axelrod and Cooper, *St. Martin's* 442). The means of review and analysis of that information include paraphrasing, summarizing, examining figurative language, logic, and the author's credibility.[1]

In another of their texts, *Reading Critically, Writing Well*, Axelrod and Cooper present "reading for meaning" (xix), an orientation toward the text that asks students to engage it from their own perspectives, which the authors recognize as socially "influenced." Like Axelrod and Cooper, Bazerman emphasizes the active role readers must take as they encounter new texts, a gesture that suggests that he also recognizes and attempts to help students understand the *generative* nature of active critical reading. Axelrod and Cooper encourage students to "read *with a critical eye*, not just comprehend passively and remember what you read but also scrutinize it actively and evaluate it" (*St. Martin's* 442; emphasis in original); although they focus on presenting students with discursive strategies, they also recognize the need for students to examine the assumptions they bring to the texts they are reading, noting that, as readers, they must be willing to challenge their own beliefs.

Bazerman's description provides a more elaborated description of the nature of this understanding of active critical reading:

> Real intellectual exchange begins when we *react* to what we read. . . . But if we swallow our reading whole, without thought, we will only be accepting empty phrases. We may parrot those phrases on an examination or at a cocktail party, but those memorized words will never affect our own thinking or lead us to say anything new. They will simply replace our thinking process with mimicry. . . . Unless we fit the words we read into everything else we think and know, we are only pretending to read. (19)

Bazerman's description bears a striking resemblance to the Bakhtinian belief that readers must make an alien word their own through an active engagement with it. What Axelrod and Cooper, Bazerman, and dozens of other compositionists suggest by discussing critical reading and presenting writing strategies in this fashion is that only by actively engaging texts do students make meaning. Memorization and mimesis gain students nothing in terms of their work at becoming more informed and more educated. Like Volosinov, these compositionists also suggest through their textbooks that "[o]nly active understanding can grasp theme—a generative process can be grasped only with the aid of another generative process" (Volosinov, *Marxism* 102). Clearly, Bazerman, Axelrod and Cooper emphasize the need for students to examine their own relationship with and reaction to a given text.

The second school of thought on critical literacy is characterized by the work of such scholars as Paulo Freire, Henry Giroux, Peter McLaren and Colin Lankshear, and Ira Shor who propose that critical literacy entails not only an active engagement with text and the questioning of personal beliefs, but also, and more importantly, a questioning of institutional ideological assumptions. Such a questioning of institutional ideological assumptions leads students, ideally, to recognize, reject, and ultimately subvert and transform oppressive institutional or political practices. Through its pedagogy, critical teaching in the United States presumes and strives to enact the beliefs

> that American citizens should understand, accept, and live amicably amidst the realities of cultural diversity—along axes of gender, race, class, and ethnicity—that are the hallmarks of American society. It presumes that people are entitled to fairness in their social and economic lives. It presumes that a critical citizenry, willing as well as able to take responsibility for the nation's future, is preferable to a passive, unengaged citizenry that lets government, business, and mass media do its thinking. Finally, it presumes that no one group is exclusively entitled to the privilege of representation, but that each has a right to tell its story, critique other stories, and participate in forming a community responsive to the needs of all its members. (Knoblauch and Brannon 6)

One of the issues left unaddressed by Knoblauch and Brannon's description and overlooked by critical pedagogy scholars is the great dissensus among an engaged American citizenry regarding the nature of rights, participation, fairness, or the route the nation should take in achieving a sound economic and social future for its citizens. The unexamined assumption among these scholars is that people who take the time and make the effort to become informed will necessarily turn to critique what the critical pedagogues themselves define as injustice, discrimination, or oppression.

### Ideological Becoming and "Good" Writing

As critical pedagogy scholars suggest, however, composition pedagogy must not ignore the contextual nature of critical reading and writing as it is situated within the vexing set of relationships among students, teachers, subject matter, and institution. For example, to characterize as deficient or recalcitrant students who are unable or unwilling to engage texts critically is to characterize them without examining *why* they respond to texts as they do. Critical reading enacted in a classroom, like any discursive production, is defined by institutional practices and expectations, a student's authority, and the relationship between her experiences and the reading she's being asked to undertake. Bazerman, Axelrod and Cooper, for example, represent critical reading as an encounter between reader and text, ignoring the complications of the encounter that occur as a result of the institutional context in which it takes place. As Knoblauch and Brannon warn, to ignore the *politics* of literacy and representation—"how things are named" and "who has the authority to do the naming and who doesn't" (5)—is to ignore the very events that shape the goals of education.

Coming to critical awareness (and with it critical reading and writing ability) is a process constrained by social forces and institutions. To name critical reading and writing as part of a process and make it an explicit part of a pedagogy is to define a fundamental role for writing instruction in the university. Critical literacy should aim to transform both the student and her culture and might begin by examining the subject position of students in the classroom.[2] Such transformations, Bakhtin reminds us, are achieved only through engagement, struggle, negotiation, and dialogue. We must redefine and contextualize students' "inability" to think or write critically. We must impress upon ourselves and our students the generative nature of reading and writing and their crucial role in ideological becoming, for "[t]he person who understands must not reject the possibility of changing or even abandoning his already prepared viewpoints and positions" (Bakhtin, "From Notes" 142). At the same time, we cannot predict the route those transformations will take. Some students, rather than question the authority of the institution to determine their futures through its fiscal policies and educational mandates, may become more firmly convinced of the *necessity* of the institution to direct, even mandate students' educational decisions. Unlike critical pedagogies, which are informed by a leftist ideology, a pedagogy of possibility recognizes that the role of literacy education is not to dictate outcomes but to provide students with opportunities for, and assist them in, developing skills that will make them active participants in a democratic society regardless of their political affiliations. A pedagogy of possibility strives to silence no one and empower everyone, even at the recognized risk of empowering further those who are already fully represented.

Bakhtin posits in *Toward a Philosophy of the Act* a "non-alibi in Being" (40), which requires responsibility of all people for the ways they live their lives and answerability to others for their actions. This phrase is also applicable to learning, for to state that there is no alibi for living is to argue that all persons must be thoughtful and engaged, that they must make a commitment to learning and not fall into the pattern of what Bazerman refers to as "pseudo-boredom," "when you feel you just cannot be bothered to figure out what all the new information and ideas mean; the mind backs away from a real and demanding occupation." The "only cure for pseudo-boredom," Bazerman continues, "is to become fully and personally involved in the book . . . in front of you" (20). To be engaged actively in living and learning is a difficult, time-consuming, and tiring task. Yet, only through active critical reading, and by engaging the ideological discourses they encounter, will students work toward "ideological becoming," that "process of selectively assimilating the words of others," of struggling to gain "hegemony among various available verbal and ideological points of view, approaches, directions, and values" (Bakhtin, "Discourse" 341, 346).

Ideological becoming entails constructing not only generative readings but also what I call "productive" discourse: situated discourse that engages the texts it encounters. Language, Bakhtin writes, "becomes 'one's own' only when the speaker populates it with his own intention, his own accent, when he appropriates the word, adapting it to his own semantic and expressive intention." And "although born of another or dynamically stimulated by another, [one's own discourse and one's own voice] will sooner or later begin to liberate themselves from the authority of the other's discourse" ("Discourse" 293–94, 348). As we might expect, the heteroglot word is made up of contradictory languages and ideological positions with regard to any given subject, and because of these inevitable tensions and contradictions, a person must actively choose her orientation among them. The mandate for ideological becoming emanates from the word itself, with its intense and unrelenting ideological struggle.

Given this understanding of the word and a person's need to orient herself among the various ideological positions, "good" critical reading and writing might be defined as *situated* writing through which a student struggles to engage and orient herself and her beliefs and, at the same time, recognizes her right to her "own" word. It is, Nancy Welch reminds us, "by orchestrating— not by repeating, not by silencing—that polyphony that the writer makes meanings heard" (495).[3] As students read and write, they must neither simply repeat the words of the other as authoritative nor ignore or silence them. The generative nature of reading and writing are made manifest in the *orchestration* of the words of others alongside their own. By encouraging students to "converse with, rather than retreat from, those alien voices that subvert their initial meanings," Welch initiates a call for critical literacy, for critical reading and writing that entails active engagement, constructing meaning out of texts that have become, to use a Bakhtinian phrase, "internally persuasive" (501). "Good writing" defined this way pushes a student to reflect on, engage, and contend with her ways of knowing, engaging her in the process of ideological becoming, "growth and commitment" (Ronald 27). A writing teacher then, Welch argues, has a dual mentoring role as she takes on the task of examining the "forces that have shaped who the student is" and exploring the means by which she might orchestrate those "forces," defining them not as authoritative but as internally persuasive discourses she engages rather than obeys (501).

*Active Engagement and Passive Reception*

WAYS OF ENGAGING OTHERS' WORDS

During my years of teaching, I have posed many questions to myself about students' writing, but two related questions in particular frustrated me as I reflected on my teaching of basic writing: "Why are some students unwilling to question authority?" and, concurrently, "Why are they unable to claim authority and write themselves into their texts?" Scholars and researchers who study basic writing offer insightful, but incomplete, answers to these questions. In some cases, they report that students' unsatisfactory performances may be accounted for by dialect or second language interference, learning disabilities, or an unfamiliarity with the conventions and rules governing the grammar, spelling, and syntax of Standard American English. That is, their higher interpretive and critical skills are hampered by an overriding concern for more local concerns or by a lack of fluency.

These responses helped to answer my question—to an extent. Still, many students at any of the institutions where I had taught—Yavapai College, Northern Arizona University, the University of Texas, Ohio State University—were unaccounted for: students whose grammar, mechanics, and spelling were, if not exemplary, at least acceptable; students who had mastered traditional academic writing tasks—comparison/contrast, definition, or argumentative essays—and all in the ubiquitous five paragraph format. These were students whose writing lacked voice, as Donald Stewart might put it. I heard my colleagues and myself lamenting, "These students keep telling me that they 'can't find topics to write about'; they 'have nothing to say'; 'nothing worth writing about has ever happened' to them; or they 'can't get an angle on the topic.'" I could see the result of some larger problem right there on the page, one not discernible as error or linguistic interference. The problems that all of these writers faced, I have come to believe, might be represented as a function of *un*critical thinking, reading, and writing, of an unwillingness or inability to combat "pseudo-boredom." However, these students, in many cases, were very successful in employing strategies like those outlined by Bazerman or Axelrod and Cooper; they could paraphrase and annotate in classroom exercises, yet when it came to generating their own discourse, they were unable to claim for themselves the right or privilege to speak. So I began investigating, though not successfully at first, the question of authority.

I became interested in the possibility of using the Bakhtinian constructs of authoritative and internally persuasive discourse in relation to students' writing when I first read "Discourse in the Novel." There, I found the point from which to begin to address the question of authority, not by asking "Why do some students write this way?" but by inquiring, "How do these students perceive texts and what stances do they take in relation to discourse and the institution that prevent them from writing effectively and authoritatively?" The answer I formulated in response to my own question was this: Students are conditioned to receive knowledge and discourse passively; they do not actively engage them.[4] Until they actively engage others' discourses they will be unable to produce their own effective responses.

## Authoritative Discourse

By authoritative discourse, Bakhtin means a discourse so powerful, so commanding, that it inspires only adoration and respect, and thereby functions as a centripetal force that maintains the status quo. Authoritative discourse is often intended by its users, and usually perceived by its hearers or readers, as untouchable, removed, and distanced; its binding authority seems unquestionable. Bakhtin defines authoritative discourse as that which

> demands that we acknowledge it, that we make it our own; it binds us, quite independent of any power it might have to persuade us internally; we encounter it with its authority already fused to it. The authoritative word is located in a distanced zone, organically connected with a past that is felt to be hierarchically higher. It is, so to speak, the word of the fathers. Its authority was already *acknowledged* in the past. It is a *prior* discourse. It is therefore not a question of choosing it from among other possible discourses that are its equal. It is given (it sounds) in lofty spheres, not those of familiar contact. Its language is a special (as it were, hieratic) language. It can be profaned. It is akin to taboo, i.e., a name that must not be taken in vain. (Bakhtin, "Discourse" 342; emphasis in original)

That is not to say that authoritative discourse cannot be analyzed or interpreted, but despite such commentaries, it remains remote and static. In her reading of Bakhtin, Julia Kristeva equates authoritative discourse with "God, 'History,' Monologism, Aristotelian logic, System, Narrative" (58).

Authoritative discourse takes many forms, but it often addresses political, ethical, moral, or religious issues. It is the monologic word of parents, elders, or teachers. It commands "unconditional allegiance" (Bakhtin, "Discourse" 343). Nancy Welch associates authoritative discourses with the act of "'reciting by heart' the static language of remote authorities" (495).[5] One cannot overlook the power attributed to authoritative discourse by its recipients. The authority of such discourses is granted not by its innate value but by generic, cultural, or religious tradition. It is, in other words, canonical knowledge or belief. A reader who views a discourse as authoritative does so not only because of the text itself, but also because of what surrounds that text, culturally, socially, or educationally.

When a reader reads a text authoritatively, that reader's voice, authority, and subjectivity are undermined. This model of reading valorizes the text and the power of the author and establishes a seemingly objective meaning. Those who read authoritatively do not achieve a dialogic understanding of a text. An authoritative text insists on only one reality—its own. This is a dangerous prospect for people in marginalized positions (e.g., students, women, people of color), because authoritative texts are created almost exclusively by and for (white) men and are in "complicity with" the "patriarchal ideology" about which Patrocinio Schweickart writes.

This authoritative approach to texts, as Judith Fetterley argues, is problematic, for it removes the text from the reader's grasp: "When only one reality is encouraged, legitimized, and transmitted, and when that limited vision endlessly insists on its comprehensiveness, then we have the conditions necessary for that confusion of consciousness in which impalpability flourishes" (xi).[6] Authoritative texts are held in such high esteem they become untouchable; they speak their "truths" with such power that readers no longer question the text's assumptions. As a responsive corrective, readers "can accurately name the reality they [literary works] do reflect and so change literary criticism from a closed conversation to an active dialogue" (Fetterley xxiii). By calling into question the covert universality of texts, readers reveal the relativity of the authoritative perspective represented in the text and set that perspective in dialogue with the reader. As Elizabeth Flynn and Schweickart point out, Fetterley also claims that "everyone, men and women alike, learns to read like a man," and reading in this manner is "to adopt the androcentric perspective that pervades the most authoritative texts of the culture" (Schweickart and Flynn xv).

Students, as a result, must learn to read otherwise—against the grain, in defiance of authority—because to do otherwise, to read passively (androcentrically, in Fetterley's terms), is to read *with* a text rather than against it; to grant it, in Bakhtinian terms, "authority." Authoritative texts and passive readings of them implicate readers in their own disempowerment, an act through which readers in effect *will* their right of sovereignty to the author, the expert, "within whose competence a particular segment of the horizon is thought to lie" (Percy 401). Readers who do not engage authoritative discourse that "aspires to the monologic . . . [and] attempts to fix meaning across situations and for all speakers and hearers" (Cooper 534) can do nothing but repeat the authoritative word, an act that is neither epistemic nor generative. By reading instead "under the sign of the 'Resisting Reader,'" as Schweickart suggests, readers begin to realize their goal of disrupting the "process of imasculation" and loss of sovereignty, for a resisting reader exposes texts to consciousness by "disclosing the androcentricity of what has customarily passed for the universal" (42). By reading actively and treating texts not as authoritative but as internally persuasive, students begin the task of generating their own word from, against, or alongside those texts.

As I mention briefly above, Bakhtin implies that the authority of a discourse is not inherent in the discourse itself. But I want to make that point explicit. No discourse commands the reverence and allegiance of all readers.[7] To be sure, some discourses hold a larger captivated audience than others, such as with the Koran, the Bible, the Declaration of Independence, a statistical study, or a scientific report. That authority is not, however, inherent in the text but in the authority attributed by a reader or a culture to its author; literary tradition; genre; or political, cultural, intellectual, or religious tradition. Thus, it is more useful to talk about *dispositions toward* discourse than about authoritative or internally persuasive discourse. Because authoritative discourse demands "unconditional allegiance" and is untouchable, existing in a "distanced zone," its authority *appears* inherent (Bakhtin, "Discourse" 342–343).

Students very often view the subjects about which they write, the people who have written about those subjects, and the instructors delivering the lecture or evaluating the essay as authoritative and unquestionable. A college sophomore writing about educational methodology, for example, may accept without question the discourses of her professors, the authors of her textbooks, and her cooperating teacher. If these experts disagree, however, she faces a dilemma. She must decide how to place herself within the debate. She may continue to view all of the opinions as more powerful than her own, in which case she will find some middle ground that allows her—however unsatisfactorily—*not* to enter the discussion, or she will engage the various approaches on her own terms and with regard to her own experiences, interacting with the previous positions as internally persuasive. For texts to become internally persuasive does not mean that the student cannot accept the approach to teaching expository writing championed by one of those whom she's read, but it does mean that she has become consciously aware of her position and its attendant ideological consequences. The discourses she engages are no longer remote; she enters into a dialogue with these previous utterances and with their authors to present her own utterance, her own contribution to the ongoing dialogue about teaching practices.

### Internally Persuasive Discourse

Bakhtin posits in contrast to authoritative discourse a resistant form of discourse—what he refers to as the "internally persuasive." Internally persuasive discourse, unlike authoritative, is proximate, dynamic, and closely connected to and assimilated with a person's own words. The internally persuasive word exists on the borders between two speaking subjects, achieving meaning through their repartee, through intertextuality and dialogism. Internally persuasive discourse does not demand allegiance but encourages creativity. Meaning-making is achieved by continuously and cooperatively sharing discourses. Like centrifugal forces that "decentralize," "disunify," and "stratify," internally persuasive discourse questions and denies the preeminence of the authoritative word and centripetal force. The internally persuasive discourse is "tightly interwoven with 'one's own word.' . . . Its creativity and productiveness consist precisely in the fact that such a word awakens new and independent words, that it organizes masses of our words from within, and does not remain in an isolated and static condition" (Bakhtin, "Discourse" 345). The feminist criticism described by Fetterley, like internally persuasive discourse, "represents the discovery/recovery of a voice, a unique and uniquely powerful voice capable of canceling out those other voices . . . which spoke about us and to us and at us but never for us" (xxiii–xxiv).

Bakhtin describes the importance of the internally persuasive word in ideological becoming by noting its

> decisive significance in the evolution of an individual consciousness: consciousness awakens to independent ideological life precisely in a world of alien discourses surrounding it, and from which it cannot initially separate itself; the process of distinguishing between one's own and another's discourse, between one's own and another's thought, is activated rather late in development. When thought begins to work in an independent, experimenting and discriminating way, what first occurs is a separation between internally persuasive discourse and authoritarian enforced discourse, along with a rejection of those congeries of discourses that do not matter to us, that do not touch us. ("Discourse" 345)

Here, as well, Bakhtin articulates the process of individuation as struggling for a separation that occurs "rather late in development."

The centripetal forces that inform the authoritative word—whether political, linguistic, or social—enforce conformity and conservatism and promote the status quo. A reader who reads a text as authoritative reaffirms that text's power and dominance over her. Conversely, centrifugal forces humor no dominance; instead, they encourage parody and subversion. Reading from an internally persuasive perspective entails making new meaning out of the text despite its authority. Kristeva defines centrifugal discourses in terms of "Practice, 'Discourse,' Dialogism, Correlational logic, Phrase, Carnival" (58). The centrifugal valorizes process, conversation, connection, intuition, and disorder, while the centripetal esteems product, lecture, autonomy, reason, and order. It is, I believe, easy to create a biological male/female dichotomy, as Kristeva seems to do, when dealing with such pairs of constructs as centripetal and centrifugal discourses, and I want to suggest instead that the dichotomy is rather one of empowerment/disempowerment on any axis (e.g., race, class, gender, ethnicity, expertise). The struggle to receive another's text may be difficult and is always politically charged.

Here feminist criticism like Kristeva's or Fetterley's supplements Bakhtinian assumptions.[8] Reading is an issue of power, and because women historically have been disempowered, resistant reading is a women's issue. The powerlessness of a woman's reading "derives from not seeing one's experience articulated, clarified, and legitimized in art, but more significantly the powerlessness . . . results from the endless division of self against self," estranging a woman from the text and from her own experiences and constantly reminding her that she is "other than"—other than male, other than that which is legitimately American—for "to be universal, to be American—is to be *not female*" (Fetterley xiii). What becomes clear with regard to Bakhtin's work and any attempts I make to redefine authoritative and internally persuasive discourse as constructs useful to feminist discussions of reading is that, as Schweickart suggests, "gender will have a prominent role as the locus of political struggle" (39).

Like anthropologists in foreign cultures, students reading, writing, and learning are urged to understand that seeing (interpreting) in new ways, from alternative positions, generates new and possibly unexpected insight into a subject. The dialogic movement from one to the other is generative. "A meaning," Bakhtin writes,

> only reveals its depths once it has encountered and come into contact with another, foreign meaning: they engage in a kind of dialogue, which surmounts the closedness and one-sidedness of these particular meanings, these cultures. We raise new questions for a foreign culture, ones that it did not raise itself; we seek answers to our own questions in it; and the foreign culture responds to us by revealing to us its new aspects and new semantic depths. Without *one's own* questions one cannot creatively understand anything other or foreign (but, of course, the questions must be serious and sincere). Such a dialogic encounter of two cultures does not result in merging or mixing. Each retains its own unity and *open* totality, but they are mutually enriched. ("Response" 7)

The task this sets out for the student is formidable, for it requires that she encounter the subject of her study, a "foreign culture," with questions already in mind. Without questions guiding her, she will come away with no further insight, and she and the subject she encounters will come away unchanged.

### EXTENDING THE DISCUSSION: ACTIVE ENGAGEMENT AND PASSIVE RECEPTION

> This reliance on authoritarian discourses is not unexpected—nor is it unproductive. Although we want students to come to see that some discourses might seem to be correct only because they are the traditional, or authoritarian, ones, they will not be able to see authoritarian discourse as authoritarian until they write it down and see how it operates in a context where it comes in conflict with other discourses.
> —Marilyn Cooper and Cynthia Selfe, "Computer Conferences"

As the brief discussion above suggests, compositionists recognize the need to urge students to engage texts in what might be called a dialogue. In this discussion, compositionists call upon theorists and researchers other than Bakhtin to support an active role for students as they negotiate their authority as readers and writers. The following list illustrates the range of sources that I use in developing the constructs of passive reception and active engagement, the dispositions toward discourse that inform a pedagogy of possibility.

Two Dispositions Toward Discourse

| *Passive Reception* | *Active Engagement* |
| --- | --- |
| Authoritative Discourse | Internally Persuasive Discourse |
| The authoritative word is "religious, political, moral; the word of a father, of adults, and of teachers, etc." (Bakhtin, "Discourse" 342). | The internally persuasive word exists on the frontier between two subjects; it is "half-ours, half-someone else's" (Bakhtin, "Discourse" 345). |

With its authority, it "demands our unconditional allegiance. . . . [I]t remains sharply demarcated, compact, and inert" (Bakhtin, "Discourse" 343).

An internally persuasive discourse encourages creativity, "awakens new and independent words . . . and does not remain . . . isolated (Bakhtin, "Discourse" 345).

### Centripetal Reading

"Centripetal reading conceives of a text in terms of an original intention located at the center of the text" (Scholes 8).

### Centrifugal Reading

Centrifugal reading "sees the life of the text as occurring along its circumference, which is constantly expanding, encompassing new possibilities of meaning" (Scholes 8).

### Basic Dualism

"Right Answers for everything exist in the Absolute, known to Authority whose role is to mediate (teach) them" (Perry 9).

"Knowledge and goodness are perceived as quantitative accretions of discrete rightness to be collected by hard work and obedience" (Perry 9).

### Commitment to Relativism

"[T]he student experiences the affirmation of identity among multiple responsibilities and realizes Commitment as . . . ongoing" (Perry 10).

"[K]nowing the world means understanding what has been rendered important by one's family, friends . . . and interests" (Bizzell, "William Perry" 448).

### Silence or Received Knowledge

The silent "feel passive, reactive, and dependent" (Belenky et al. 27).

Women "equate receiving, retaining, and returning the words of authorities with learning" (Belenky et al. 39).

### Constructed Knowledge

At this stage, "women come to the basic insights of constructivist thought: *All knowledge is constructed*, and *the knower is an intimate part of the known*" (Belenky et al. 137).

"[C]onstructivists establish a communion" (Belenky et al. 143).

### Believing

"Belief involves merging" and correlates with "acquiescence" (Elbow, *Embracing* 264).

### Doubting

"Doubting is the act of separating or differentiating" and "correlates with resisting authority" (Elbow, *Embracing* 264).

These two dispositions must work in consort, for both reception and engagement are, to varying degrees with various texts, necessary in achieving, maintaining, and creating knowledge. Selzer reminds us that

[s]ometimes readers are "passive"; in the terminology of communication theory, they are "receivers," uncritical receptacles for taking in messages. In one sense,

this view of communication sees messages as objects to be consumed and digested in the same way that a computer dispassionately takes in and stores information. In another sense, this view sees writing as a script and reading as a process of accepting cues spelled out, implicitly or explicitly, by a text. Whatever the metaphor, the reader becomes one who passively "processes" a piece of writing. While recent developments in critical theory, reading, and cognitive psychology have quite properly undermined this view of reading, it remains true that to read relatively passively remains an option for readers in certain circumstances. At times it makes sense to subordinate oneself to the text, to try to "process" the text as much as possible.[9] (170–71)

Given the sheer number of texts available, it is impossible to engage actively every one encountered, but Selzer goes beyond this impossibility of consumption to argue that passive reading is sometimes desirable.[10] Active engagement is the preferred form, an important *end* of education, but passive reception provides readers a necessary base from which to form their own interests and beliefs. Selzer continues:

But most often, of course, readers and reading are more active. . . . At the very least, reading means bringing to the text knowledge and experience that enable people to recognize connections and fill in omitted information. At most, reading means shaping the outcome of an encounter with a text—not "processing" but "making meaning." Someplace in the middle it means negotiating meaning—*negotiating* in both senses of the term—with the author through the text. (171; emphasis in original)

Selzer's statement includes an understanding of the active nature of reading as described by Bazerman or Axelrod and Cooper in that he distinguishes between "processing" (recognizing the significance of) the term and "making meaning" (dialogically and actively engaging it).

### Robert Scholes: Centripetal and Centrifugal Reading

Scholes presents two forms of reading that coincide with Bakhtin's concepts of authoritative and internally persuasive discourses, using "centripetal" and "centrifugal" to characterize the two forms. Centripetal reading aims to retain the original meaning granted to a text by its author; it "conceives of a text in terms of an original intention located at the center of the text." Centrifugal reading works away from that original intention, struggling against its boundaries. Scholes defines centrifugal reading as that which "sees the life of the text as occurring along its circumference, which is constantly expanding, encompassing new possibilities of meaning" (8). Both Scholes and Bakhtin attribute to centripetal forces an authority that readers are compelled to obey, and those attitudes toward knowledge generally and discourse specifically characterize an authoritative paradigm. Both writers also propose that, by interacting with another's word responding to it, readers may productively and actively engage knowledge and discourse. The act of reading centrifugally is not, however, as utopian as either Scholes or Bakhtin implies, for reading against the boundaries of a text is always a struggle—particularly for readers disempowered by the text.

### *William Perry and Mary Belenky et al.: Ethics and Epistemology*

In reporting their findings from a longitudinal study of Harvard undergraduates, William Perry and his associates created a scheme that describes the range of students' intellectual and ethical development, from seeing the world in terms of a basic duality, through the ability to entertain multiple points of view, to a kind of ethical relativism. Each stage in the process represents a different epistemological mode or stance through which students progress in their roles as learners.

Like authoritative discourse, Basic Dualism, the first of Perry's categories, characterizes a person's attitude toward knowledge as dependent upon the absolute word of authority. The world is made up of polarities of right and wrong, good and bad. The learner, Perry notes, associates with the good and right versus the wrong or the bad and perceives learning as passively gathering and retaining the word of authority. In addition, Perry contends that a student will fail who persists in regarding education as a process by which teachers impart knowledge and truth to students who simply receive and memorize it. Among these students I would place the basic writers about whom I was concerned when I first entertained authoritative and internally persuasive discourse—those students who not only passively receive knowledge but also approach writing as a matter of right and wrong. At the other end of Perry's scheme lies Relativism. By adopting a relativist world view, students both accept multiple and conflicting world views and establish their identities and ideologies within those worlds. In the end, a student who is a committed relativist realizes that existing productively in the world entails making ethical choices, which in turn entails actively engaging discourse and placing herself in relation to it.

Unlike Perry who found no student dualists, Mary Field Belenky, Blythe McVicker Clinchy, Nancy Rule Goldberger, and Jill Mattuck Tarule did. In what might be considered a companion study to Perry's, they investigated the patterns of women's acquisition of knowledge. The authors' category of Received Knowledge, as the previous list indicates, contributes to an understanding of passive reception and may be equated with centripetal and authoritative discourse and basic dualism, while their Constructed Knowledge joins centrifugal and internally persuasive discourses and Perry's Commitment to Relativism in forming a disposition of active engagement.[11] Like the basic dualists in Perry's study, women who see the world in terms of Received Knowledge understand learning as collecting, remembering, and reiterating information given to them by teachers. But, contrary to the young men in Perry's study, who associated themselves *with* Authority (with the right and good), Belenky et al.'s female subjects continued to perceive themselves *apart* from Authority and knowledge.

In the stages of basic dualism and received knowledge, the authors report, subjects played one of two roles. Young men tended to lecture, espousing the authoritative line, while women listened, reaffirming their subservience and obedience to authority. In both tendencies—lecturing and passively listening—the students model learning practices that promote their dependence on authority and passive reception of knowledge and reinscribe a patriarchal institutional hierarchy. In contrast to Received Knowledge, Belenky et al. posit Constructed Knowledge, another component of active engagement. By viewing knowledge and learning as social constructs, learners realize and take responsibility for building their own self-knowledge, achieving a sense of autonomy and individual voice, a sense of independent choice within a socially constructed world. And in an unusually Bakhtinian turn of phrase, Belenky et al. write that "constructivists establish a communion with what they are trying to understand" (143). That is, the constructivists the authors studied demonstrated an awareness of and closeness to the subjects of their inquiry.

Similarities exist among the terms of Bakhtin, Scholes, Perry, and Belenky et al., as I have noted. There is, on the one hand, a sense of absoluteness and authority that students are compelled to obey, and those attitudes toward knowledge generally and discourse specifically characterize a disposition of passive reception. On the other hand, by interacting with another's word and by responding to it, students may productively and actively engage knowledge and discourse.

Like Bakhtin, Perry and Belenky et al. also recognize "[i]nterpretation as the discovery of a path to seeing (contemplating) and supplementing through creative thinking" (Bakhtin, "Toward a Methodology" 159). Interpretation through reading and writing—contemplation that engages students in creative thinking and ultimately creative understanding—does not "renounce itself," its own position or culture (Bakhtin, "Response" 7).[12] At this point, the differences between a pedagogy informed by Bakhtinian theory and critical pedagogy become most distinct: Critical pedagogy aims to transform oppressive institutional and social structures; a pedagogy informed by a Bakhtinian creative understanding is not, as Cooper and Selfe argue, concerned about

> [w]hat particular discourse they [students] find internally persuasive . . . and it is not something we [teachers] can dictate in any case. Any discourse that matters to them can be adopted and adapted by students as internally persuasive, particularly when they are encouraged to bring in a variety of discourses. (866)

The *process* of coming to creative understanding (not the outcome) concerns Bakhtin, Perry, and Belenky and her coauthors.

*Active Engagement and Passive Reception*

*Peter Elbow: Doubting and Believing*

The process of critical reading, defined as an inquiry into one's relationship with a text and its hero, entails both passive reception and active engagement, although passive reception is clearly subordinate, functioning as an initial stage in the process of active engagement. In addition to resembling Scholes's, Perry's, and Belenky et al.'s constructs, Bakhtinian authoritative and internally persuasive discourses resemble later formulations of Peter Elbow's believing and doubting. Elbow describes the characteristics of doubting and believing this way:

> Doubting is the act of separating or differentiating and thus correlates with indi-
> vidualism; it permits the loner to hold out against the crowd or even—with logic—
> to conquer. Belief involves merging and participating in a community; indeed a
> community is created by—and creates—shared beliefs.
>   Doubting correlates with resisting authority; believing with acquiescence. . . .
> (*Embracing* 264)

Doubting aligns itself with an active disposition toward discourse and believing (in its acquiescence) with passive reception. Elbow himself recognizes the tandem of doubting and believing as a dialogic means of effective problem-solving, self-exploration, and social interaction. They are means of inquiry—"artificial, systematic, and disciplined uses of the mind" (258). Doubting and believing become "equally necessary" contraries in literary interpretation, the writing process, and the search for truths. Elbow maintains distinctions between the two methods, neither denying their individuality nor claiming one or the other as the privileged method of inquiry.[13]

In the final chapter of *Embracing Contraries*, Elbow develops a dialogue between the self and the internalized other, between doubting and believing that does not appear in his earlier work. This later version of doubting and believing recalls LeFevre's category of internally dialogized invention and moves toward a more social orientation to language. In the doubting and believing game, the interindividual territory on which meaning is negotiated is internalized; meaning is reached through the contrary activities of doubting and believing. Believing affirms the articulated thought on a particular topic; doubting questions and denies it.

Although doubting and believing are introduced in *Writing Without Teachers* and *Writing with Power* as two alternatives to response and evaluation, Elbow depicts them in *Embracing Contraries* as more political and ideological by suggesting their powers of consensus and dissensus.[14] This politicized doubting and believing game leads Elbow still closer to a Bakhtinian dialogic. A comparison of the two affirms the increasingly social nature of Elbow's method. Centripetal and centrifugal forces, like believing and doubting, represent the forces of consensus and dissensus respectively. An individual, through believing, speaks in unison and in harmony, or, through doubting, she speaks in dissonance with others. Whatever the case, she responds to the discourses that have preceded hers, believing and accepting the validity and persuasiveness of some, doubting and rejecting the claims of others. The audience to whom she directs her discourse is also instrumental in the construction of her discourse. The audience in turn believes or doubts—acquiesces to or resists—her discourse and, with it, her ideological position.

To study and analyze centripetal and centrifugal tendencies in a given utterance would no doubt prove a difficult task. The difficulty of separating and distinguishing the various conditions, influences, and voices giving rise to an utterance makes heteroglossia a difficult concept to describe, but not impossible, as Bakhtin suggests when he writes that "[i]t is possible to give a concrete and detailed analysis of any utterance, once having exposed it as a contradiction-ridden, tension-filled unity of two embattled tendencies in the life of language" ("Discourse" 272). Among the texts that most clearly embody the push and pull of centripetal and centrifugal forces, John Edlund and Nancy Welch argue, are the texts of student writers who struggle to attain the standard, centripetal discourse while retaining markings of centrifugal discourses in the forms of nonstandard dialect, other nonstandard linguistic characteristics, and/or ideological positions.[15] A basic writer's text, with all of its textures, makes apparent the linguistic and the ideological struggle that writers face as they work with the tensions between centripetal and centrifugal forces.[16] Every utterance is dialogic and contains both centralizing and decentralizing tendencies. Like the language of characters in a Dickens novel, an utterance composed by a student embodies "one point of view opposed to another, one evaluation opposed to another, one accent opposed to another" (Bakhtin, "Discourse" 314). The student's text often does not effectively conceal the struggle between centralizing and decentralizing forces—a characteristic that in many ways is *more* representative of the nature of writing, which is, according to the Bakhtinian understanding of language, inherently tension-filled, textured, and even contradictory.

In this sense, the text that is coherent and clear is one that has been clarified, made clear from the muddiness of its earlier form. Because of this, students' texts may provide one of the richest and most compelling points of departure for initiating the "concrete and detailed analysis" of which Bakhtin speaks. Nancy Welch provides such a point of departure when she discusses the work of Linda, a student in a colleague's first-year writing course. Linda's essay, which relates childhood experiences surrounding the naming of her mother's alcoholism, is at once awkward, confusing, and affecting. Rather than dismiss the apparent problems with the tensions between content and form, Welch argues that the tensions might be more productively read as "arising from the interaction of authoritative and internally persuasive voices, as a necessary step in the complicated process of making the word one's own" (497). John Edlund makes a similar observation regarding an essay by a male Korean student whose text, he suggests, "contains clear examples of hybrid constructions and heteroglossia" (61). The heteroglossia is not, however,

> entirely under the author's control. There is still a dialogue, but often the voices seem not to be listening to one another. In such texts, a word will be thrown out to stand for a concept that has not been sufficiently negotiated among the parties to the dialogue. Such a word has been appropriated, but not assimilated. The attempt of the writer to employ the word is premature, in that the ideological system of the writer has not restructured itself to accommodate the new word and the meanings and opinions it entails. In this case, new meanings are *not* created, unless they are accidental or extraneous ones. (61)

In examining the essays of Linda and the Korean student, Welch and Edlund neither valorize nor vilify the diversity of voices that appear, however problematically orchestrated or represented.[17] Instead, they use the apparent confusion and tensions as a means of working with the students to recognize and therefore begin the process of making authoritative discourses internally persuasive.

## BASIC WRITERS AND DISPOSITIONS TOWARD DISCOURSE

As I demonstrate above, the notions of authoritative and internally persuasive discourse are helpful in analyzing basic writers' work. I sensed among a fair number of students in my classes a disposition of passive reception characterized by their tendency to view texts as authoritative and removed, see the world as consisting only in polarities of right and wrong, and view education as a process of learning what others tell them is important. Although characterizing basic writers as passive receivers may have named the attitude they held, it did not tell me *why* they saw authority (theirs and others') and discourse in the way they did.

Other scholars, including Mike Rose in *Lives on the Boundary*, offer some insight into basic writers' attitudes by suggesting that their literacy backgrounds contribute a great deal to their dispositions toward learning and texts. Rose intimates that negative attitudes toward, distance from, limited involvement with, or rejection of texts affect placement in basic writing courses almost as much as any other factor. Consider the ways that Rose's terms echo the others that define passive reception: distance, involvement, and attitude recur as key factors in a person's relationship with discourse. By recasting Rose's comments in terms of dispositions toward knowledge and discourse, a few years ago I posited a working definition of basic writers as those students whose literacy backgrounds include, among other factors, a strong and crippling sense of textual authority. Basic writers—to a larger degree than more proficient writers— seemed to see the texts they encountered as authoritative and distanced; they had not yet questioned the authority of academic discourse.

David Bartholomae, like Rose, addresses issues of authority and discourse with regard to basic writers. I agree with Bartholomae when he argues that basic writers must struggle to make sense of academic discourse without knowing its conventions, objectives, or history. As a result, Bartholomae suggests, these students must insinuate themselves into the academic community by claiming authority. But consider, if you will, the difficult task facing writers who perceive academic discourse as removed and dominating. They attempt to mimic and reproduce a discourse that they have never actively engaged, as Edlund suggests. It is no wonder that they create such seemingly illogical prose. If students do not break away from a passive disposition toward discourse, if they do not work through a relationship to knowledge as other than dualistic or received, they cannot actively engage discourse, integrate it as internally persuasive, relate to knowledge as relative or socially constructed, or generate their own texts. Academic discourse, and all of the knowledge it holds, remains a static object of study external to them. When students write from this subordinate position, they produce essays in which they claim no authority of their own.

Basic writers' passive disposition toward discourse and their reliance on authority are reflected in their writing processes, which often include, in the early stages, an excessive concern with local error. Because their dispositions toward discourse, and even their own discourse to some extent, are framed in terms of polarities of right and wrong, basic writers continue to focus throughout the drafting process on discernible, objectifiable problems. Theses, ideas, proof, and argument are replaced by what Bartholomae has referred to as the power of the cultural commonplace. On a more general level, basic writers may avoid altogether problems not easily solved or issues that have no clear or correct answer. When they do approach controversial issues, they do so as if there were only one right answer. In using others' texts as sources, basic writers often quote insufficiently or incorrectly, allowing entire passages to stand independently, sharply separated from their own words. Paraphrases may retain too much of the original passage, organization, sentence structure, and word choice reflecting it too closely. They sense that only *those* words, not their own, accurately and adequately address the topic. Students' passive reception of discourse cannot account for every case of plagiarism we encounter, but it offers an alternative perspective on a problem with student writing that until now has been treated as a purely mechanical difficulty or moral shortcoming.

Joy Ritchie and Deborah Mutnick explicitly address in Bakhtinian terms the issues of authority in the basic writing classroom and the basic writer as a user of discourse. As they demonstrate, Bakhtin's work is nicely suited to a study of basic writers, whose texts and experiences with discourses are situated on the borders of various discursive communities. The Bakhtinian concern for dialogism, competing discourses, and authoritative texts, Ritchie and Mutnick argue, elucidates our understanding of these students, their perceptions of discourse, and the texts they produce.

However, by singling out basic writers as we do, Ritchie, Mutnick, and I risk further marginalizing them by claiming that their processes of coming to know are different from, or deficient when compared to, those of others. As I continued to teach writing and explore the issue of authority, I realized that the difficulty with claiming authority was not confined to basic writers. Some student(s) in all of my writing courses—from first-year writing through graduate courses in rhetoric and composition—had trouble situating themselves in their writing. In many cases, in fact, the characteristics of the writing among advanced undergraduates, graduate students, and my own writing were strikingly similar to those exhibited by basic writers whose passive dispositions toward discourse first caught my attention. Most notable was the heavy reliance on "linear" direct quotation and a sharp distinction between others' discourses and those of the authors. Although I continue to believe that compositionists benefit from understanding basic writers as existing on the borders of cultures, as at once included in and excluded from the academy, I cannot help but argue that the same is true—to greater and lesser degrees, of course—for any number of us. To treat as homogenous all basic writers (as Ritchie, Mutnick, and I tend to do) on the basis of some perceived subordinate relationship to the academy or arrested critical development does nothing more than redefine them as deficient and continue their marginalization.

If, on the other hand, I generalize from dispositions toward discourse, constructing them as processes rather than problems, and examine their roles in developing the critical and ideological becoming of all people, I avoid branding basic writers. Carolyn Ericksen Hill argues similarly that, like beginning writers, more advanced undergraduates struggle to speak languages of the academy in which they are not yet fluent and that they are hampered as much by social and political hurdles as cognitive ones. Similarly, John Edlund argues that the rhetorical situations that students face in writing classes force them to "attempt to use appropriated language before it has been completely assimilated." That is, writing classes often "attempt to hasten and *direct* the appropriation/ assimilation process," ostensibly for the students' benefit. Edlund notes that "one predictable result is unintentional heteroglossia and garbled internal dialogue" in the students' writing like that described by Nancy Welch or Thomas Recchio (61; emphasis added).

That students are unable to create assimilated arguments in assimilated language is in part a function of the composition classroom and the university instructional system of quarter-, trimester-, or semester-long courses. Couple the time constraints with these new intellectual contexts, conventions, and generic demands, and it becomes surprising that any student manages to construct productive, situated writing in a single term.

Bakhtin is rather pragmatic about discursive contexts that find people out of their linguistic or social element:

Many people who have an excellent command of a language often feel quite helpless in certain spheres of communication precisely because they do not have a practical command of the generic forms used in the given spheres. Frequently a person who has an excellent command of speech in some areas of cultural communication, who is able to read a scholarly paper or engage in a scholarly discussion, who speaks very well on social questions, is silent or very awkward in social conversation. Here it is not a matter of impoverished vocabulary or of style, taken abstractly: this is entirely a matter of the *inability to command a repertoire of genres* of social conversation, the *lack of a sufficient supply of those ideas about the whole of the utterance* that help to cast one's speech quickly and naturally in certain compositional and stylistic forms, the *inability to grasp a word promptly*, to *begin and end correctly* (composition is very uncomplicated in these genres). ("Problem of Speech" 80; emphasis added)

Although Bakhtin shows a bias toward the academic as a privileged discursive sphere, he makes a compelling point regarding the motivations for or causes of silence, garbled discourse, or a passive disposition toward authoritative discourse. (One wonders, however, if he would make the opposite argument, that a person who speaks comfortably in social conversation but is silent or confused by scholarly papers, discussions, or social issues is so not because of an "impoverished vocabulary or of style" but because of a short supply of generic and discursive convention.) Like Bartholomae, Hill, and Edlund, Bakhtin recognizes that as we gain "command of genres, the more freely we employ them, the more fully and clearly we reveal our own individuality in them" (80). That is, as students become accustomed to writing in particular forms of the academic essay, as they begin to gain some confidence in these genres, they are more likely to construct discourses that engage the alien word.

## NEGOTIATING THE HETEROGLOT WORD

The process of negotiating authoritative and internally persuasive discourse and determining dispositions toward discourse continues as readers of all educational levels and achievement encounter new texts in new contexts, as they work to place themselves self-consciously and ideologically among the competing discourses they encounter. This heteroglossic phenomenon is not confined to basic writers, ESL students, or even struggling students. A short passage from Ohio State University sophomore Christian Zawodniak's essay, "'I'll have to help some of you more than I want to': Centralized Power, Student Pedagogy," serves as an example of how a competent, compelling student text bespeaks the tension-filled dialogic, heteroglossic nature of authority, and how a discourse itself demonstrates that tension.

Chris begins his essay with a narrative analysis of his experiences in a first-year writing class, arguing that the role the teacher takes in the classroom is fraught with political and pedagogical implications. In the passages immediately preceding the one quoted below, Chris relates how he grew increasingly dissatisfied with the consequences of his teachers' actions. He continues,

Since my class with Jeff,[18] I have had several different teachers who have had different approaches to writing instruction. The ways of writing that they have taught me have lasted longer and proven more beneficial than the fear of judgment I experienced in Jeff's class, which had the effect of constraining my writing. I am a Post-Modernist, and I'm not faking it, the way Jeff was, and the way I was faking it with him. While I no longer operate under Jeff's pedagogy or his paradigms, my current studies only make me more aware of how delicious a temptation those reductive paradigms can be. It seems so pretty and easy, the notion that *we can just follow the rules and everything will work out*. But it is the most destructive thing we can do to the voices of students. In Freshman Composition—and in all writing courses—we students need to create our own identities, and only through our own voices can our own identities emerge, not by pretending foreign voices are our own. This idea may not be very easy to fulfill, but it's the only way to achieve growth. Students cannot fake a discourse and have it contribute to long-term writing growth, if only because faking discourse robs us of our own voices. Moreover, we students know when teachers are "lying." It sometimes takes us a long time—I am an example—but we do find it out. Then the unlearning of poor instruction can be difficult, but we do unlearn and relearn. Rather than Jeff's tricky compositional hoop-jumping, teachers should help students find their own voices from the start. This can be dangerous, and is probably always difficult, but not more so than overcoming another teacher's poor instruction. (underlined emphases added)

In this passage, Chris speaks from at least three perspectives, each of which entails its own ideological perspective on writing and writing instruction. The passage reveals a general "we" of an informed body of people: "It seems so pretty and easy, the notion that *we can just follow the rules and everything will work out*." In this first construction, Chris speaks from the most general of "we's"; this statement is a commonplace against which he is reacting, a commonplace that as a postmodernist he has come to distrust. At the same time, as a preface to his passionate statements as a student speaking for students, he speaks as a teacher: "But it [leading students to believe that following the "rules" is the most productive approach to writing instruction] is the most destructive thing *we* can do to the voices of students" (emphasis added). In the passages marked above by a single underline, he writes as a student speaking for students; in these passages "we" marks the collective responses of students who "need to create [their] own identities," yearn to speak "through [their] own voices," are able to discern "when teachers are 'lying,'" and are capable of unlearning and relearning despite their teachers' actions.

When Chris came to me with the draft of this essay, asking for assistance as he prepared it for publication, I was almost immediately struck by the shifts in pronoun reference. But I was struck less by the problematic nature of the "we's" than by what they revealed to me about the perspectives Chris was taking as he drafted the essay, the way he negotiated those perspectives, and what the text revealed about his various concerns about writing instruction. On one front, Chris struggles as a student and a thinking person with the foundational and objectivist notions that following the rules is the single most important element in writing. On another, Chris allies himself with teachers of writing, warning his colleagues (and himself by association) of the consequences of their actions. On a third, he speaks as a student, from his most immediate experiences in the expository writing classroom. Because he studies writing and rhetoric, Chris's experiences with the composition classroom are quite varied; he *sees* the classroom as both student and teacher. As a result, his essay about writing instruction reveals these positions. And, I would argue, the essay is made more successful by those various textures.

In a composition classroom in which pedagogy is informed by a sense of writing as seamless and consistent, an instructor might simply encourage Chris to correct the shifts in pronoun reference and to choose among them, without examining the *logic* behind the shifts. In fact, asking Chris to make the references consistent implies that they are not logical. I chose not to do this in my meeting with Chris, for I felt that strategy would only elide what I saw as the richness of the text—its multivoicedness and its struggle to assimilate the words as internally persuasive. I instead spoke with Chris about what I saw happening. I pointed out the shifts in meaning from one "we" to the next and asked Chris to talk about them. He was intrigued by the implications of his use of the language, and together we began to interpret the shifts as moments at which he was struggling to come to terms not only with the topic and his purpose, but also his place in the classroom and in the discipline. He was in an unusual position as an undergraduate student who has presented at national conferences and is publishing a piece in a collection of essays intended for writing instructors and graduate students. Thus, he was neither *just* a student nor *entirely* a teacher, and his shifting use of "we" reflects that tension, as well as his attempts to negotiate his position in terms of his own authority, subject, and audience.

Chris's paper illustrates that language and its forms (both centripetal and centrifugal) are the products of prolonged discursive exchange among members of a given speech community. An utterance like Chris's finds language already prepared for use. Previous discourses provide the material for the utterance and set constraints on the utterance's possibilities. Volosinov reminds us that what is characteristic for a given utterance specifically—its selection of particular words, its particular kind of sentence structure, and its particular kind of intonation—is the expression of the relationships between the speakers and of the whole complex set of social circumstances under which the exchange of words takes place. When a student uses language inappropriately (relative to a standard, centripetal dialect or discourse), writing instructors should not assume that she is behaving irresponsibly; instead, we might consider that she is rehearsing, learning, and applying a script determined in part by her social and educational circumstances.

Chris Zawodniak is not a lone example of a successful writer whose prose reveals unresolved tensions or a difficulty negotiating among various ideological positions. Mutnick notes, for example, her own struggles as a college student, a "harsh social critic who fervently wanted social acceptance," a "mystified and distressed" student for whom language was elusive. She was engaged, as Chris is, "in what Bakhtin describes as a process of conflict and struggle in which external authoritative discourse becomes internally persuasive" (xviii). As I reflected on the implications of a broader understanding of authoritative and internally persuasive discourses, I began to reexamine my own reading and writing history as a graduate student.

At some point after first reading *Marxism and the Philosophy of Language* and *The Dialogic Imagination*, when composing the first draft of my dissertation, I felt compelled to stop and consider my reading process because I was having trouble writing about what I had read. When stumbling through writing the section of my dissertation that explicated some of Bakhtin's concepts, I thought I was facing a case of writer's block, and when I questioned the cause of the block, I attributed it to lack of comprehension. So I began rereading, secretly hoping that careful reading—noting important concepts and topic sentences, and underlining and looking up unfamiliar words as my elementary and high school teachers had suggested—would bring me better understanding. I found as I reread Bakhtin that my trouble wasn't lack of comprehension; I could reel off neat definitions and thorough explanations—that is what passing my Ph.D. orals was all about. The trouble was, I wasn't contributing anything. My writing was passive, empty. Paragraph after paragraph did nothing but paraphrase and quote Bakhtin and his commentators, allowing them a monologue in my text.

Some writing teachers might argue that I began writing too soon or that I hadn't spent enough time pre-writing and formulating my own opinions about the material, and this is probably true to some extent. My difficulties resulted more from my sense of myself as a reader and novice theorist competing with Bakhtin as a writer, "master" theorist, and authority. What I encountered in my reading process is what I believe many students experience, particularly those designated "developmental." Teachers, textbook authors, counselors, administrators, parents—by virtue of their position in the educational hierarchy—command and sometimes demand respect. Many students respond to this seemingly innate authority by unquestioningly accepting their mentors' ideas. I read Bakhtin's texts acceptingly, and while I may at first have read from this posture because I was reading strange and distant texts, I continued to read with little criticism even after gaining control over the content. Like Dale Bauer, who writes that her "first reaction to Bakhtin was to become seduced by his theory of dialogism," I also found myself seduced (Bauer qtd. in Mutnick 18).

As I first encountered Bakhtin's work, I read authoritatively. I took in his words and accepted them uncritically. I held his words in highest esteem; I believed and accepted his conditions and constructs. This acceptance was reflected in my own prose as I wrote about Bakhtin. His words, his phrasing, his ideas overshadowed my own. His words were written as if they existed on a plane above my own. This same tendency is, I believe, visible in our students' writing and may be interpreted as uncritical acceptance of another's words, letting those words stand alone, as if they need no comment or interpretation.

For some time Bakhtin's words dominated my own, and in this respect one might justifiably argue that my disposition toward Bakhtinian discourse lagged well behind Chris's growing active engagement with the discourses of composition pedagogy. As I began to gain confidence with Bakhtin's work, I questioned. I first tried to accommodate his words, to integrate them into my discourse, but the words began not to fit well, and slowly my words took over. I began to read subversively, searching for ways to reframe and recast his concepts, subordinating his ideas to mine, using my interpretations of his ideas to inform the process I propose here. I was not the ideal active or resisting reader, but I strived to reach that characterization as Fetterley presents it. "Clearly," she writes,

> the first act of the feminist critic must be to become a resisting [active, doubting] reader rather than an assenting [passive, believing] reader and, by this refusal to assent, to begin the process of exorcising the male mind that has been implanted in us. The consequence of this exorcism is the capacity for what Adrienne Rich describes as re-vision—"the act of looking back, or seeing with fresh eyes, of entering an old text from a new critical direction." And the consequence, in turn, of this re-vision is that books will no longer be read as they have been read and thus will lose their power to bind us unknowingly to their designs. (xxii–xxiii)

I queried myself: "What do I, as a reader, want to take away from these texts?" and shifted the focus from the text to myself as a reader. My responses to my own question varied. As a teacher of writing, I thought that I had found a theorist who could revolutionize composition studies. The concepts of dialogism, heteroglossia, and carnival all seemed appropriate and valuable to writing instruction in the academy.

When I revised my initial question to "What do I, as a compositionist, want to take away from these texts?" my reading took on a new and revitalized focus. I no longer read to comprehend alone but to interpret. Bakhtinian notions were important to me *as a teacher*, so I began to reread as a teacher, as a reader with a particular agenda, interacting with the alien word, attempting to find ways of co-opting the materials to support a way of reading that could empower composition pedagogy from a corpus that valorizes literary texts. It was as I reread that I returned to authoritative and internally persuasive discourse. My intent became not to salvage Bakhtin but to explore those elements of his work useful in discussions of critical reading and writing.

My response to Bakhtinian texts is clearly bifurcated. Reading, as a compositionist, a text intended as a celebration of literature, I found that I necessarily resisted and redefined Bakhtinian models of discourse. My reading is perhaps best described by what Schweickart describes as a dual hermeneutic that includes both "a negative hermeneutic that discloses their [texts'] complicity with patriarchal ideology, and a positive hermeneutic that recuperates the utopian moment—the authentic kernel—from which they draw a significant portion of their emotional power" (43–44). But even before I could resist, I began my reading *with* Bakhtin, treating his text as authoritative. I struggled for some time before engaging a negative hermeneutic that designated the critical point at which Bakhtin *does not* introduce rhetoric as a concern of his sociological linguistics. But I still hoped to recuperate from Bakhtin that "authentic kernel." In employing a positive hermeneutic, I enlisted the commentaries of Julia Kristeva and Dale Bauer, two scholars who adopt Bakhtinian concepts in their feminist criticism. After convincing myself that I could use Bakhtinian ideas without betraying my convictions, I began to review authoritative and internally persuasive discourse. Like Bauer and Kristeva, I employ Bakhtinian notions to promote my agenda, for I find in Bakhtin the means by which to encourage an empowering process of reading.

By reading internally persuasively, I valorize my own experience, my own interpretations of the texts in front of me. And in valorizing my own experiences and interpretations, I validate myself and who I am as a reader. To borrow the words of Pamela Annas, a reader who approaches a text internally persuasively "does not necessarily have to accept the given topic (or the assumptions underlying a topic) but can reframe it to suit" herself (365). As I read Bakhtin, I am free to recast his words in terms of my own, not bound to accept and repeat the resonance of his words. I make new meaning by reading this way, for I have engaged Bakhtin in a new conversation, one that extends beyond the boundaries of the *The Dialogic Imagination*. My intuition and this anecdote tell me that many, if not all, of my past reading and writing experiences proceeded through two stages, from a first stage at which I deferred to the authority of the author to a second stage at which I questioned the author and began to formulate my own interpretations in response to that text.

When attending conferences I speak both formally and informally with colleagues and friends about my own reading experiences, and I find that many people relate similar experiences and describe their "coming to know" in their fields of study in a similar fashion—as an unquestioning belief followed (sometimes years later) by doubt or resistance. I was not surprised to find, then, that other academics write about their own processes of ideological becoming. Deborah Mutnick, in addition to citing Dale Bauer's tale of seduction at the word of Bakhtin, reflects on her own struggle to rectify the

> disparity between my assumption of entitlement as a middle-class person and my discovery that I was ignorant of social codes that other more privileged, freshman seemed to know intimately. . . . I was a harsh social critic who fervently wanted social acceptance. (xviii)

I found comfort in the knowledge that my descriptions held validity for others. Most recently, at the end of a quarter in which I taught a graduate seminar on

"Bakhtin and Composition Studies," I encountered a striking narrative from Rebecca Taylor, a Ph.D. student in rhetoric and composition at Ohio State. Her words and the process they describe are hauntingly familiar to me:

> As a graduate student in a seminar devoted to the study of Bakhtinian texts and their influence upon composition studies, I underwent a series of reading and writing processes that alternately conjoined me with and distanced me from Bakhtin's work. As I first read *Marxism and the Philosophy of Language*, I desperately highlighted passage after passage, terrified that I would miss a key concept and convinced that if my classmates marked the same passages, I had achieved a successful reading of the text. I placed all authority outside of myself—I was brought closer to understanding only when my comprehension "matched" that of others. This practice continued as I read "Discourse in the Novel" and selections from *Speech Genres*. I became entrenched in Bakhtin's language, giving up on the notion of highlighting text that spoke to my own concerns, and instead marking those passages that seemed "Bakhtinian" somehow. Interestingly, when I was asked to summarize a Bakhtinian text that was not on our syllabus, and then present my interpretation of the implications of that text to my peers, I sensed a shift in my own stance as a reader. I was responsible for representing the words of another to people who had not read the text. (In Bakhtinian terms, I was developing a sense of my own words as answerable utterances.) I needed to both represent Bakhtin's text fairly and to account for the rationale behind that reading. While my summary was peppered with quotations from the text, I chose where and when to include those quotations. I was the decision-maker and Bakhtin became authoritative only when I chose to orchestrate his authority. After enveloping myself in *Freudianism: A Critical Sketch* in order to write a summary, I took a critical step back to prepare my oral presentation, which required me to forge connections across multiple texts. Seeing larger patterns across texts involved distancing myself from them: I had to determine how and why Bakhtin spoke most powerfully to *me*, to *my* concerns. I had to impose my own terms, my own frameworks, upon his text. As a result, when I reported back to my classmates, Bakhtin's terms coupled with my own and he and I shared authority as we spoke about the new text we had created together—a text which, by virtue of their responses to it, my classmates coauthored as well.
>
> Clearly the process I describe above is lengthy, complicated, and occasionally painful as well as exhilarating. In pedagogical terms, it involves asking students to take a series of positions toward potentially authoritative, alien discourses as they attempt to make those discourses a part of their own language use. (emphasis in original)

Rebecca's and my reflections demonstrate a need for us to see the Bakhtinian word in relation to our own. Both of us report a turning point, an elemental shift in how we imaged the text and named our authority in relation to it. And in both cases, our authority was not in mastering Bakhtin, in becoming an expert over his word, but in claiming a self-defined sovereignty from a particular position *outside* (yet simultaneously in terms) of Bakhtin's work.

*Active Engagement and Passive Reception*

*Composition Pedagogy and Creative Understanding*

Rebecca's further commentary on her experiences reading and writing about Bakhtin does not ignore the difficulty of making the authoritative word internally persuasive. She writes that

> if this process of assimilating the words of others is so complicated for me, a Ph.D. student in Rhetoric and Composition who supposedly reads and writes about the words of others for a living, how must the process feel to my students, in particular, to the basic writing students that I will teach next fall? How are they able to maintain any sense of themselves as writers when faced, often for the first time, with the voices of other writers who seem to hold such power over the act of writing itself? Beginning composition students (including basic writers) are bombarded with the voices of others in the composition classroom.

Rebecca's concerns are not without foundation, as both Edlund's and Welch's discussions of student texts suggest. Students at any level will, when facing foreign contexts for writing, have difficulty adjusting, both discursively and ideologically. Yet, her own recollections about her reading and writing processes illustrate that the "[s]tages in the dialogic movement of *understanding*" articulated in Bakhtin might serve as a pedagogical paradigm for instructing students in developing an actively engaged disposition toward the discourses they encounter. Because he is concerned in "Toward a Methodology for the Human Sciences" with articulating processes of generative knowledge and creative understanding, Bakhtin presents in this essay a starting point for examining possible strategies for actively engaging students in their reading, writing, and learning that includes the familiar mode of comparison (the "warmth of love") and contrast ("the coldness of alienation") and entails several "[s]tages in the dialogic movement of *understanding*: the point of departure, the given text; movement backward, past contexts; movement forward, anticipation (and the beginning) of a future context" (162). The reader begins with "the point of departure, the given text" then, with a "movement backward," investigates the historicity of that text and its "past contexts." This reading process places the text in a social, cultural, and intellectual context, thereby situating it as constructed and not inherently authoritative. From this leap to the past, the reader then moves forward in "anticipation (and the beginnings) of a future context" for the words she will generate from the now internally persuasive word (161–62). This back and forth movement allows students to encounter the text both on its own terms, as a product of a given historical and ideological moment, and on their own terms, purposely detaching it from its own history and infusing it with a sense of "own-ness."

I agree with Gregory Clark, who claims that Bakhtin, perhaps more than any other theorist, compels us to investigate the social nature of all discourses and promote the necessary interaction of reading and writing in the formation of knowledge. It is not enough, however, to claim that reading and writing are related skills, or that as students read more they stand a better chance of becoming better writers. Certainly, as students experience more discourses as readers they also gain a sense of generic difference, patterns, conventions, or strategies that may help them become better writers. But simply *consuming* more texts will not assist them in creating a place for themselves within the academic community. Only by letting go of a passive disposition toward discourse and knowledge and, conversely, by actively engaging and approaching discourse as open to question and appropriation on their own terms, will students orient themselves to knowledge in the academy in ways that allow them to generate meaning out of its texts. And from this new orientation to discourse—with the diminishing authority of the text—students may gain a sense of their own increasing authority.

# FIVE

# The Politics of Reported Speech
# and the Ideology of Form

It is sometimes extremely important to expose some familiar and seemingly already well-studied phenomenon to fresh illumination by reformulating it as a problem, i.e., to illuminate new aspects of it with the aid of a set of questions that have a special bearing upon it. It is particularly important to do so in those fields where research has become bogged down in masses of meticulous and detailed—but utterly pointless—descriptions and classifications.

—Volosinov, *Marxism and the Philosophy of Language*

The phenomena under study in the present chapter, pedagogical representations of and instruction in paragraphing and quotation, have undergone little change in the past one hundred years despite significant and even paradigmatic shifts in composition pedagogy during that same time. The arrival of process pedagogy of the 1960s and 1970s, and social epistemic pedagogies in the 1980s and 1990s, which together proved powerful enough to redefine the very nature of composition pedagogy, had little effect on instruction in paragraphing and quotation, which survived nearly intact. One might logically argue that instruction in these elements of composition has gone largely unchanged and unchallenged because they are being taught effectively. In many respects, I have no quarrel with such an argument. Certainly, students learn to construct functional, even compelling, paragraphs, and they also develop skill in the mechanics of quotation under current pedagogical practice. The same was said, however, of most elements of composition when current-traditional approaches to writing instruction were challenged. What remains problematic, of course, is that instruction in these elements of composition remains tied to current-traditional, objectivist (even scientistic) notions of language, reality, and knowledge. Volosinov's invitation for a renewed observation is then made even more intriguing; studying anew an event or subject normally taken for granted may reveal it as something more significant. In the case of paragraphing and quotation, such an illuminating study reveals these phenomena as dynamic, social exchanges in the construction and life of a discourse.

## PARAGRAPHING IN THE CURRENT-TRADITIONAL PARADIGM

Although they disagree as to the nature of the influence, most historians of composition acknowledge that a small group of nineteenth-century pedagogues (John F. Genung, A. S. Hill, Barrett Wendell, Fred Newton Scott, and Joseph V. Denney) largely determined, through their theories of writing and textbooks, the basis of instruction in American college composition courses well into the twentieth century.[1] Among the elements of composition that received extensive attention among the group was the paragraph. Sharon Crowley notes in *The Methodical Memory: Invention in Current-Traditional Rhetoric* that the current-traditional "preoccupation" with the paragraph as a central unit of discourse may be traced in large part to Alexander Bain's *English Composition and Rhetoric*, the first modern textbook to treat paragraphs in a significant fashion.[2] The characteristics and "rules" for paragraphs that informed Bain's work, for example, inform the later texts of Scott and Denney in the 1890s and those of Taft, McDermott, and Jensen and McCrimmon in the 1940s and 1950s.

Bain defined the paragraph in terms of its "organic" relation to the whole discourse and articulated coherence, "parallel construction," topic sentences, logical relationships among sentences, unity, and proportion as the "requirements" for the paragraph (Crowley, *Methodical* 127). Later authors like Scott and Denney followed suit in their own textbooks, although most made minor changes in Bain's methods of paragraph development, with Genung and Wendell settling on three—unity, coherence, and proportion or emphasis.[3]

Of all of the requirements of the paragraph established by Day, Bain, Scott and Denney, and others, unity seems to have been the most important among current-traditionalists; cited by Crowley as a "self-evident principle of discourse," unity "came to be conceived as an end in itself to which the flow of all parts of the discourse, even sentences, was to be subordinated" (*Methodical* 129–30). Scott and Denney, for example, eschewed digressions within paragraphs, noting that unity of discourse is achieved only through proper and complete selection of relevant details. Generally speaking, current-traditional textbook authors also followed Bain by presenting induction and deduction as two patterns of unified paragraph development, leading Crowley to argue that what classical rhetoricians developed as methods of inquiry became for current-traditionalists organizational and developmental principles. "In a sense," she writes, Bain's "principles of the paragraph . . . shift[ ] the ultimate responsibility for the ordering of discourse away from the steps gone through during inquiry and onto the way that discourse is supposed to look on the page" (128). Arrangement rather than invention, presentation rather than inquiry, become primary concerns for writing instruction.

Although over fifty years removed from the publication of Bain's *English Composition and Rhetoric* and Scott and Denney's *Paragraph-Writing*, textbooks throughout the early- to mid-twentieth century repeated time after time the theories and requirements set out in these texts. Crowley notes, for example, that Norman Foerster and J. M. Steadman's 1931 textbook, *Writing and Thinking*, bears the hallmarks of a current-traditional understanding of the paragraph. Edward P. J. Corbett is perhaps too hopeful in his assessment of the influence of current-traditional practice with regard to the paragraph when he writes that patterns of development (which he rightly notes are "adaptations of the classical topics"), the topic sentence, and concern for "unity, coherence, and emphasis" "disappeared from our classrooms and our textbooks" at about the same time Foerster and Steadman's textbook was published (627). Two other textbooks—Taft, McDermott, and Jensen's *The Technique of Composition* and James McCrimmon's *Writing with a Purpose*—demonstrate the degree to which textbook writers (and assumably classroom teachers) continued to depend upon a current-traditional understanding of the paragraph. These textbook authors, like scores more during the 1940s, 1950s, and 1960s, discuss the paragraph in terms of unity, function, structural aesthetics, and the needs of a reading audience, defining it through comparison to the sentence and essay.

Taft, McDermott, and Jensen rely in their text entirely on a current-traditional understanding of the paragraph. The definition of the paragraph itself is reminiscent of Bain's "collection of sentences with unity of purpose" (qtd. in Crowley, *Methodical* 126–27): "[A] paragraph is a group of sentences related to one another by the fact that each sentence in the group is concerned with the same idea or the same part of an idea" (Taft, McDermott, and Jensen 396). They also argue that the principle of unity demands that sentences not be distributed willy-nilly throughout an essay; rather, "[a]ll of a single part of a thought should be brought together in the same paragraph" (397).

In most of their descriptions of the paragraph, Taft, McDermott, and Jensen turn to readers' (in)abilities to comprehend a discourse as a justification for unity and focused scope. Students must take care, they warn, to "present one thing at a time," avoiding "needlessly" jumbling "[s]everal or more large units of thought . . . together in the same paragraph" (399). The topic sentence also ensures readers' ease of understanding. The authors also describe the paragraph in terms of the sentence, noting the similar functions of both units. The paragraph, like the sentence, eases readers' consumption of the text by dividing it into digestible units. Defining paragraph length and completeness according to readers' abilities to process text is a common tendency among later current-traditionalists, who encourage students to consider the "limits of readers' ability to endure hardship" when encountering lengthy paragraphs (Crowley, *Methodical* 131). True to current-traditional form, *The Technique of Composition* also takes up each successively larger unit of discourse in order—

sentence, paragraph, entire essay—suggesting the authors' staunch belief that the skills learned and applied with the smaller units of discourse may be applied later when the larger units are introduced.

One of the most striking elements of *The Technique of Composition* is the emphasis Taft, McDermott, and Jensen place on the "visual balance" of paragraphs and essays. They clearly subordinate the subject of the discourse, purpose of the paragraph, and author's goals to aesthetic considerations, arguing, for example, that "any work which contains an overabundance of long paragraphs seems heavy and dull, whether it is or not" (400). Taft, McDermott, and Jensen acknowledge that paragraphs may range from only a few words to a few hundred, but they nevertheless emphasize a conventional length as a defining feature of successful paragraphing:

> Although the length of a paragraph is actually determined by the emphasis the writer wishes to place upon an idea or upon the importance of one idea when compared to other ideas in the same piece of work, the modern expository paragraph will average about 125 words. (401)

They go so far as to argue that an essay unbalanced by a significantly larger paragraph of two hundred words in a sea of sixty-word paragraphs indicates that "there is probably something wrong" with the essay (403). They base this judgment solely on paragraph length, offering this additional piece of advice: "No mechanical rule can ever be followed entirely if one is to write paragraphs that are just as long as they should be, and no longer" (403).[4] Taft, McDermott, and Jensen are not alone in their current-traditional representations of the paragraph. They remain, in fact, in the mainstream with their descriptions and advice.

James McCrimmon's *Writing with a Purpose*, one of the most long-lasting and influential composition textbooks of the twentieth century, entered the textbook market as a part of the long established current-traditional paradigm of writing instruction characterized by Taft, McDermott, and Jensen, Scott and Denney, Bain, and others. McCrimmon's text, however, altered that tradition when it diverged from the current-traditional practice of introducing students to the smaller units of discourse first and then moving to the essay in latter portions of the textbook. In part 1 of *Writing with a Purpose*, McCrimmon moves from "choosing a subject" (not to be confused with the invention of later process pedagogies) through patterns of essay development, details, and outlining before introducing paragraphs and sentences in chapters 5 and 6 respectively, arguing that the instruction in this part of the text is applicable to any type of writing the student might undertake. Although this shift in the organizing principle is far more than cosmetic, it demonstrates a fundamental shift in compositionists' understanding of how students are best introduced to the act of writing. McCrimmon, however, makes no further significant changes to the established current-traditional paradigm.

Like Bain, and Taft, McDermott, and Jensen before him, McCrimmon argues for the necessity of paragraphing on the basis of the audience's need for assistance in reading, characterizing the initiation of a new paragraph as a "signpost" that marks the "structural units of a piece of writing" (113). Other requirements for the paragraph articulated by current-traditionalists remain central features of McCrimmon's discussion as well: "completeness, unity, order, and coherence," for example, determine the success of a paragraph, which McCrimmon describes as "an organic microcosm of the essay," a "miniature composition" (114). In discussing development ("completeness"), he warns students against constructing long paragraphs because of their unsightly physical appearance. Unity plays as important a role for McCrimmon as it did for Bain, Scott, and Denney; paragraphs must demonstrate a unity of purpose, subject, and focus. To stray risks losing the reader. Digression, he argues, simply betrays "uncontrolled thinking" (117); no hint here that digression, purposeful or otherwise, might rather be a result of the complexity of a subject or its inherent resistance to linear development. The unified paragraph also generally follows a deductive order, moving from the omnipresent topic sentence through its detailed and specific elaboration. The author's goal, McCrimmon notes, is to construct the paragraph in such a way that readers sense it, not the sentence, as the fundamental discursive unit. Sentences are not, in other words, to call attention to themselves, as the paragraph becomes for McCrimmon the central unit of discourse.[5]

I take these few pages to characterize briefly the nature of paragraph instruction in Taft, McDermott, and Jensen, as well as in McCrimmon, as a way of introducing some of the features of the paragraph that have come to the composition classroom through the textbooks of current-traditionalists. The requirements of the effective paragraph as presented by McCrimmon ("completeness, unity, order, and coherence"), the overriding concern with a reader's ability to navigate the paragraph, and rule-bound discussions of paragraph length and variety have all gone unquestioned, and remain largely intact, in composition textbooks written nearly a half-century after McCrimmon and a full century after Bain.

## The State of the Paragraph in the 1990s

My goal in this portion of the chapter is to demonstrate, through analyses of multiple examples from several different types of expository writing textbooks, that compositionists—despite poststructuralist influences on composition theory and pedagogy—continue to rely largely on a current-traditional understanding of the paragraph as a "'collection of sentences with unity of purpose'" (Bain qtd. in Crowley, *Methodical* 127). Crowley, for example, characterizes Anthony Winkler and Jo Ray McCuen's *Rhetoric Made Plain* as a "very-current-traditional textbook," one that follows lockstep the previous century's depiction of the paragraph (130–31). In the analyses below, I extend Crowley's observations about Winkler and McCuen to suggest that not only "very-current-traditional textbooks" but also textbooks that reflect a variety of epistemological positions on the nature of discourse and knowledge continue to rely on a current-traditional understanding of the paragraph as a unit of discourse.

*Definitions of the paragraph.*[6] Consider the following definitions of the paragraph, all taken from expository writing textbooks published between 1994 and 1996, and all of which rely on a current-traditional understanding of the paragraph:

> An essay is written not in large, indigestible lumps, but in *paragraphs*—small units, each more or less self-contained, each contributing some new idea in support of the thesis or main point of the essay. (Kennedy, Kennedy, and Holladay 370)

> A . . . paragraph is a block of sentences that presents a statement about a fact, an opinion, or an experience, or in some other way treats a topic that is an important part of the subject of the entire text. (Harris and Cunningham 569)

> Most paragraphs . . . include a number of sentences that develop and clarify one idea. (Reinking, Hart, and Von der Osten 186)

The paragraph remains for these textbook writers a group of sentences that presents a single idea. Kennedy, Kennedy, and Holladay's definition bears a stronger resemblance to current-traditional descriptions than the others, for it explicitly notes the paragraph as "self-contained." To describe the paragraph in this manner is to imply that it may stand alone as an independent discursive unit, much like the essay. A further implication of these definitions is that all paragraphs work for the common good, in support of a thesis or important element of the essay. The paragraphs in an essay, like the sentences in a paragraph, work collectively to ensure the unity, coherence, and development of the whole. There is no room here for dissension, digression, or dialogue to surface (intentionally or unintentionally) and play a role in the paragraph or essay.

*The paragraph in relation to the sentence and essay.* Current textbooks do far more than imply structural and functional similarities between sentences and paragraphs, and paragraphs and essays; they state the affinities explicitly. Like current-traditionalists of the last century, contemporary compositionists rely on comparative statements to define the role and structure of paragraphs. Harris and Cunningham are quite frank about the analogy: "A paragraph is a miniature essay. It is a self-contained unit that develops a limited idea similar to the way a larger text develops a more comprehensive subject" (568). Their description repeats almost verbatim McCrimmon's description of the paragraph as a "miniature composition" (114). Looking back to the sentence, Harris and

Cunningham also inform students that the sentences in a paragraph illuminate and support the topic sentence "much the same way that the base clause of a sentence is developed and modified by other phrases and clauses" (568). By next looking forward to the essay, Kennedy, Kennedy, and Holladay argue that students may simply return to earlier advice on topic sentences when composing thesis statements for essays, implying that the topic sentence functions as a "thesis" for the paragraph. Although these kinds of comparative statements on the nature and function of paragraphs might seem helpful to students, the advice also suggests that, given these comparative definitions, to compose successful essays students simply have to reapply the rules governing sentence and paragraph structure and function.

*Requirements for effective paragraphs.* Reinking, Hart, and Von der Osten—like McCrimmon and current-traditionalists before him—name unity, adequate development, a clear pattern of organization, and coherence as the "characteristics of effective paragraphs" (186–99).[7] The current-traditional requirements remain a central informing feature of the presentation of paragraphs in a range of college composition textbooks, as the following quotations suggest:

> *Each paragraph should possess a single main idea, usually expressed in the topic sentence.* That topic or design controls the arrangement of all the information in the paragraph. Everything that is included should develop and support that single idea, without digressions. (Spatt 379; emphasis in original)

Spatt, like Scott and Denney, demonstrates no tolerance for digressions that work against the design and control that a unified paragraph strives to achieve. For Axelrod and Cooper, who are even more fervent in their representation than Spatt, unity again achieves the prominence that it enjoyed with Henry Noble Day and Bain in the nineteenth century:

> If any rule for paragraphing is truly universal, it is this: paragraphs should be focused, unified, and coherent. That is, the sentences in a paragraph should be meaningfully related to one another, and the relationships among the sentences should be clear. (*St. Martin's* 471)

What Crowley noted as a "self-evident" principle among the current-traditionalists has become in Axelrod and Cooper a "truly universal" tenet. The requirements for good writing, then, might also be defined in these terms: focused, unified, and coherent. No room for digression, circumlocution, or alternative forms of argumentation outside established and immediately recognizable patterns of development. The watchword is control. The paragraph in each of these representations serves as a confining structure that must take care to admit only those ideas relevant to the subject at hand, with no advice on how to determine relevancy.

*The role of the reader in paragraph structure.* In addition to representing the paragraph as a defined and unyielding structure of confinement, expository writing textbooks continue the current-traditional practice of defining paragraphs as necessary to "help guide readers through longer pieces of writing" (Reinking, Hart, and Von der Osten 186). Note the paternalistic nature of Kennedy, Kennedy, and Holladay's characterization of the function of paragraphs with respect to readers: "Paragraphing effectively means taking your readers by the hand and not only telling but also *showing* them, with plenty of detailed evidence, exactly what you mean. It means providing signposts to guide your readers through what you say" (370). The reader, like a toddler, must be led by the hand and given explicit and specific information if the author expects his meaning to be understood. Of course authors must consider the consequences of their choices on readers' understanding of a text, but descriptions like this one infantilize readers, by severely underestimating their interpretive abilities, and place an uncompromising burden on the author to ensure that readers read accurately. This insistence on signposts, clarity, and cohesion all reveal an objectivist understanding of meaning: texts that are clear, concise, and detailed are more likely to be read accurately. However, as poststructuralist theory has taught us, accurate reading is itself a myth.

*Patterns of development and paragraph length.* Although they no longer rely solely on deductive and inductive forms of development in their discussions, textbook authors have done little to advance discussions of the patterns of development present in texts published during the late 1940s and early 1950s. Taft, McDermott, and Jensen, for example, name development through example, definition, analysis, analogy, or a combination of these, and McCrimmon elaborates on the chronological, spatial, and analytical as three fundamental patterns of development.[8] Contemporary compositionists make very few alterations to these categorizations. Harris and Cunningham, for example, discuss narration, description, exemplification, and comparison/contrast. To Harris and Cunningham's list Reinking, Hart, and Von der Osten add process analysis, classification, cause and effect, and argument, nearly all of which had been articulated by Taft, McDermott, and Jensen and McCrimmon by 1950.

Aesthetic appeal and internal wholeness, which played significant roles in current-traditional discussions of paragraph length, remain a concern among contemporary compositionists, but the role of aesthetics is now contextualized rhetorically. Hairston and Ruszkiewicz write, for example, that determining paragraph length "depends on who your readers are, what you're trying to accomplish, what kind of writing you're doing, what kind of style you've chosen to write in, and other factors" (162).[9] Paragraphs must be pleasing to the eye, but the appeal of the form also reflects a deeper discursive dilemma:

> Paragraphs may look bad because they are so long that they discourage readers;
> they may also look bad because the writer has jammed together several points that
> should be presented in a list. A series of short paragraphs may also look bad be-
> cause they chop ideas into too many small parts and make it hard for the reader to
> see connections. (145)

Hairston and Ruszkiewicz urge students to consider the effect of paragraph
length on readers' sense of structure and argument, not merely on their aesthetic sensibility, even though their metaphors urge students to avoid paragraphs that "look bad." Paragraph length is no longer purely a matter of aesthetics, and students are not urged to vary paragraph length primarily on the
basis of "visual presentation."[10] Instead, textbook authors also call upon context (newspapers, pamphlets, business reports, college essays, scholarly articles), audience, purpose, and convention as defining elements in determining
paragraph length.

### THE PARAGRAPH AND THE IDEOLOGY OF FORM

Certainly, the textbooks I have reviewed here—Axelrod and Cooper's *Read-
ing Critically, Writing Well* and *St. Martin's Guide to Writing*, Hairston and
Ruszkiewicz's *The Scott, Foresman Handbook for Writers*, Harris and Cunningham's *The Simon & Schuster Guide to Writing*, Kennedy, Kennedy, and Holladay's *The Bedford Guide for College Writers*, Lester's *Writing Research Papers*,
Reinking, Hart, and Von der Osten's *Strategies for Successful Writing*, and
Spatt's *Writing from Sources*—are not poorly conceived or executed texts.[11]
They do represent, however, a habit in composition studies to rely on current-
traditional approaches to the paragraph.

There are a few bright moments, however. Hairston and Ruszkiewicz, for
example, demonstrate an incredulity and self-reflexivity almost entirely absent
from composition textbooks when they present to students the standard definition of the paragraph: "A paragraph is, after all, *supposed* to develop an idea—
that is, to consist of a group of sentences that focus on, explain or illustrate a
point" (161; emphasis added). More important in terms of instruction, they
also recognize the dilemma students face as they begin to examine their own
paragraphs, admitting that paragraph definitions do little to assist students as
they consider paragraph structure:

> Conventionally, textbooks define a paragraph as a unit of writing that develops a
> single idea. A neat definition, but unfortunately when you are the writer, it's not al-
> ways easy to decide when you have developed an idea and when you need more
> than one paragraph to do so. Nor is it always easy to decide where to break a para-
> graph and where to start a new one. (145)

Unfortunately, when Hairston and Ruszkiewicz give advice to students regarding development and focus, they merely return to the current-traditional topic

sentence and patterns of development. They go no further in addressing the inherent circularity of the problem of paragraph structure, focus, and length.

Beyond a few remarks like those from Hairston and Ruszkiewicz, compositionists are not self-reflexive about instruction in paragraphing. Because instruction in the paragraph has gone unquestioned for so long and is so entrenched in teachers' and students' understanding, the possibility for significant change is probably quite remote. It is, nevertheless, important to reimagine this element of instruction, for the picture of the paragraph these and so many other textbooks paint is nothing less than confining, even oppressive. We suggest to students that paragraphs that lack unity or coherence must be fixed because they appear to readers as out of control.

In no composition textbook that I reviewed did I find any suggestion that students *engage* the messiness and the disjunction rather than try to repress or rectify it, as if messiness were an unnatural state of thought, and clarity and certainty a natural state. Messiness is, of course, always associated with "bad" discourse and clarity with "good." This is a fundamental philosophical difference between current-traditional and postmodern or Bakhtinian perspectives on the nature of the subject of discourse as it is represented in the paragraph. The desire to repress and rectify disjunction relies on an understanding of the subject and discourse as something to be handled or mastered. Conversely, emphasizing engagement with the discourse in its messiness and disjunction implies a dialogic relationship between author and subject.

Presentations of paragraphing in composition textbooks ignore the dialogic nature of the paragraph, a condition that Volosinov's commentary on the paragraph addresses: "To say that a paragraph is supposed to consist of a complete thought," writes Volosinov, "amounts to saying absolutely nothing" (*Marxism* 111). This iconoclastic statement works against commonly held current-traditional beliefs about the paragraph and contradicts textbooks that describe the paragraph as expressing a complete thought or being similar to syntactic structures. Volosinov's explicit statement, that "[w]ere we to probe deeper into the linguistic nature of paragraphs we would surely find that in certain crucial respects paragraphs are analogous to exchanges in dialogue" (111), provides the point from which to begin to redefine the paragraph as dialogic.

*Redefining the Paragraph*

Like current-traditionalists and contemporary compositionists, Volosinov recognizes that paragraph length varies greatly and that the sentences that make up a paragraph range from fragments to much more complex syntactic constructions. But, to rely on sentences and paragraphs as fundamental segments of discourse, Volosinov argues, is preposterous. The utterance, which is not defined in terms of discursive structure, is the basis of a Bakhtinian theory of language, and focusing on sentences and paragraphs as units of central concern in discourse draws attention away from the more concrete utterance. It follows for Volosinov, then, that the paragraph (like the sentence or essay) cannot be considered a complete thought simply *because* of its structure as a paragraph, for only an utterance may be defined in this fashion. "What is needed, after all," Volosinov continues, "is definition from the standpoint of language, and under no circumstances can the notion of 'complete thought' be regarded as a linguistic definition" (*Marxism* 111). Volosinov, of course, ascribes completion only to the utterance, which resists definition on the basis of discursive structures. Volosinov does not dismiss the necessity of paragraphs; what he reacts against is the notion that the structure of the paragraph (like the sentence) has led theorists to treat it, *ipso facto*, as a complete whole.

The notion of the paragraph as expressing a complete thought, moreover, serves to undermine the very dialogic nature of discourse. To argue that a paragraph represents a complete whole denies its dialogism, its addressivity, and answerability. The unified whole is a myth borne of monologism: "The paragraph is something like a *vitiated dialogue worked into the body of a monologic utterance*" (*Marxism* 111). A paragraph can never stand on its own. What we might see if we were to look carefully into the paragraph under construction are the negotiations among author, audience, and subject.

Even Volosinov's comments on structure demonstrate his continuing concern with the dialogic nature of the paragraph. Note the inherent dialogism in the substance of each of the following "classic" paragraph types he mentions: "question and answer (where question is posed and answer given by the same author); supplementation; anticipation of possible objections; exposition of seeming discrepancies or illogicalities in one's own argument, and so forth" (*Marxism* 111). Each type is inherently dialogic and demands that the substance of a paragraph be defined not in terms of its own unique and whole contribution but in terms of its relationships to others' discourses. Question and answer, for example, requires an explicit statement of a problem for which the author proposes a response. Supplementation, like question and answer, relies on previous discourses in its formulation. "Anticipation of possible objections" and "exposition of seeming discrepancies," on the other hand, are oriented more obviously toward addressivity and answerability, toward the responsiveness of others' words.

Volosinov's categories are not exhaustive, but they suggest a way that compositionists might begin to reemphasize the dialogic nature of patterns of development. Hairston and Ruszkiewicz define analogy, for example, as "an extended comparison" in which the author explains a more difficult or less familiar concept in terms of a less difficult or more familiar concept (156). The example they offer, a paragraph from John Wheeler's "Black Holes and New Physics," defines black holes by drawing an analogy to traffic jams at sports arenas. The gases circling a black hole, like the traffic around a busy sports arena, become more and more compact as they come closer to the black hole.

In a very real sense, Wheeler's paragraph is an amalgam of at least two distinct voices that, when brought into contact with one another, create meaning through their dialogic relationship.

## *(Re)presenting the Paragraph: Implications for Pedagogy*

Representations like those I have cited from contemporary composition textbooks are clearly designed to introduce students to the fundamentals of the discursive structure and purpose of the paragraph. Students are advised to avoid digression and focus their writing by composing and developing topic sentences through clearly defined organizational patterns (e.g., narration, cause and effect, analysis, exemplification). These descriptions are far from satisfactory from a Bakhtinian perspective, however, for they assume that the author retains full responsibility for and control over the development and presentation of the text. The reader, while a major consideration in the author's deliberations about the length of paragraphs, serves in no way as a coauthor. He is, rather, a glorified translator through whom the discourse passes. The subject of the discourse does not come into play; that is, there is no recognition that some subjects might inherently resist linear organizational patterns or Western notions of logic and argumentation that inform the sanctioned patterns of paragraph development. In the end, the representation of the paragraph remains rather linear and simplistic. To argue that students must, as they write, present all of the material on one issue in one paragraph and then move on to the next misses the complexity of thought, utterance, and development that enrich any piece of writing. Moreover, and perhaps most important from a pedagogical perspective, the discussions of paragraphs do not instruct students on how to work productively from draft to essay.

The question then becomes how to instruct students in paragraphing in a way that (1) foregrounds the dialogic nature of their writing, (2) enables them to write paragraphs that do not oversimplify the complexity of their thought, and (3) allows their paragraphs to achieve the goals they've set. One answer is in the approach. Take, for example, what Hairston and Ruszkiewicz describe as "paragraph sprawl." This "internal" problem in paragraphing is characterized by unfocused sentences that lack coherence or a sense of logical organization. In advising students to tighten such paragraphs, Hairston and Ruszkiewicz suggest that students construct topic sentences or "downshift" (Francis Christensen's term) by utilizing different levels of generality in their paragraphs (147–48, 149–50). As I have mentioned before, what Hairston and Ruszkiewicz do not provide students is a method by which to determine the main idea(s) of a paragraph or negotiate the relationships among them. The portion of Christian Zawodniak's essay I presented earlier illustrates how insisting on unity and coherence works *against* the richness and complexity of a student's ideas. Here, again, is the passage from Chris's essay:

Since my class with Jeff, I have had several different teachers who have had different approaches to writing instruction. The ways of writing that they have taught me have lasted longer and proven more beneficial than the fear of judgment I experienced in Jeff's class, which had the effect of constraining my writing. I am a Post-Modernist, and I'm not faking it, the way Jeff was, and the way I was faking it with him. While I no longer operate under Jeff's pedagogy or his paradigms, my current studies only make me more aware of how delicious a temptation those reductive paradigms can be. It seems so pretty and easy, the notion that *we can just follow the rules and everything will work out*. But it is the most destructive thing we can do to the voices of students. In Freshman Composition—and in all writing courses—we students need to create our own identities, and only through our own voices can our own identities emerge, not by pretending foreign voices are our own. This idea may not be very easy to fulfill, but it's the only way to achieve growth. Students cannot fake a discourse and have it contribute to long-term writing growth, if only because faking discourse robs us of our own voices. Moreover, we students know when teachers are "lying." It sometimes takes us a long time—I am an example—but we do find it out. Then the unlearning of poor instruction can be difficult, but we do unlearn and relearn. Rather than Jeff's tricky compositional hoop-jumping, teachers should help students find their own voices from the start. This can be dangerous, and is probably always difficult, but not more so than overcoming another teacher's poor instruction.

This paragraph, at nearly three hundred words, would immediately raise concern among teachers for whom "long" paragraphs are problematic.[12] Some teachers might characterize the paragraph as uncontrolled and scattered, trying to take on too much, and in working with Chris, might urge him to divide the paragraph into chunks of related ideas according to patterns of development, or as part of an extended argument:

Comparison of teaching methods:

Since my class with Jeff, I have had several different teachers who have had different approaches to writing instruction. The ways of writing that they have taught me have lasted longer and proven more beneficial than the fear of judgment I experienced in Jeff's class, which had the effect of constraining my writing.

Statement of a pedagogical and theoretical problem:

I am a Post-Modernist, and I'm not faking it, the way Jeff was, and the way I was faking it with him. While I no longer operate under Jeff's pedagogy or his paradigms, my current studies only make me more aware of how delicious a temptation those reductive paradigms can be. It seems so pretty and easy, the notion that *we can just follow the rules and everything will work out*. But it is the most destructive thing we can do to the voices of students.

Call for alteration in pedagogy:

In Freshman Composition—and in all writing courses—we students need to create our own identities, and only through our own voices can our own identities emerge, not by pretending foreign voices are our own. This idea may not be very easy to fulfill, but it's the only way to achieve growth. Students cannot fake a discourse and have it contribute to long-term writing growth, if only because faking discourse robs us of our own voices.

### Implications of a revised pedagogy:

Moreover, we students know when teachers are "lying." It sometimes takes us a long time—I am an example—but we do find it out. Then the unlearning of poor instruction can be difficult, but we do unlearn and relearn. Rather than Jeff's tricky compositional hoop-jumping, teachers should help students find their own voices from the start. This can be dangerous, and is probably always difficult, but not more so than overcoming another teacher's poor instruction.

These four sections, which range in length from about fifty to ninety words, are much more "unified" segments of discourse than the larger single paragraph. With more clearly defined topic sentences, additional detail, exemplification, and explanation, they could be developed a bit more and separated into four paragraphs. Such a revision would make the passages more reader-friendly, but that friendliness comes at a significant cost.

In contrast to this rather current-traditional approach to working with Chris to revise the passage by dividing it into chunks unified around an explicit or implied topic sentence, a teacher who recognizes the inherent dialogism of discourse might urge Chris to name the several voices he has engaged in the passage, focusing on the diversity of opinion inherent in the subject and revealed through the complexity of the draft. In response, Chris might note that he speaks as a(n)

### postmodernist:

I am a Post-Modernist, and I'm not faking it, the way Jeff was, and the way I was faking it with him. While I no longer operate under Jeff's pedagogy or his paradigms, my current studies only make me more aware of how delicious a temptation those reductive paradigms can be. It seems so pretty and easy, the notion that *we can just follow the rules and everything will work out.*

### student of rhetoric:

Since my class with Jeff, I have had several different teachers who have had different approaches to writing instruction. The ways of writing that they have taught me have lasted longer and proven more beneficial than the fear of judgment I experienced in Jeff's class, which had the effect of constraining my writing. . . . In Freshman Composition—and in all writing courses—we students need to create our own identities, and only through our own voices can our own identities emerge, not by pretending foreign voices are our own. This idea may not be very easy to fulfill, but it's the only way to achieve growth. Students cannot fake a discourse and have it contribute to long-term writing growth, if only because faking discourse robs us of our own voices.

educator:

But it is the most destructive thing we can do to the voices of students.

composition student:

Moreover, we students know when teachers are "lying." It sometimes takes us a long time—I am an example—but we do find it out. Then the unlearning of poor instruction can be difficult, but we do unlearn and relearn.

informed commentator:

Rather than Jeff's tricky compositional hoop-jumping, teachers should help students find their own voices from the start. This can be dangerous, and is probably always difficult, but not more so than overcoming another teacher's poor instruction.

In addition to these voices, behind the text stand Jeff, Chris's classmates, and other faculty, whose acts and utterances inform how Chris has come to think about writing instruction. Rather than ask Chris to dissect the existing paragraph with an eye toward clarifying and distinguishing among the various themes or even voices, thereby dividing them and taking them out of their rich and combative proximity, an instructor might ask Chris to name and make more explicit those combative relationships, and even to engage them. In effect, this approach will work *from* the sense of frustration and confusion Chris felt and examine the process by which he came to understand and interpret his classroom experiences with Jeff. Rather than gloss over or ignore the different opinions expressed in the paragraph, or contain and quarantine them in their own compartments, an instructional approach that encourages students to dwell on and revel in the contradictions will lead to a piece of writing that does not back down from or oversimplify the complexity of the problems described. As the second analysis above demonstrates, the paragraph is far from (and at the same time far more than) a whole or complete thought or a separate statement existing apart from, yet in service of, the larger structure. Chris's paragraph is, instead, a rejoinder in the conversation. Chris has neither exhausted everything he has to say on the issues of pedagogy or postmodernism nor concluded his debate with Jeff and his other writing instructors.

I do not mean to suggest that we not give students advice about writing or that we tell them that paragraphs are miniature dialogues and cut them loose. Rather, I argue that what we tell them about paragraphs be informed by a Bakhtinian philosophy of language that recognizes the dialogic nature of language and that unified and cohesive paragraphs are informed by, emerge from, and very often ignore or vitiate a diversity of voices. What this means, of course, is that we take the time to describe the process by which students might most productively compose paragraphs that serve their purposes and maintain

*The Power and Politics of Pedagogy*

the complexity of their ideas, as I have briefly suggested in outlining an alternative approach to responding to Chris's paragraph.

## QUOTATION IN COMPOSITION TEXTBOOKS

As he closes his discussion of the paragraph in *Marxism and the Philosophy of Language*, Volosinov suggests that as a "seemingly already well-studied phenomenon," the practice of reporting the speech of others also deserves close examination and reformulation as a sociological and ideological phenomenon (112). The bane of existence for many students in expository writing courses, the conventions of quotation must seem a composition teacher's particular form of torture. Unfortunately, because convention is such a significant element of quotation, composition textbooks wallow in page after page of rules and examples, ignoring the very powerful political nature of direct and indirect quotation in discourse.[13] Although textbook authors recognize the social nature of quotation by acknowledging that, as Kennedy, Kennedy, and Holladay write, "[q]uoting is reproducing an author's exact words" (714), they rarely acknowledge that the act of presenting another's words—even through accurate, direct quotation of another's exact words—is an act of representation and interpretation.

The general guidelines are rather standardized: When researching a paper and quoting material, students are advised to use timely and authoritative sources relevant to the focused subject of their essays. Determining what and whether to quote material directly from a source is nearly always depicted as a stylistic or rhetorical consideration, as it is for Axelrod and Cooper:

> As a general rule, quote only in these situations: (1) the wording of the source is particularly memorable or vivid or expresses a point so well that you cannot improve it without destroying the meaning; (2) the words of reliable and respected authorities would lend support to your position; (3) you wish to highlight the author's opinions; (4) you wish to cite an author whose opinions challenge or vary greatly from other experts'. (*St. Martin's* 594)

"[Q]uotation should be a last resort," Spatt advises. "If the phrasing is unique, if the presentation is subtle, if the point at issue is easily misunderstood or hotly debated, quotation may be appropriate. When in doubt, paraphrase" (141). To these fairly standard lists, Hairston and Ruszkiewicz add using a direct quotation as a "focal point" for an essay (571), and Harris and Cunningham advise quoting only shorter passages. Too great a reliance on quotations, Reinking, Hart, and Von der Osten claim, suggests that a student has not understood his sources. Lester is even more blunt in his characterization of the risks of excessive quotation:

> The overuse of direct quotations from secondary sources indicates either (1) that you did not have a clear focus and copied verbatim just about everything related to the subject, or (2) that you had inadequate evidence and used numerous quota-

tions as padding. Therefore, limit quotations from secondary sources by using only a phrase or a sentence.[14] (Lester 126)

Students are also warned to integrate smoothly (yet in diverse fashion) the quotations they select. Integrating quotations (or "framing" them as Hairston and Ruszkiewicz call it) is, like much of the advice regarding the selection of quotations, also largely a matter of stylistic concern; students are urged by Axelrod and Cooper, for example, to refrain from integrating quotations of more than four lines into their own sentences. Methods of introducing integrated quotations are presented as matters of punctuation and sentence structure, with most of the concern placed on the type of punctuation mark required with the various forms of introduction and a premium placed on avoiding awkward sentence structure. Only Brenda Spatt makes the helpful (and singular) distinction between two types of direct quotations, what she refers to as "separated" and "integrated" direct quotations, acknowledging in effect that each type of direct quotation reflects a particular relationship between reported and reporting discourses. Separated quotations carry heavy and decisive punctuation (comma or semicolon) and mark a sharp distinction between the reporting discourse and reported discourse. Integrated direct quotations, on the other hand, require no introductory punctuation because the reported discourse and its ideas are fully integrated into the sentence structure of the reporting discourse.

Commentary on indirect quotations often accompanies discussion of direct quotations and is nearly always relegated to a single example or series of related examples. Hairston and Ruszkiewicz define indirect quotation (what they refer to as "indirect discourse") as "[t]he substance of what a speaker or writer has said, but not the exact words" (783). The indirect quotation, students are reminded, is introduced with "that" and omits the quotation marks and introductory comma. The following examples are fairly typical:

Faulty:      He told us that, we shouldn't have done it.
Faulty:      He told us that, "You shouldn't have done it."
Revised:    He told us that we shouldn't have done it. (Kennedy, Kennedy, and Holladay H:154)

The motorist said that she hated all pedestrians. (Spatt 94)

At the altar Ike told Bernice he would sue her if she didn't marry him. (Hairston and Ruszkiewicz 783)

Again Spatt makes some of the most insightful comments on the nature of quotation when she represents indirect quotation as a means of "report[ing]" others' discourses (94), a term that fits very nicely with Volosinov's designations of reporting and reported speech. Because of the possibility of confusion and difficulty of attribution, however, Spatt urges students to use indirect quotations sparingly.

SUMMARY AND PARAPHRASE
IN COMPOSITION TEXTBOOKS

Summary and paraphrase, two forms of reporting speech closely related to indirect quotation are often presented in composition textbooks as merely a preliminary exercise to test a student's reading comprehension. A student who is unable to summarize is a student who has not read carefully or with complete comprehension. The assumption here is similar to that which leads textbook authors to argue that students who quote too much or too often have not mastered the *substance* of the material they're engaging. The importance of summary for McCrimmon, for example, lies in its value as a means of determining whether a student has understood what he has read and of improving his reading comprehension "by translating it into his own words" (426–27). Skill in paraphrasing is contentious and "requires the student to master the reported discourse and make it his own" (430). The gastronomical and agonistic metaphors of consumption and mastery are not unintentional for McCrimmon, who characterizes the act of summary as a combination of consumption, digestion, and gaining advantage. For McCrimmon the significance of summary and paraphrase does not rest in its ability to assist the student in formulating an opinion about the text, which is a characteristic of later representations of paraphrase and summary. Contemporary textbook authors articulate for students these same motivations for paraphrase and also suggest paraphrasing as a method of note taking.[15]

In addition to articulating a rather limited role for summary and paraphrase, textbooks authors are fairly dogmatic in their guidelines for paraphrasing. "Paraphrase those passages," Axelrod and Cooper advise students, "whose details you wish to note completely but whose language is not particularly striking" (*St. Martin's* 594–95). Authors advise students to select, boil down, weave, condense and pare, summarize long passages selectively, focus on main points to support their opinions, and report the gist of the reported speech in their own words.[16] Clearly (and problematically), quotation is reserved for those sources that *deserve* to be heard. Paraphrase and summary, on the other hand, are intended to relay facts or "opinion that has marginal value" (Lester 119), or to explain and clarify less interesting or compelling sources. These and other textbook authors provide constructive advice when they instruct students that conscientious summary and paraphrase are productive means of engaging and understanding texts, yet they vilify the paraphrased texts at the same time, as Lester's advice that sources of "marginal value" be paraphrased suggests.

Nevertheless, to argue that paraphrase and summary alone *and not direct or indirect quotation* are capable of reporting another's discourse in a critical manner is to misunderstand the potential that direct and particularly indirect quotations have as centrifugal, dialogic forms of representation and interpretation. My own experiences in reading Bakhtin suggest that coming to a stronger sense of autonomy as a reader is not simply a matter of stepping *away* from direct quotation and toward paraphrase. Indeed, one may maintain a subordinate position in paraphrase just as easily as one may in directly quoting a source. In other words, its not the *form* that the reporting discourse takes that determines its orientation toward the reported discourse but the *style* of that reporting discourse. Once again Volosinov's *Marxism and the Philosophy of Language* proves a productive starting point for a discussion of what I refer to as linear (following Volosinov) and ludic styles of reporting discourse.

## REPORTED SPEECH IN THE BAKHTINIAN CANON

Volosinov warns that the site of quotation, of reported speech—what he refers to as the "reporting context"—is made up of "dynamic relations of high complexity and tension" (*Marxism* 119); if teachers do not engage and examine the relations between reporting and reported discourses when presenting quotation and paraphrase to students, they ignore the vital and volatile nature of that reporting context. Just as readers take either an authoritative or internally persuasive stance toward the discourses they read, writers, in reporting the speech of others, use either a linear or pictorial style. In other words, people not only work in dialogue with others' utterances as they read; they also work dialogically as they write.[17]

In *Marxism and the Philosophy of Language*, Volosinov problematizes and politicizes the practices of quoting and paraphrasing by focusing not on the conventions of reporting discourse but on the possible orientations between reporting and reported discourses. Volosinov argues, for example, that no writer can use another's words within a new and ideologically bound context (the reporting discourse) without commenting on or responding to those (reported) words. A writer cannot simply present another's words without *valuing* them, valorizing or denigrating them, even in direct quotation. Every act of reporting discourse—relating another's words as "direct," "indirect," or "quasi-direct" discourse in Volosinov's terminology—carries with it stylistic, rhetorical, and ideological consequences.

Reported speech—a phrase used by Volosinov to refer to the patterns by which an author (re)presents another's utterances, as "speech within speech, utterance within utterance, and at the same time also *speech about speech, utterance about utterance*" (*Marxism* 115)—provides the basis for reexamining the manner in which quotation and paraphrase are represented in composition textbooks and interpreting the ways that students use reported discourses in their writing. That is, the ways that compositionists represent forms of reported discourse to students as well as the ways that students in turn report others' discourses suggest a great deal about cultural and political expectations for students as they engage discourses. In discussing reported speech in *The Material Word*, Silverman and Torode emphasize this same point, citing the following passage from *Marxism and the Philosophy of Language*:

What we have in the forms of reported speech is precisely an objective document of this reception. Once we have learned to decipher it, this document provides us with information, not about accidental and mercurial subjective psychological processes in the "soul" of the recipient, but about steadfast social tendencies in an active reception of other speakers' speech, tendencies that have crystallized into language forms. (306–7)

It is through reported speech, they suggest, that Volosinov identifies various sociological tendencies within a given cultural era. What may be revealed, then, by analyzing composition textbooks and student writing is not so much a single author's or student's orientation toward particular reported information, but a larger cultural understanding and presentation of authority, knowledge, and texts. In short, composition textbooks, in their convention-bound discussions of quotation, and limited understanding of reporting discourses generally, maintain a hierarchical relationship between reported and reporting discourses, between expert and novice, with the reported expert discourse being privileged.

Reported speech may take a number of forms, each of which reflects a different relationship with and a different reception of the reported utterance. The two forms I am most concerned with as part of this argument are direct and indirect quotation, which are analogous to Volosinov's direct and indirect discourse.[18] Direct discourse, like direct quotation, presents another's words within quotation marks as if it were a line of dialogue. Indirect discourse, on the other hand, reports another's words. The following passage from Dostoevsky's *The Brothers Karamazov*, quoted by Volosinov, gives examples of both discursive forms:

> Though filled with the profoundest respect for the memory of his ex-master, he nevertheless, among other things, declared that he had been negligent toward Mitja and had *"brought the children up wrong. The little child without me would have been eaten alive by lice,"* he added, recounting episodes from Mitja's earliest years. (*Marxism* 132; emphasis added by Volosinov)

In this example, of course, the italicized passage illustrates a form of direct discourse, the exact words spoken by the character. The short passage that precedes it, "that he had been negligent toward Mitja and had," is an example of indirect discourse in which the narrator reports what had been previously said. The direct form of this indirect discourse might have been "I have been negligent toward Mitja."

### Linear and Ludic Styles of Quotation

In addition to distinguishing between direct and indirect discourse, Volosinov recognizes the centripetal and centrifugal possibilities of both forms. The two forms can take on what Volosinov refers to as "linear" or "pictorial" styles of reporting speech. Linear tendencies in the reporting speech strive to "demarcate," to "maintain its [the reported discourse's] integrity and authenticity," thereby preserving and accentuating the differences and borders between the author's words and those reported (*Marxism* 119). The reported word remains bounded, in many cases impenetrable. Although both direct and indirect quotation can serve either centripetal or centrifugal ends, composition textbooks provide, almost exclusively, examples of a linear style of reporting discourse, which valorize the reported discourse, distancing it from the reporting discourse and making response and retort more difficult. Consider the following examples from textbooks, each of which clearly privileges the word of the reported discourse:

> Shakespeare wrote, "Some are born great, some achieve greatness, and some have greatness thrust upon them." (Kennedy, Kennedy, and Holladay H:152)

> *In 1896, Woodrow Wilson, who would become Princeton's president in 1902*, declared, "It is not learning but the spirit of service that will give a college a place in the public annals of the nation." —Ernest L. Boyer (Hairston and Ruszkiewicz 575; emphasis in original)

> Similarly, Duncan Turner asserts, "As matters now stand, it is unwise to talk about communication without some understanding of Burke" (259). (Axelrod and Cooper, *St. Martin's* 598)

> I agree with Hawthorne's views expressed in *The Blithdale Romance*, that we Americans rarely meet with women that have really feminine qualities.

> I agree with Hawthorne in *The Blithdale Romance*, when he says, "We seldom meet with women now-a-days, and in this country, who impress us as being women at all."
> *or*
> As Hawthorne says, "We seldom meet with women now-a-days, and in this country, who impress us as being women at all." (Taft, McDermott, and Jensen 373)

> In *The Second Sex*, Simone de Beauvoir describes such an experience as one in which the girl "becomes as object, and sees herself as object" (378). (Axelrod and Cooper, *St. Martin's* 597)

> As Wabash notes, "The threat to our enviroment [*sic*] comes from many directions." (Reinking, Hart, and Von der Osten 322; correction in original)

In each case, the reported discourse remains in a privileged, valorized position, set off from the reporting discourse that ushers in the privileged word. The reporting discourse does not resist or question its authority. Quite the contrary, the reporting discourse does everything it can to valorize the reported speech. Shakespeare, Wilson, and Turner are called upon to make authoritative statements that the author represents as truth, or at least fact. Certainly, this sort of representation of reported discourse is a central feature of writing. Students, like academics, business people, and others, must sometimes, perhaps even frequently, engage reported discourses in a linear fashion. I am concerned, however, that this is the *only* style of reporting discourse textbooks present. What is far less frequent is a ludic style of reporting discourse. Through examples like these and through the instruction that they have received, students are conditioned not to *engage* the words of others but to *present* them, like precious gifts, to their readers. Such an orientation merely reinforces the authoritative nature of the reported discourses students encounter in their reading and writing in the university.

Volosinov describes the second style of reporting discourse, the pictorial, as a *conscious* linguistic means of "infiltrating reported speech with authorial retort and commentary" that strives to "resolve it, to obliterate its boundaries" (*Marxism* 120). The pictorial (what I prefer to call the ludic, a term that speaks more directly to the centrifugal and subversive nature of this reporting style), unlike the linear, speaks *against* the reported discourse.[19] Klancher notes that paraphrase is particularly suited to the pictorial style of reporting because of the "inevitable misrepresentation" that leads to a "strategic transfer of power" from the reported to the reporting discourse "[a]s it departs from quotation, periphrasis introduces an irreversible element of *parody* into the writer's language" (87). Klancher is, I believe, correct in acknowledging the relative ease with which paraphrasing reported discourse takes a ludic style; nevertheless, I do not wish to ignore the fact that the ludic style is possible with direct quotation, as well.

The linear and pictorial styles, like most of the concepts in the Bakhtinian corpus, may be categorized in dialogic relation to one another. The two styles, Todorov points out, may also be aligned with the two stylistic lines of the novel. Linear styles of reporting discourse are characteristic of the first stylistic line and are centripetal, conservative, and present dialogue *in absentia*, with heteroglossia as a dialogizing backdrop absent from the actual text. Pictorial styles of reported discourse, on the other hand, incorporate heteroglossia—with its clashing and mixing of alien languages—directly into the utterance. The result of this heteroglossia *en praesentia* is a breaking down of the borders between authorial, or reporting, and reported discourse through commentary and evaluation. In addition to this rather grammatical and stylistic distinction between the two styles, Volosinov notes that linear styles seek to maintain the original intention of the reported discourse while the pictorial more often retorts and parodies reported discourse.

Spatt and Hairston and Ruszkiewicz provide examples of the ludic (pictorial) style of reporting discourse, which demonstrates to students a means of questioning, exposing, or evaluating reported speech. Spatt's and Hairston and Ruszkiewicz's examples—which demonstrate that the direct quotation is not incapable of presenting a reported discourse in a ludic style—remain two of only a few examples of the ludic reporting style I found in my review:

Worst of all is the overwritten prologue, about John Lennon's death and its impact in Liverpool: "The ruined city, its abandoned river, its tormented suburban plain, knew an anguish greater than the recession and unemployment which have laid Merseyside waste under bombardments more deadly than Hitler's blitz." A moment's thought should have made Norman and his publishers realize that this sort of thing, dashed off in the heat of the moment, would quickly come to seem very embarrassing indeed.[20] (Spatt 90)

But as soon as we mention the words "value" and "purpose," we run into one of the most firmly entrenched taboos of twentieth century science. Hear the voice of Jacques Monod, high priest of scientific rationality, in his book *Chance and Necessity*: *"Any mingling of knowledge with values is unlawful, forbidden."* (Hairston and Ruszkiewicz 573; emphasis in original)

These passages—unlike the other short quotations above that serve merely to place the word of Shakespeare, Wilson, or Turner in front of the reader for consumption—immediately call upon the reader to question, interrogate, or even dismiss the reported discourse. In the first passage, the reader is conditioned to read the reported discourse with a critical eye toward its stylistic excesses; in the second, the reader is asked to take a skeptical stand against Monod's words.

By not distinguishing between linear and ludic styles of reporting discourse (direct and indirect quotation), and therefore privileging the linear in the examples presented to students in expository writing textbooks, compositionists imply rather clearly that students should subordinate their own opinions and positions to the discourses of more authoritative persons. It will come as no surprise, then, that, like Volosinov, I prefer the ludic form of reporting discourse, which leads me to make one further comment on its importance with regard to writing instruction. Reporting others' discourses is an important part of a great deal of essay writing in the university. Students undertaking researched reports, writing analyses, interpreting literary texts, and responding to the opinions of others are asked to engage the discourses of others within their own writing. If Volosinov is correct—if indeed reported discourse reflects cultural and societal tendencies and not individual ones—then the ways that our students respond to and report on texts tells us much about the academic institution and its writing instruction, as well as our students' relationships to learning and knowledge. If we continue to offer instruction in quotation and paraphrase that privileges linear forms, we continue to condition students to privilege the authoritative word and treat it as distanced and definitive.

Charles Bazerman's *The Informed Writer* is singular in acknowledging the rhetorical *and* ideological elements of quotation, paraphrase, and summary. Bazerman's understanding and explanation of authorial voice and its relationship to the sources it reports are uncommon and bear a striking resemblance to Bakhtinian understandings of authorship and reported speech. Bazerman assumes that sources—the "voices" of others—necessarily interact with and inform a student's authorial voice and are explicitly represented in discourses through direct and indirect quotation. He recognizes, in other words, that *all* forms of reporting discourse, both paraphrase and quotation, are a "retelling in one's own words" (Bakhtin, "Discourse" 341). In the reporting discourse that surrounds a direct quotation, for example, Bazerman recognizes that the writer creates a particular way of reading the quoted material. Thus the writer influences how the reader interprets the quotation, retaining control of the reported discourse, making it serve the overall meaning of the reporting passage. Indirect quotation, Bazerman suggests, allows the writer even greater control over the other person's words because he has more freedom to select particular emphases and details. Many textbook authors recognize the conversational nature of writing (particularly source-based writing) and the role of higher education in preparing students to engage in the conversations underway in their cultures, but unlike Bazerman, they have not yet brought this knowledge to bear on their discussions of quotation and paraphrase.

## ACTS OF REPRESENTATION: REPORTING THE SPEECH OF OTHERS

In presenting quotation and paraphrase as matters of convention and grammatical correctness, textbooks miss the opportunity to provide students a means of constructing a self-consciously dialogized reporting discourse. Such an understanding of the power of discursive structures is not absent from composition studies; it simply has not made a significant impact on the classroom through its textbooks.

Like Volosinov, who prefers the active, present heteroglossic nature of the ludic, Bartholomae in "Inventing the University" privileges essays in which students place "themselves both within and against a discourse, or within and against competing discourses," and work "self-consciously to claim an interpretive project of their own, one that grants them their privilege to speak" (158). Although he does not write directly with regard to reporting discourse strictly defined as quotation and paraphrase, Bartholomae outlines in this essay one of the most crucial elements of ideological becoming and language use. Those students whose writing is reproduced in "Inventing the University" have each accepted one of two general postures toward their culture; they naively accept the cultural commonplaces that inform their writing (an authoritative orientation), or they present these commonplaces and then examine or criticize them (an internally persuasive orientation). As Bartholomae's examples demonstrate, only after students begin to appropriate a new discourse by first mastering a previous discourse and then criticizing it as naive can they begin to move beyond imitating a new discourse and toward appropriation and then parody.

Bartholomae stops short, however, of suggesting that this process of imitation-appropriation-parody can apply to academic discourse as well as the discourse of the cultural commonplace. Returning to Bakhtin here is helpful, for parody plays a central role in his notion of internally persuasive discourse and in my understanding of a ludic style of reporting discourse. The ways that students present information and report the ideas and word of others suggest their individual and collective stances toward that information and those ideas. In other words, in the writing of students who simply accept cultural norms as fact, we may find clichéd phrases of common knowledge like those Bartholomae finds in the excerpts from an essay on a young man's job as a mechanic: "there's always someone trying to take advantage of you"; those who don't succeed fail from a "lack of pride" (137). Students who report others' language critically (in a ludic fashion), on the other hand, who present it skeptically, articulate their own contributions among and against the contributions of others.

Nevertheless, many students are not able (or willing) to work against discourse, for much discourse—especially that of experts and academicians whom students often cite in their researched writing—is perceived as too authoritative to engage. Textbooks, lectures, lab sessions all speak monologically to them. Knowledge remains objectifiable and inert, passed on from the expert to the novice, a process of coming to know that they demonstrate in their writing and through their use of reported discourse. To question is to presume equality, and equality is something students often assume they don't have, especially when it comes to writing and expressing their opinions in opposition to, or even alongside, the opinions of privileged others.

As we begin to work with our students on their own discourse, in presenting others' utterances in both linear and ludic styles, and in constructing their own contributions to the ongoing conversations that they are entering as members of an academic community, we must be careful, as Bartholomae points out, to define for them what kinds of contributions we expect. Again, Volosinov provides a helpful backdrop for this observation. If compositionists understand all discourse as dialogic, for example, we cannot present to students an organic model of composing in which each person is responsible for presenting his contribution as independent and original because that depiction of discourse is antithetical to dialogism. Bartholomae echoes these same warnings, reminding his readers that "alongside a text we have always the presence of 'off-stage voices,' the oversound of all that has been said (e.g., about girls, about English). These voices, the presence of the 'already written,' stand in defiance of a writer's desire for originality and determine what might be said" (Bartholomae, "Inventing" 142–43).

The measure of an effective discourse, then, is neither in the level of its originality nor in the extent to which it says something new, but rather in the extent to which it recognizes, entertains, manages, and contends with those "off-stage voices," the extent to which it effectively reports others' discourses in a ludic style. As Klancher acknowledges, this ludic or "parodic tone often remains unconscious or at least inexplicit" in student writing, yet "the kind of writing many of us [teachers of composition] reward with an 'A' is the kind that recognizes and boldly accentuates the parodic intention that most students suppress in fear of censure" (87).

Many compositionists respond to statements like Klancher's by arguing that we cannot expect the discourses of students just entering the university to reach such a level of social and ideological self-awareness. They are right in many respects. Compositionists cannot hope to bring every student to an informed and considered understanding of his position in his social, cultural, and political surroundings. Every person moves at a different pace in his ideological becoming. That does not mean, however, that composition classes should not strive to engage students in discussions and introduce them to discursive forms that encourage ideological becoming. Encouraging students to work beyond their perceived abilities, as Bartholomae and Petrosky's textbooks demonstrate, proves a most effective pedagogical approach. Like Mike Rose, who refers to his encounters with writers and thinkers as a "dialogue" that he and his fellow underprepared students were "encouraged to enter, to consider, to take issue" with (*Lives* 58), Bartholomae and Petrosky recognize what most textbook authors fail to implement in their discussions of quotation and paraphrase: Every discursive choice has ideological implications.

Redefining paragraphs as dialogic and reexamining quotation and paraphrase as ideological constructs are not the most crucial issues facing composition studies, but such a revisioning suggests that the details of common (and very often unexamined) practices such as these cannot be ignored as compositionists work to theorize and enact postmodern pedagogies.

# SIX

# Toward a Pedagogy of Possibility

In his May 1994 "From the Editor" column in *College Composition and Communication*, Joseph Harris writes briefly about the various approaches the contributors to that issue use to "push against or beyond the limits of conventional scholarly prose" (161). Harris's point, at least in part, is to challenge compositionists to redefine the terms of disciplinary discussions of academic discourse and pedagogy. "Indeed," he continues,

> the whole argument over whether we should teach "personal essays" or "academic discourse" strikes me as misleading and debilitating—since the opposition between the two tends quickly to devolve into a stand off between belletrism and pedantry, sensitivity and rigor, and thus turns both into something that most students I have met have shown little interest in reading or writing. . . . I think we need to stop taking sides on this opposition and to try to move beyond it instead. (162–63)

Like Harris, I have long been uncomfortable with the direction that discussions about the nature of scholarly discourse have taken. In casual conversations, seminars, and at symposia, graduate students have asked me time and again where I stand on the issue of academic discourse. I hedged in my responses, suggesting that no one model of academic discourse existed or that we might ask students to adopt academic discourse critically for their work within the academy. But with either of these responses—or any of the many others I have given in the past couple of years—I felt uncomfortable, uneasily occupying positions that I found problematic and distasteful. When faced with a decision either to acknowledge that, "Yes, we need to teach our students academic discourse for their own good," or "Yes, our students have a right to their 'home' language, and we have a responsibility to maintain this," I bristled. Neither alternative suited me.

Only as I came across some of bell hooks's comments on the academy in *talking back* did I realize that our discussions in composition studies about the nature of academic discourse are informed by an inherently problematic and debilitating dichotomy. Recalling the "conflict and contradiction" of her own life as a poor black woman and as a Stanford undergraduate, hooks writes that the

> insistence on choosing between the world of family and community and the new world of privileged white people and privileged ways of knowing was imposed upon me by the outside. It is as though a mythical contract had been signed somewhere which demanded of us black folks that once we entered these spheres we would immediately give up all vestiges of our underprivileged past. (*talking back* 80)

She, not the dominant culture, hooks continues, was able to "formulate a way of being that would allow me to participate fully in my new environment while integrating and maintaining aspects of the old." Citing Freire's distinction between "adaptation" (assimilation, absorption) and "integration" (the "capacity to adapt oneself to reality plus the critical capacity to make choices and transform that reality"), hooks reminds us that adapting or resisting are not the only options available to students outside the dominant discourse (qtd. in hooks 67).[1] Adapting, assimilating, or absorbing a dominant culture entails a passive acceptance of it as an unquestionable, remote, and static authoritative structure. Integrating into a culture—in the Freirean sense that includes a critical awareness—entails entering it with the intent of interanimating one's own words and discourses with those already in use within the structure. To argue about academic discourse in terms of "home" versus academic literacy leads us to a "kill or be killed" conclusion that serves no one. The dichotomy between home and academic discourse is itself a construction that colonizes, banishes, or exterminates the resistant, the subversive, as Patti Lather and other feminists remind us.

## THE CONTINUING DIALOGUE, CONTINUING THE DIALOGUE

We might best begin to investigate current renditions of academic discourse through terms set out by Benedict Anderson and cited by Mary Louise Pratt in "Arts of the Contact Zone." In summarizing Anderson's theory of "imagined communities" as they contribute to nationalism, Pratt sets out "three features that [Anderson uses to] characterize the style in which the modern nation is imagined." The community "is imagined as *limited*, by 'finite, if elastic, boundaries'"; as "*sovereign*"; and as "*fraternal*" (37). What is perhaps most problematic about this rendition of a community is that it assumes that "principles of cooperation and shared understanding are normally in effect," the "situation is governed by a single set of rules or norms shared by all participants," and "all participants are engaged in the same game and that the game is the same for all players" (38). "Often [the situation] is" the same for all, Pratt continues, "[b]ut of course it often is not, as, for example, when speakers are from different classes or cultures, or one party is exercising authority and another is submitting to it or questioning it" (38). The latter is true of students writing in and for the academy who often enter what Deborah Mutnick terms an "alien" culture.

A case in point is David Bartholomae's explanation of a student's acquisition of academic discourse that not only assumes the sort of "imagined community" within the academy that Anderson ascribes to nations but is also informed by a colonial attitude toward literacy:[2]

> The student has to appropriate (or be appropriated by) a specialized discourse, and he has to do this as though he were easily and comfortably one with his audience, as though he were a member of the academy or an historian or an anthropologist or an economist; he has to invent the university *by assembling and mimicking* its language while finding some compromise between idiosyncrasy, a personal history, on the one hand, and the requirements of convention, the history of a discipline, on the other. *He must learn to speak our language.* ("Inventing" 135; emphasis added)

The student who learns to speak "our" language might be empowered to some degree through her nominal admission to the academy, but she suffers a far greater disempowerment through the concurrent silencing of her other discourses, as Giroux suggests. Bartholomae describes in telling detail the kind of discursive conventions students must work "within and against" as he relates that a former teacher urged him to "use the following as a 'machine' for producing a paper: 'While most readers of —— have said ——, a close and careful reading shows that ——' " (153). The form, while perhaps not universal, functions as a template for argumentation. Text-based, Western, and agonistic, such discourses privilege academic and cultural commonplaces. Contrast Bartholomae's narrative and advice with that of Elizabeth Ellsworth as she quotes Audre Lorde:

> "The master's tools will never dismantle the master's house," and to call on students of color to justify and explicate their claims in terms of the master's tools— tools such as rationalism, fashioned precisely to perpetuate their exclusion—colludes with the oppressor in keeping "the oppressed occupied with the master's concerns." (305)

Although I am certainly not comfortable with the essentialism of oppressor/ oppressed expressed in Lorde's or Ellsworth's claims, they do point out the inherently problematic dichotomous nature of our discussions of academic discourse.

Clearly, Bartholomae's descriptions rely on insider/outsider, initiate/initiator metaphors and binaries. Carol Severino has examined and critiqued such metaphors of exclusivity, suggesting that they deny the possibility of a "common ground" from which students might begin to write. Marginalized students, she suggests for example, are "in some ways more experientially ready for, and indeed are active participants in, some of the inquiries into comparative cultural study and contrastive language study that occur in history, anthropology, political science" and other disciplines (9). To critique the exclusivity of the club metaphor and its attendant insider/outsider binary, I need only mention again bell hooks's comments regarding her own educational experiences, or to turn to Freire who himself has warned us against distinguishing the underprivileged or underprepared as "marginal":

> The truth is, however, that the oppressed are not "marginals," are not people living "outside" society. They have always been "inside"—inside the structure which made them "beings for others." *The solution is not to "integrate" them into the structure of oppression, but to transform that structure so that they can become 'beings for themselves.'* (55; emphasis added)

Freire's solution is both revolutionary and commonsensical.[3] If an institutional or cultural structure oppresses some citizens, the answer is not to change the citizens to fit the continually oppressive structure, but to change the structure so that it no longer oppresses. We might make an analogous argument with regard to academic discourse: If genres of academic discourse are oppressive to students, the answer is not to change students to meet the expectations of the discourse but to challenge the discourse to adapt to students. In effect, this argument recognizes the inherent intertextuality and mutual answerability of both student and institutional discourses.

Rather than rely on Freire's terms of adaptation and integration to describe writing instruction, however, I would like to call on the notions of proficiency and productivity that might provide a more distinctive terminology, one that allows us to understand academic discourse as a site for the interanimated nexus of dominant (institutional) and subordinate (student) discourses. As a dialogic, internally persuasive and interanimated discourse, an academic discourse defined in terms of proficiency, productivity, and possibility exists on the borders between university and student. It does not demand allegiance but encourages creativity from students. Meaning-making is achieved by continuously and cooperatively sharing texts or discourses. Many scholars, particularly those within the critical pedagogy movement, rely on conflict metaphors—struggle, competitiveness, resistance—to describe the collision of discourses, world views, and material existences that occur as students write themselves into the academy. Certainly such struggle takes place, but to define heteroglossic texts only in terms of competing discourses is to overlook the possible, probable, even inevitable end of the "collision" of languages: interanimation, which can and does work beyond simple agon to a newly formed productive and generative discourse.

I propose we shift the terms of this argument about academic discourses to accommodate hooks's critique, first by examining the consequences of the present debates about academic discourse and then by redefining and reconstructing academic discourses as sites of an interanimation of proficiency and productivity that attends to both the centripetal and centrifugal tendencies in discourse. Scholars like Giroux, as Peter McLaren points out, extend the post-structuralist critique and argue that educational institutions serve both cultural tendencies. The same is true of academic discourses; they, too, might be defined as "complexes of dominant and subordinate cultures"; such a definition compels us to move away from oppositional rationalist and humanist binaries of home and academic discourses, or personal and scholarly writing.

The consequences of the present state of the discussion about academic literacy are palpable. The academic/home discourse binary essentializes and hierarchizes, maintaining rather than subverting privileged institutions, conventions, and forms. To insist on the binary of home versus academic discourse essentializes both terms, necessarily privileges one over the other, and relies on defining academic discourse in terms of humanistic and romantic notions of the stable, congruous individual.[4] The academic/home discourse binary also overlooks the myriad of other discourses that impinge upon, inform, and populate a given utterance. By defining these two positions as the only alternatives, we overlook the differences that exist within and across academic discourses.[5]

Composition studies also relies on metaphors of exclusivity that reinforce colonial notions of the exotic Other—outsider, marginalized, deviant, deficient—and metaphors of confrontation—struggle, resistance, agon. As compositionists discuss academic discourse, we continue, inadvertently perhaps, to define power as property, which situates the instructor as the "agent of empowerment" (Gore 56) and ignores Foucault's constructions of power as a "relation" (Orner 82). "[T]o accept a view of one's work as giving power (as property) to others/Others," writes Jennifer Gore, "is to overly simplify the operation of power in our society" (58), and, I would add, to overly simplify the construction of academic discourses.

## A TURN IN THE CONVERSATION

> Dialogism is the characteristic epistemological mode of a world dominated by heteroglossia. Everything means, is understood, as part of a greater whole—there is a constant interaction between meanings, all of which have the potential of conditioning others.
> —Michael Holquist in Bakhtin, *Dialogic Imagination*

As the preceding chapters of *A Pedagogy of Possibility* demonstrate, dialogism, which Holquist describes in the epigraph above, remains for me not only a characteristic mode of reality but also a central and defining feature of composition pedagogy. At each and every level of discussion, compositionists benefit from a dialogized understanding of the discipline, pedagogy, and classroom instruction. Composition studies benefits, for example, when historiographers recognize the dialogic relationships among pedagogies and describe their contingent natures and the interrelationships among them. Acknowledging and acting upon the inherent complexities of and dialogic relationships among author, audience, and subject provide composition theorists a basis from which to construct and enact pedagogies that seek to engage students in productive discourse. Teachers of expository writing can then begin the work of constructing classrooms that engage students in examining and understanding the contingencies and politics of language and encourage them to claim a language of their own.

In the case of composition studies, scholars have not been remiss in theorizing their positions—Berlin, for example, is explicit about the assumptions and biases that inform his work—but most scholars have overlooked the implications for classroom pedagogy of the conceptual frameworks they claim. The structure of Berlin's taxonomy compels writing teachers to align themselves with particular camps—objectivists, expressivists, or transactionalists.[6] Yet, in practice, most writing teachers rely on elements of all three approaches in their pedagogies. The distinctions among the schools work, in theory, to describe epistemological dispositions, but epistemology alone does not drive pedagogy. How do we move beyond the constructs that now dominate our thinking in composition studies? In many ways, the will to move beyond is an easy but crucial step in that it acknowledges the shortcomings of the previous way of thinking. Constructing an alternative is, however, much more difficult.

As I noted in part 1, Sherrie Gradin defines herself as "trapped by the language of category and dichotomy" (15) as she undertakes a critique of the field, yet she and others investigating and questioning the value of current taxonomies have not yet moved beyond categories and dichotomies. They are, in effect, confined by the structures that define the discipline, just as the discipline has, in the past, been confined by the process/product models, subjective/objective dichotomies, and student- and teacher-centered classroom constructs. If composition studies is to take yet another step away from the divisiveness of these taxonomies and toward an interanimation of pedagogies and academic discourses, the discipline must begin to imagine writing instruction in other terms altogether.[7] Just as Young and Berlin shifted the discipline away from the process/product paradigm to the objective/subjective/social, we must move beyond their paradigm. So, rather than define our discipline along taxonomic lines, I propose an alternative architectonics informed by dialogue and the performative nature of pedagogy—the interanimated acts and scenes of teaching and learning, what I call a "pedagogy of possibility."

## THE ARCHITECTONICS OF A PEDAGOGY OF POSSIBILITY

In his introduction to Bakhtin's *Art and Answerability*, Michael Holquist defines "architectonics" as "concerned with questions of building, of the way something is put together." Later, Holquist notes, architectonics provides Bakhtin a framework from which to read and interpret texts and to criticize "his opponents [who] have not completely theorized their position" or provided an "overarching conceptual framework" for their work (x). I invoke the notion of architectonics here because it gives me a way to discuss not only those structures that have so dominated the field but also that which I believe promises to reimagine the existing structure of composition studies.

I am concerned in this chapter with laying the groundwork for such an architectonics, an overarching conceptual framework of pedagogy in composition studies based neither on epistemological categories or the subjective/objective dichotomies that Kate Ronald and Hephzibah Roskelly note undergird taxonomies of the field nor on discussions of academic discourse that pit home versus academic discourses. By traversing taxonomic categories and introducing new influences on composition studies, Irene Ward, despite her partial reliance on Berlin's categories, illustrates how we might begin to forge this alternative architectonics. Ward examines the construct of dialogue as it functions in expressivist, social constructivist, and radical pedagogies, as well as postmodern theories of discourse.[8] By focusing on dialogue as the central feature of her argument, Ward rejects traditional Western epistemological categories as the basis for defining pedagogy. She in turn characterizes meaning not as static or wholly unified but as interactive.

Ward takes an important step away from established taxonomies in composition studies by traversing them, ignoring subjective/objective dualities, and focusing on the contributions of each pedagogy to building a fuller understanding of dialogue in composition studies. Such an eclectic approach to the field allows Ward to compare the claims and assumptions of the pedagogies, engage alternative ways of seeing writing instruction, and avoid a confining pedagogical, theoretical, or epistemological position. A dialogic understanding of reality in fact mandates that compositionists recognize that knowledge, and therefore pedagogy, is constructed from multiple and conflicting knowledge claims, and that purist ideological frames limit understanding. Just as our language is already someone else's, so, too, are our pedagogies. They are not static; not *pure*, except in the abstract, but dependent, dialogic, working from, across, and through one another.

As a dialogic enterprise, composition studies, like other disciplines, is subject to both centripetal and centrifugal forces—opposing forces that at once attempt to "maintain the kind of separate identity and uniformity of thought that leads to stability, and . . . allow for communication with other groups and for the necessary innovations that come from without that lead to productive change" (Cooper 531). Dialogue is, however, only a starting point for a pedagogy of possibility, not an end. Dialogism names the process by which knowledge is generated; it does not account for the specific nature of the debates and conflicts in composition studies, and largely ignores issues of (in)equity within dialogic relationships. A pedagogy of possibility, though based epistemologically on dialogism, nevertheless recognizes the limitations of dialogue as a defining metaphor for composition studies. Power relations within and around the classroom, for example, undermine the nature of dialogue among students and between students and teachers. Who speaks (or writes) and whether others respond with creative understanding—a central feature of dialogism—remain problematic in expository writing classrooms, particularly those constructed without a self-consciousness about the political nature of the classroom and pedagogy.

### FEATURES OF A PEDAGOGY OF POSSIBILITY

> We should require in our writing classrooms activity, not passivity. As Ong has put it, the writing classroom needs kinesis more than anything else. . . . The textbook-bound classroom as it now often exists—in spite of Ohmann, Rose, and other critics—promotes passivity.
> —Kathleen Welch, "Ideology and Freshman Textbook Production"

Welch's quotation serves as a useful epigraph here because it names one of the central assumptions of a pedagogy of possibility: learning is (inter)active. No person learns or generates knowledge from a passive posture. This is, of course, another way of saying that a pedagogy of possibility assumes active engagement as a necessary condition for learning. A pedagogy of possibility may be defined by this and several other central features: an architectonic structure characterized by dialogism; an understanding of author, audience, and subject redefined in Bakhtinian terms; a belief in the necessity of both proficiency and productivity, and reciprocal interaction and critique between them. A pedagogy of possibility also espouses a maieutic approach to writing instruction and recognizes teaching as an addressed and answerable act in which students serve as coauthors and heroes.

The both/and of a pedagogy of possibility—a pedagogy that recognizes the need for both proficiency and productivity—has its roots in Bakhtinian linguistic principles of monologism/dialogism and cultural principles of centripetal/centrifugal forces. Proficiency is informed by any or all of the following orientations toward discourse, knowledge, learning, and students: an assumption of certainty; emphasis on centripetal cultural and polemic rhetorical ends; passive reception of knowledge and authoritative reception of discourse; instruction in and production of normal, preservative discourses; development of linear styles of reporting discourse; an overriding concern for convention and form.[9] Productivity, on the other hand, is informed by an assumption of ambiguity; emphasis on centrifugal cultural and parodic rhetorical ends; active engagement of knowledge and internally persuasive reception of discourse; instruction in and production of abnormal, investigative discourses; development of ludic styles of reporting discourse; and a concern for content. Productivity is centrifugal; it works away from that original intention, struggling against boundaries and convention.

As important as the features that inform a pedagogy of possibility is the manner in which these features are related. That is, the singular and most central feature of a pedagogy of possibility is an architectonic structure characterized by dialogism, by a belief that "highlights possibilities of reciprocal interaction between and among" the elements of the construct (Code qtd. in Ward 194). Such a *reciprocal interaction* between proficiency and productivity strives to work against the either/or of traditional western epistemology, assuming the both/and of Bakhtinian dialogic epistemology. Every discourse, for example, is made up of both polemic and parodic linguistic tendencies; every discourse functions both as normal and abnormal discourse, as preservative and investigative. Similarly, pedagogies are at once centripetal and centrifugal, functioning both to support and undermine institutional conventions, norms, and structures. It is not enough, from a dialogic perspective, to argue that the centrifugal depends upon the centripetal for its existence; the two always already exist within the utterance. Understanding a pedagogy of possibility as presenting its features as reciprocal and interactive also allows for what Nancy Welch refers to as "reciprocal critique" through the transformative dialogue of the features. Investigative discourse, for example critiques the preservative, and the preservative critiques the investigative in the recursive process of development and change characteristic of dialogism.

A pedagogy of possibility also assumes that pedagogy is best defined as and through the act of teaching, with "act" imbued with all of the characteristics of the utterance articulated by Bakhtin. Implied in a Bakhtinian understanding of the utterance as an act is the notion of "answerability," an ethical imperative developed by Bakhtin in two texts, the abbreviated "Art and Answerability" and *Toward a Philosophy of the Act*. In these texts Bakhtin constructs an ethics of action and, by extension, discourse, noting that speakers and writers must be "answerable," or individually accountable, for composing their discursive acts, using their lived experiences in an effectual manner, and living in an active and self-evaluative mode.[10] If we redefine the architectonics of the rhetorical situation of the classroom dialogically and imbue that understanding with Bakhtinian notion of coauthorship, the classroom becomes a site where encoder/decoder/reality are not only intrinsically related and many of the differences among them elided, but also equally responsible for constructing a pedagogy. Pedagogy becomes a "performative act" through which a teacher "calls everyone to become more and more engaged, to become active participants in learning" (hooks, *Teaching* 11).

In short, pedagogy entails *answerability*. Defining pedagogy as addressed and answerable to an audience acknowledges students as always already the coauthors and heroes of our classrooms, an understanding lacking in much current educational theory—including critical pedagogy (outside of Freire)— which often overlooks students' coauthorship of pedagogy. Like meaning, which is constructed between and among individuals within a particular cultural context, pedagogy is enacted not by a teacher alone but in consort with students.

In addition to defining pedagogy as a construct coauthored by instructors and students, a pedagogy of possibility recognizes that pedagogy is not static, cannot be defined solely on synchronic terms, and is more productively characterized as a constant interaction of different pedagogies diachronically arranged. Like meaning, which is perfected only at the moment of the utterance, a pedagogy is determined only at the moment it is constructed, enacted, and meets with creative response. Two pedagogical dichotomies in composition studies—the process/product debate and student-centered/teacher-centered pedagogies—have defined expository writing instruction by contrasting privileged (process, student-centered) and vilified (product, teacher-centered) terms. When asked, most compositionists would likely define themselves as process-oriented and student-centered in their teaching. It is even difficult for us to imagine a process-oriented classroom that is not student-centered. But these terms, and the debates about them, have done little to investigate how students coauthor pedagogy. Compositionists simply do not discuss pedagogy in these terms.

Sharon Crowley has come the closest, perhaps, to articulating the consequences of the egocentricity (and teacher-centeredness) of *all* pedagogies, when she notes in *A Teacher's Introduction to Deconstruction* that students, particularly when compared to teachers, do very little writing in their classes. This phenomenon suggests what most composition instructors would probably admit: students do not coauthor the courses and are not engaged in their development, arrangement, or performance. They generally are not actively engaged in constructing the syllabus, for example.[11]

A pedagogy of possibility, which understands teaching as an answerable act, is critical both for the construction of classroom practice and for the evaluation of that practice. By imagining and investigating students' reception (answerability, respons-ibility) of pedagogy, we might begin to answer not only local, individualized concerns about why classes (don't) work but also larger, collective concerns about the reception of entire approaches to writing instruction. By seeing pedagogy as an answerable act, we

1. shift the focus on pedagogy from what we *do* (and what our intentions are in "doing" teaching the way we do) to how our teaching is received, which, in turn, allows us to examine the *ethics* of teaching;
2. begin to examine pedagogy as practice, pedagogy in action—not pedagogy in theory;
3. see differently the reticence, resistance, and accommodation of students;
4. enlarge the responsibilities and contributions of students to pedagogy and the successes of classroom practice.

To this final end, a pedagogy of possibility is a student-generated (not simply student-centered) pedagogy in which students are given and expected to bear responsibility for the construction of the classroom and its goals.[12] That is, a pedagogy of possibility depends upon students engaging discourse and pedagogy in a responsive manner as they strive to construct internally persuasive discourse.

A colleague of mine, who had been a recreational golfer for many years—a person who golfed every few weeks with a group of friends—last spring began golfing several times a week. After the first few weeks of being reintroduced to the game, he commented that his understanding of his game had shifted significantly. He noted that he had enjoyed golfing for many years, even felt comfortable enough to play once a week during the summer without thinking seriously or consciously about the *process* of golf. As his interest increased, however, he became dissatisfied with the hit or miss inconsistency of his game. So he made a decision to begin thinking consciously (and conscientiously) about the need to understand why he made the choices he did as he golfed. He was no longer satisfied with a good shot or puzzled by a bad one; he yearned to know *why* the shot worked or didn't work, what he did right or wrong and how to begin to improve his game and achieve some level of consistency and proficiency. He needed a sense of how to go about making choices. Students, like my colleague, must make a conscious effort to achieve, and as a writing instructor, I have a responsibility to encourage that achievement. The relationship between us is a mutually answerable one; I am answerable to them for constructing a course that affords them the opportunity to achieve, and they are answerable to me insofar as they must make a committed and concerted effort to achieve.

> The rooms I visited felt alive. People were learning things, both cognitive and social, and doing things, individually and collectively, making contributions, connecting ideas, generating knowledge. . . . People were encouraged to be smart. . . . These young people were acting as agents in their own development. And that agency became an essential force in sustaining the classroom.
>
> —Mike Rose, *Possible Lives*

Rose's comments on his travels through America's public school classrooms strikes a resonant chord for me. The "consciousness of possibility" that informs his philosophy of education also informs the pedagogy of possibility I outline here. Central to both Rose's and my visions of the classroom and education at large is a need for students and teachers to share responsibility for creating a productive learning environment, one in which students and instructors become critical "co-investigators" (Freire 87). Certainly, because Freire's term was initially scripted for Brazilian peasants seeking empowerment in a political democracy, it is problematic when applied to composition studies in North America.[13] A teacher cannot escape the inevitable authoritative nature of her institutional discourses, her contextualized right to name reality within a particular educational setting and under particular circumstances. Yet, because authoritative discourse is neither monolithic nor static, a teacher's authority is not absolute.

Moreover, teachers and students—despite potential significant differences in age, culture, ethnicity, or personality—do not always move in entirely different cultural, social, or political spheres. They sometimes share languages, cultural experiences, even ideologies. Although within the institutional discourses of the classroom, the teacher's words may remain authoritative to some, or even most, students, they become internally persuasive to others, or else, John Edlund writes, "teaching would be an impossible and useless activity" (62). A teacher serves, for example, as an interpreter, bringing the authoritative words of others into contact with students. These alien words of others, if encountered in another context without the teacher or with a different teacher, might have remained authoritative (or ineffectual) had it not been for this teacher's mediation. By mediating authoritative discourses and encouraging students to engage alien discourses as internally persuasive, compositionists are enacting a maieutic pedagogy, yet another central feature of a pedagogy of possibility.

A maieutic pedagogy appears in one of its earliest forms in the Platonic dialogues. In the early portions of the *Theaetetus*, Socrates refers to himself as a midwife and to the art of drawing out knowledge as midwifery, *maieutikos*. A maieutic pedagogy, then, is synergistic as opposed to agonistic. It is a cooperative and interactive undertaking in which a student gives birth to ideas as the teacher and other students assist as part of an on-going intellectual conversation. These processes of coming to know are informed by dialogism and heteroglossia.

In *Problems of Dostoevsky's Poetics*, Bakhtin himself refers to Socrates and midwifery in setting out a strategy for attaining truth. Like the form of the Socratic dialogue itself and the generation of knowledge, a maieutic pedagogy is dialogic, for it encourages the search for knowledge, not the passive acceptance of authority. Socrates, Bakhtin recalls, brought students together in a fashion that required them to investigate collaboratively the nature of truth, for "[t]ruth is not born nor is it to be found inside the head of an individual person, it is born *between people* collectively searching for truth, in the process of their dialogic interaction" (110). In a like manner, students in expository writing classrooms encounter colliding opinions as they search for and find their own positions with regard to others' authoritative or internally persuasive discourses. A maieutic pedagogy also recognizes the collaborative, performative nature of pedagogy. Carolyn Ericksen Hill makes a similar argument with regard to the role of others in the writing classroom when she notes that in "authoring" a text, students rely on readers, who "enter into the birth of new texts (or children) [and] contribute some genetic material" (42). The words of others, then, become midwives as well—the catalysts through which students determine themselves and their discourses.

If students are unable to engage consciously and actively the discourses of others, they will be unable to respond creatively or formulate self-conscious positions with regard to conflicting knowledge. They may become proficient in reciting what others have said, but they will be unable to construct productive discourse in response to others. As a result, they generate no new knowledge. The teacher must address students' lack of generative discourse by helping them to recognize those forces that have shaped who they are and how they write as a consequence of being in the world. Once the teacher demonstrates to students that other discourses inform their writing (and their selves), she can then work with them to begin to "reshape and transform those forces to create a discourse that is internally persuasive and publicly meaningful" (N. Welch 501) and work to effect a student's desired personal, ideological, institutional, or cultural transformation.

The goals of a pedagogy of possibility emerge from the central features outlined above. These goals are lofty, even idealistic. When we articulate the goals of any pedagogy, of course, we recognize that not all teachers or students will achieve all of the goals and some may reach none of them. Rather, we articulate goals as a means of defining what our intentions and beliefs are regarding teaching, learning, students, and education.

*A pedagogy of possibility seeks to engage students in responding to monologic discourses, to work their way out of subservience to those authoritative discourses.*[14] A restatement of the argument presented in chapter 5, this pedagogical goal seeks to assist students as they adapt internally persuasive texts in a creative fashion. The "creativity and productiveness" of an internally persuasive discourse, Bakhtin writes,

> consist precisely in the fact that such a word awakens new and independent words, that it organizes masses of our words from within, and does not remain in an isolated and static condition. It is not so much interpreted by us as it is further, that is, freely, developed, applied to new material, new conditions; it enters into interanimating relationships with new contexts. ("Discourse" 345–46)

The newly wrought word is itself made "productive" by its responsiveness, creativity, and answerability. At the same time they engage the internally persuasive word, students must acknowledge their reliance on all previous discourses, even the ineffectual and monologic.[15]

*A pedagogy of possibility seeks to alert students to the restrictions on their language and the potential of their voices* by introducing them to the contingencies of language and its supportive and restrictive nature. Examining the linguistic and material conditions that inform, support, and restrict their voices grants students a fuller understanding of their situatedness within an institution or culture. The classroom itself, Jones suggests, might become the site that students examine.[16] By developing an ability to read the classroom and its discourses and determine the monologic and dialogic nature of inquiry, knowledge, production, and reception, students will be in a position to analyze and then respond in an appropriate fashion to the monologic or dialogic expectations of other academic and cultural contexts.

*A pedagogy of possibility seeks to define writing as an act* for which students are individually responsible. Despite the social construction of knowledge and discourse, individual discursive acts are the word of a given individual. Although theorists like Bakhtin and Volosinov, who embrace poststructuralist notions of authorship and language, call the ownership of language into question, individual responsibility for those words cannot be deferred.

*A pedagogy of possibility articulates claiming languages as a primary goal of first-year writing.* Students who undertake an intensive and conscientious study of social languages and their informing qualities may begin the task of constructing and claiming their own languages.

*A pedagogy of possibility seeks to engage students in purposeful resistance.* Once students have understood the nature of languages to influence and inform their ways of seeing and constructing the world, students are in a position to release themselves from the power of the authoritative word. Jones notes, however, that the mere "relief of release" from the authoritative word does not in and of itself "necessarily engender learning" (17). A student's claimed languages and freedom from the authoritative word simply prepare her for the larger task of purposeful resistance. That is, her discourses must not simply name and reject the authoritative word but must generate answerable utterances that provide alternatives to or improvements upon those conditions she sees as unsatisfactory.

## AN INTERANIMATED PEDAGOGY: PROFICIENCY AND PRODUCTIVITY

In a 1990 interview with Terri Gross on National Public Radio's "Fresh Air," ambient musician Brian Eno noted that creativity often wanes as musicians allow proficiency to lull them into a "lack of alertness" about their craft and that musicians must always strive to "surprise" themselves out of the complacency that often accompanies proficiency. As I listened to the Eno interview, I was struck by the similarities between musicians and students in expository writing courses. Like the musicians Eno was describing, students, too, can be lulled into a sense of complacency and comfort that affects their writing. Without some means of surprising them out of that complacency, students run the risk of both taking their skills for granted and losing them. Unless students continue to challenge themselves as writers by surprising themselves, their writing will begin to degenerate.[17] Pedagogies that require students to generate only academic discourse (abstracts, reports, or researched essays, for example) very likely encourage students into complacent attitudes about their writing.

By itself, then, proficiency is, in its oppression, as Freire points out, *domesticating*.[18] Taken alone, that is, without a sense of the importance of productivity, pedagogies that posit proficiency as an end resemble what Kurt Spellmeyer calls a "pedagogy of ascetic self-reformation." As a pedagogy based on canonical texts and knowledge, as existing in and through "authorized" institutional practices, ascetic self-reformation privileges "knowledge over the learner" (*Common Ground* 50). Pedagogies that emphasize proficiency, and with it privilege authoritative approaches to discourse and learning, are a growing trend among courses in writing in the disciplines. Marilyn Cooper argues, for example, that

> As Foucault has explained so clearly, the institutional constraints we work under fairly consistently enact a notion of disciplinary knowledge, where the only valid form of knowledge is the accumulation of a stable set of ideas and data through the use of disciplinary conventions, and where knowledge is transmitted to neophyte members of the discipline as they learn conventions.[19] (532)

In first-year writing courses that emphasize proficiency, students are expected to accumulate knowledge about writing or some other content, not test or question the assumptions behind that knowledge. Regardless of its pedagogical orientation, a writing course that does not *encourage* students to critique their learning is a course that promotes proficiency. The end is to train students to write effective discourse, not question why a particular kind of writing is considered good writing. David Bartholomae, for example, promotes a pedagogy of proficiency when in "Inventing the University" he suggests that students learn the patterns of academic discourse as an entree into the university. Ward notes that Bruffee, borrowing from Rorty, claims that "normal discourse" must be the "primary task of composition instruction" (Ward 69). Like Ward, I am bothered by Bruffee's (and Bartholomae's) disregard for the importance of abnormal discourse in students' ideological becoming and for students' abilities to construct abnormal discourse. Constructing normal discourse is *not* enough to allow members a full place in the dialogue of a given language group. Normal discourse, as centripetal, conventional, preservative, and validated, remains monologic, distanced, and authoritative. People become full, card-carrying *dialogized* members of a group only when they *actively* participate in *producing*, not simply replicating, their own self-consciously constructed versions of that discourse.

The motivations for adopting the patterns and ideology of academic discourse, as Don Bialostosky points out, is quite strong. In many cases, students and instructors alike measure success by how well students comply with and meet institutional expectations. And it is not easy, hooks concurs, to write against the grain in a "consumer culture where we are all led to believe that the value of our voice is not determined by the extent to which it challenges, or makes critical reflection possible, but rather whether . . . it (and sometimes even we) is liked" (*talking back* 16). Let me reiterate, though, that proficiency like that which Bartholomae posits is a necessary part of the process of composing productive, performative discourse that questions, tests, and even resists those academic forms. Proficiency is not all bad. It becomes problematic when it acts as an end in itself rather than as a means to an end.

Toni Morrison elaborates on the problematic nature of proficiency and its political consequences in the introduction to *Race-ing Justice, En-Gendering Power*, an edited collection of essays on Anita Hill and Clarence Thomas, when she writes of *Robinson Crusoe* and the linguistic fate of the rescued Friday. Her comments are, I believe, analogous to not only Clarence Thomas as an African American "rescued" by Anglo-culture, but also to many first-year writing students—women and minorities in particular—whom we ask to adopt academic discourse through a mastery of convention and genre in place of a "mother tongue":

> [I]nternalizing the master's tongue is the problem of the rescued. Unlike the problems of survivors who may be lucky, fated, etc., the rescued have the problem of debt. If the rescuer gives you back your life, he shares in that life. But, as in Friday's case, if the rescuer saves your life by taking you away from the dangers, the complications, the confusion of home, he may very well expect the debt to be paid in full. Not "Go your own way and sin no more." Not "here, take this boat and find your own adventure, in or out of your own tribe." But full payment, forever. Because the rescuer wants to hear his name, not mimicked but adored. (xxv–xxvi)

Like Friday and Clarence Thomas, whom Morrison describes as "condemned first to mimic, then to internalize and adore, but never to utter one single sentence understood to be beneficial to their original culture" (xxix), many students rescued by the academy privilege academic discourse and revere academic practices at the expense and degradation of alternative discourses and cultural practices. Bell hooks argues similarly when she suggests that "today's black students have been encouraged to believe that assimilation (to make similar, to be absorbed) is the way to succeed. . . . yet is "at its very core dehumanizing" (*talking back* 67). And like Robinson Crusoe, academicians—and even to a great degree critical educators—do not learn, and are not required to learn, the language of the "rescued," and thus reinscribe their institutional positions of power over their students.

Bell hooks also examines and critiques the violent consequences of insisting upon and promoting a rationalist notion of academic discourse:

> [I]t was disturbing to me that intellectual radicals who speak about transforming society, ending the domination of race, sex, class, cannot break with behavior patterns that reinforce and perpetuate domination . . .
>
> . . . One of the clear and present dangers that exists when we move outside our class of origin, our collective ethnic experience, and enter hierarchical institutions which daily reinforce domination by race, sex, and class, is that we gradually assume a mindset similar to those who dominate and oppress, that we lose critical consciousness because it is not reinforced or affirmed by the environment. (*talking back* 77–78)

Here hooks echoes the sentiments of Toni Morrison as she examines the costs borne by Clarence Thomas and Defoe's Friday as they mimic the language of their oppressors. Similarly, Maria Lugones, who acknowledges the risks of entering hierarchical institutions like the academy, writes that "[t]here are 'worlds,'" that "we enter at our own risk, 'worlds' that have agon, conquest, and arrogance as main ingredients in their ethos. These are 'worlds' that we enter out of necessity and which would be foolish to enter playfully" (401). The academy is one of those worlds.[20]

We become aware of the *possibilities* and power of our own discourses by actively *producing* discourses that work out of and against proficiency, seeking to make the "university and the classroom . . . a place of promise and possibility" rather than "a place of punishment and confinement" (hooks, *Teaching* 4).

### Enacting Pedagogies of Possibility

> As I see it, the writing class opens up a space in which individual ideological development can become not just the accidental outcome of encounters with the disciplinary languages but the deliberate goal of a reflective practice.
> —Don Bialostosky, "Liberal Education, Writing, and the Dialogic Self"

A pedagogy of possibility may take many forms, and for that reason I have at various points in my discussion referred to pedago*gies* of possibility. My point is this: no one approach to writing instruction ensures that students will actively engage discourses or make a commitment to their own ideological becoming. Compositionists, such as Don Bialostosky in the epigraph above, have, however, articulated a series of environmental and pedagogical preconditions for the dialogic classroom and proposed a variety of dialogic classroom approaches to writing instruction. I begin below by first proposing the consequences of "monologic" pedagogies. I then describe representations of dialogic pedagogies, those that seek to invite dialogue, diversity, and possibility.

*"Monologic" methods.* As might be expected, compositionists proclaiming the need for dialogic classrooms do not devote a great deal of time outlining those teaching practices that impede dialogism. A number of familiar teaching practices, however, often reinforce the authority of texts and therefore decrease the potential dialogue that might take place between texts and students.

1. By characterizing some texts as canonical, for example, instructors reinforce the authority of these texts as well a student's responsibility to revere, not question them. A pedagogy that distinguishes, for example, between *interpreting* a Shakespeare play and *criticizing* a peer's essay implies a distinction between those two discourses based on their implied authority and cultural value. Shakespeare's is worthy of interpretation, while the student's text warrants only criticism and correction. This is not to suggest that canonical texts should not be used, but that they must be used in such a way as to examine their acquired but seemingly inherent authority.

2. Lecture/discussion formats, when dominated by the instructor or more advanced students, establish a hierarchy within the classroom that defines knowledge as the presentation of formed thought rather than the

exploration of thought under formulation. The value of a person's contribution is also often determined by the "authority" of her word rather than her attempts to come to terms with the text from her own perspective. As Klancher and Cooper and Selfe note, this hierarchy, alongside students' passive dispositions toward academic discourse and their view of the teacher as Authority, transforms classroom discussion into a debilitating monologue that further distances texts and knowledge.

3. Not allowing students to lead discussions on published or canonical work and restricting their responses to other student texts again imply that *Tom Jones* or *Cultural Literacy* is the property of a select few who may interpret for others, while student texts can be interpreted by anyone.

4. Prescribing interpretive guidelines for student responses to published work and not for responses to student writing implies a similar hierarchy of authority among texts.

5. Methods of evaluation can also reinforce the monologic. Testing procedures that ask students to recall and reconstruct particular pieces of information without at the same time asking them to integrate that information into their own perspectives on the subject certainly reaffirms the authority of discourse. Multiple choice examinations and even short essay questions that force students to rely on distanced and external texts reinforce passive reception and acceptance of and increased reliance on those texts.

By constructing classrooms with this authoritative ethos, instructors increase the likelihood that students will passively receive authoritative discourses rather than actively engage them. Students are often very quick, in fact, in determining whether an instructor expects a passive response to the information given in a lecture or assigned in readings. I want to note, however, that a lecture, like any utterance, is a genre made up of a variety of voices, and in this it is dialogic. The form of the lecture alone, in other words, does not make it monologic; the intent of the speaker and the reception by the listeners determine whether it is *enacted* monologically.

*"Dialogic" methods.* Compositionists have posed various means of constructing a Bakhtinian or dialogic classroom that invites students to attend to their ideological becoming. In doing so, they often rely on particular classroom methods as means of ensuring that students have opportunities to contribute actively to the classroom. Nancy Welch cites alternative methods of teacher response, letters from students to instructors, student responses to writing, and peer groups; Farmer creates a series of writing assignments designed to engage students with one another and various genres of published texts; Middendorf

asks students to define and then question their notions of "good" writing; Comprone encourages collaboration; Nancy Welch and Bazerman propose writing logs or journals; and Gay urges "active" reading by encouraging students to maintain a dialogue with texts. Bialostosky gives perhaps the most specific suggestions, arguing that a teacher who constructs a classroom guided by dialogic principles

> can modify the terms of disciplinary education in the students' favor by letting them in on the secrets of genre and convention that disciplines silently observe, by sharing with students the power produced by switching genres and defying conventions, and by suspending for the sake of student's development some of the conditions of disciplinary discourse itself. ("Liberal" 16)

Bialostosky's suggestion differs from the others in its focus as well. He does not rely on particular *practices* (e.g., collaboration, journals) but on *outcomes*.

Collaboration seems a reasonable method of fostering dialogue in the classroom, for it alters the role of the instructor and provides students with a different perception of the authority of the teacher and the teacher's texts. By distributing the responsibility of response and evaluation among students, collaborative pedagogies have the potential to reorganize the relationships in the classroom. Ideally, teacher-student relationships are no longer primary; they are replaced by student-student exchanges that reinforce the cooperative sharing of texts to achieve meaning. Alternative discussion formats also encourage students to interact with a text and grant them an equal right to and responsibility for analyzing texts. Cooper and Selfe, for example, argue that computer-mediated discussions provide a means of working against traditional discussion formats that privilege some voices at the exclusion of others. Bialostosky suggests bringing an authoritative text within reach of students by having them parody its style or prepare class presentations on a novel or chapter from a textbook. In doing this, students realize the need not only to read a text and understand it but also to communicate it to others. If they can successfully communicate their responses to or evaluations of a text, they have taken a first step toward actively engaging that text.

In *Literacy, Ideology, and Dialogue*, Ward undertakes a retrospective of forms of dialogue in composition classrooms. Among the expressivists Ken Macrorie, Donald Murray, and Peter Elbow, Ward designates the helping circle, publishing student writing, freewriting, one-on-one conferencing (best characterized by Murray's conferencing approach), and the teacherless writing class as "dialogic" activities. Like Berlin, Ward acknowledges the limited nature of the expressivist dialogic as she defines it: Expressivists, she concludes, "are concerned with dialogic interaction with others only insofar as such interaction helps to promote the writer's ability to dialogue more effectively with the inner self and thereby come to know that inner self" (45). Social constructivists and collaborative learning proponents like Bruffee use students' face-to-face dialogue and reading aloud as dialogic activities "that give them [students] authentic practice in the kinds of social situations that they will encounter when they enter discourse communities beyond the educational system" (80).

Yet, these contributions to the dialogic pedagogy Ward envisions pale in comparison to social constructivists' (i.e., Bruffee's) transgressions, most important, that writing groups are just as likely to enforce conformity as independence and therefore stifle dialogue: "Along with Myers," Ward concludes, "I question collaborative learning's ability to introduce students to new discourse communities. It seems just as likely that collaborative learning will confine them to unquestioned, unexamined ideological structures" (87–88). Like Evelyn Ashton-Jones, Ward also concludes that "[c]ollaborative learning theory, at least from a social-epistemic perspective, has not yet provided an adequate description of how these [status] differences and the inevitable resulting conflicts are to be dealt with democratically" (87).

Ira Shor and Cy Knoblauch share the blows of Ward's critique in her chapter, "Dialogism and Radical Pedagogy." As I indicated in chapter 2, Ward argues that Shor's dialogism does not adequately construct students and teachers as equals or provide opportunities for students to construct meaningful public discourse. As in her treatment of Shor, Ward critiques Knoblauch for imposing his own curriculum on the students and not providing opportunities for writing for audiences beyond the classroom. Ward acknowledges that any attempt Knoblauch (or any other teacher) might make toward involving students in designing the curriculum for their course is thwarted by institutional constraints, but does so only after having already charged Knoblauch with a failure to manage somehow in spite of the constraints. Of the radical pedagogues, Kyle Fiore and Nan Elsasser's come the closest to "Returning the Dialogic to Radical Pedagogy." In Elsasser's classroom, the lives and experiences of the adult black women in the class are privileged and distinctions between academic and experiential (objective/subjective) knowledge are eschewed. Ward continues to call for giving students similar opportunities to "experience how language and action work themselves out in situations outside the classroom where written discourse has effects on people's lives" (111). In "Postmodern Views of Discourse and Dialogism," the penultimate chapter of *Literacy, Ideology, and Dialogue*, Ward articulates the function of dialogue in postmodern pedagogies. "Paralogic" rhetorics and pedagogies, which enjoy a relatively privileged status in composition studies, prove fertile ground for Ward, who unearths for a functional dialogic pedagogy synthesis journals (from Gary Olson) and dialogues (like those proposed by Bill Covino in *The Art of Wondering*).

Ward's criticism of dialogue as it functions in the work of these scholars revolves around several key characteristics she argues must be present in a "truly" dialogic pedagogy, but which are, to one degree or another, absent in their practice. These compositionists omit just those elements that inform Ward's own "functional dialogism":

- Student writing must be made public. That is, students must write not only to the teacher but also to audiences outside the classroom. Ward insists that students not simply write prose that is "never directed to anyone for any purpose other than to fulfill assignments and to receive a grade." Ward continues:

  > if students are continually asked to write in arhetorical situations, they never gain the audience-analysis skills that can act as guidelines for estimating the success of any piece of writing that they may produce. . . . They never experience their writing as part of a dialogue with an "other." (Ward 110–11)

- Students must have a substantial and defining voice in constructing the curriculum of the course. The curriculum must not be imposed by the teacher's own agenda.
- The work of the classroom must be informed by a sense of Freirean *praxis*, of reflection and action.
- The classroom must be defined by a sense of mutual understanding and respect. "[S]tudents need to know," Ward contends, "that what they say will be taken seriously as a statement of a thinking person and that the instructor and the other students will actually respond and engage in a dialogue" (117). A dialogic pedagogy, in other words, is informed by an "ethical framework that fosters and values a multiplicity of voices without invalidating differences among participants" (193).
- A dialogic pedagogy is also characterized by its epistemology, which "values more than objective knowledge and . . . recognizes that knowledge making is a collective endeavor" (193).
- Further, a dialogic pedagogy is defined by its insistence on "communicative ethics," and its belief that ethics can be determined most successfully through thorough, open and "reciprocal critique among groups of people" (200).

Ward acknowledges that one of the most formidable challenges facing teachers who wish to implement a dialogic pedagogy is developing and maintaining an atmosphere of trust in the classroom, and she faults many of the composition theorists she discusses, such as Elbow, Bruffee, Knoblauch, Covino, for "fail[ing] to address the possible ways that unequal social structures of classrooms inhibit this [dialogic] atmosphere" (184). Ward assumes that "truly democratic dialogue takes place only in an atmosphere of trust and mutual respect" (171), that the "unequal status of members within society as a whole reproduces itself in the classroom" (172), that "a trusting atmosphere is often difficult to initiate and maintain," (184), and, citing Susan Jarratt, that "dialogic composition pedagogies have the same potential as any other composition pedagogies to reinforce racism, sexism, and classism" (185). Ward turns to Lorraine Code and Sharon Welch to find "methods that can be employed to develop the necessary trust for dialogue to function effectively" (172). These methods, it appears, are themselves rather theoretical—dialogue functions effectively in contexts in which both objective and subjective knowledge are valued and in which difference is accommodated and multiple voices validated.

In part because school writing is always institutionally sponsored writing, the educational context can *never* approximate the context in which Freire worked and to which Ward aspires. So, to require, or even expect, the same sorts of "action" from our students is unreasonable. But I would argue that if we limit our understanding of dialogue to an evaluation of methodology and classroom interaction, then we will always fail to achieve "truly democratic dialogue," for we cannot assure how our pedagogies will be *received* or *enacted* by students. That the dialogic pedagogy Ward proposes is defined almost entirely in terms of classroom practices, rather than in terms of the dialogic principles at work in language use and knowledge construction, is problematic. Naming particular methods (e.g., collaboration, the helping circle) as dialogic is problematic because any method, like any discourse or act, can be interpreted or enacted monologically. By focusing on methods and speaking in terms of discrete writing tasks, Ward does not allow herself to explore some of the more theoretical and political implications of the dialogic on writing instruction. In the end, compositionists must go beyond defining methods or activities as characteristic of dialogic pedagogies and begin examining both the production and reception of pedagogy. Pedagogy is a performative, answerable, and addressed act, and as such it relies on both teachers and students for its success. Reading or synthesis journals, for example, do not ensure that students will engage texts actively. These may, in fact, simply become sites at which students continue to valorize the published authoritative word.

If teachers of writing are to find any success in mentoring students as they engage the alien word, they must recognize that they themselves, and the institution they represent, must make a fundamental shift in their views of the educational enterprise and student writing. An institution or pedagogy based on authoritative understandings of discourse and knowledge, that "does not change in response to the 'ignorant' or 'naive' uses students—or other 'outsiders'—make of it but instead acts to exclude them until they accede to its demands," is an institution that is not performing one of its most central functions (Cooper 537).

A (NOT SO) FINAL WORD

Rarely am I able to pinpoint specific passages from texts or events in my daily life that directly influence my academic and intellectual life, but in the last year, as I completed this manuscript, I have had two such experiences. The first, the Fresh Air interview with Brian Eno that I mention earlier, provided me with the notion of proficiency. I remember driving north on High Street in Columbus to pick up my daughters at day care as I listened to the broadcast. Eno's words struck me, and I struggled to find a pen and paper, eventually jotting the quotation on the back of an envelope. The second event came in the form of a quotation, this one from Deborah Mutnick's *Writing in an Alien World*. I reproduce below an extended quotation that I highlighted in my own copy of her book. Here, Mutnick cites Aronowitz and Giroux from *Education under Siege* as they describe their ongoing project of "[a]ttempting to forge a 'language of possibility'":

> Aronowitz and Giroux argue that "the concept of resistance must have a revealing function that contains a critique of domination and provides theoretical opportunities for self-reflection and struggle in the interest of social and self-emancipation" (p. 105). In this light, theories of agency and intentionality can restore a sense of hopefulness—a discourse of possibility—to critical pedagogy and counteract the pessimism of much radical analysis. Understanding that resistance can "both challenge and confirm capitalist hegemony," the authors state:
>
> > What is most important is the willingness of radical educators to search for the emancipatory interests that underlie such resistance and to make them visible to students and others so that they can become the object of debate and political analysis. (p. 108) (Mutnick 156)

This quotation from Mutnick on Aronowitz and Giroux, by recognizing the centrality of agency and intentionality, provided me with the notion of possibility as a cornerstone for the pedagogy I was imagining.

Agency, intentionality, resistance, transformation, possibility—these are the terms around which a pedagogy of possibility revolves. The student as author is an agent in her own ideological becoming, a person whose intentions and responsibility for learning determine and define what personal and cultural structures she chooses to resist and transform. Students and writing instructors who take seriously their own, and one another's, ideological development restore the possibility for cultural and political change.

# NOTES
# WORKS CITED
# INDEX

# NOTES

## PREFACE

1. Already authorship of the Bakhtinian canon becomes problematic. For the sake of clarity and accuracy of attribution, I refer to Bakhtin, Medvedev, and Volosinov as the authors of the particular texts ascribed to them. But I refer to "Bakhtin" or (when feasible) the "Bakhtinian" when making more generalized statements about ideas or terms that span texts by members of the Bakhtin Circle.

2. Existing not on the margins but being decentered is, in fact, a preferable position for Bakhtin and compositionists, as Susan Miller argues in *Textual Carnivals*.

3. One notable exception to this trend in composition theory and practice is Stephen North's *The Making of Knowledge in Composition*, a text that examines the epistemological and methodological constructs that guide scholarly and pedagogical work in the discipline.

4. See, for example, my "Of Reeling and Writhing; Or, Mixed Up Metaphors in the Teaching of Writing."

5. This term is Stephen North's. He uses the foraging metaphor to describe the work of philosophers of composition.

## INTRODUCTION: A COMPOSITIONIST READS BAKHTIN

1. I have elected to alternate pronoun references (she, he, etc.) from chapter to chapter, beginning here with "he."

2. Points of conflict between Bakhtinian ideas and composition studies do, of course, exist and are of great importance to my own understanding of the relationships I articulate in *A Pedagogy of Possibility*. Readers interested in my comments on points of conflict are invited to read two of my articles: "Starting the Dialogue: What Can We Do about Bakhtin's Ambivalence Toward Rhetoric?" and "Feminism and Bakhtin: Dialogic Reading in the Academy." Both are also reprinted in *Landmark Essays on Bakhtin*, ed. Frank Farmer. I will not replay those arguments here.

3. Bob Morgan's "Three Dreams of Language; Or, No Longer Immured in the Bastille of the Humanist Word" also makes theoretical connections between writing pedagogy and the various linguistic schools defined by Bakhtin, but does not articulate the relationships between Bakhtin and Berlin that I argue here.

4. Faigley, Cherry, Jolliffe, and Skinner acknowledge Berlin's work in *Assessing Writers' Knowledge*, citing "Contemporary Composition: The Major Pedagogical Theories" in their discussion of theories of composing. Similarly, Berlin cites Faigley, Cherry, Jolliffe, and Skinner in the final chapter of *Rhetoric and Reality*, noting that their work "considers three conceptions of the composing process" (187).

5. The four include, in addition to Berlin's *Rhetoric and Reality*, Karen Burke LeFevre's *Invention as a Social Act*, Faigley's "Competing Theories of Process," and C. H. Knoblauch's "Rhetorical Constructions: Dialogue and Commitment."

6. In a 1988 conversation, when I first brought to his attention the similarities be-

tween his taxonomies and those of Volosinov and Bakhtin, Berlin indicated that he had not read their work and was unfamiliar with their taxonomies.

7. See Berlin, "Contemporary" 767; *Rhetoric and Reality* 11; Volosinov, *Marxism* 52, 53.

8. See Volosinov, *Freudianism* 15; Faigley 534.

9. See Berlin, *Rhetoric and Reality* 11; Faigley 531; Volosinov, *Marxism* 52, 93, 94.

10. See Berlin, *Rhetoric and Reality* 15; "Contemporary" 774; Volosinov, *Marxism* 12, 98.

## PART ONE. REIMAGINING THE RHETORICAL SITUATION

1. Certainly, significant differences exist between Kinneavy's understanding of many forms of discourse—including persuasive, referential, and literary—and Bakhtin's genre theory. My goal here is to demonstrate a simple observation: Bakhtin's work supplements Kinneavy's by beginning at a similar point (by describing the elements of discourse) and moving in a different direction. Rather than classifying discourse as Kinneavy does, Bakhtin describes the way it is influenced by its situational and cultural contexts.

2. See Volosinov, *Marxism* 60; *Freudianism* 15.

## 1. REDEFINING THE STUDENT WRITER

1. Volosinov presents in *Freudianism* a particularly telling critique of Freudian psychology, one that calls into question its relatively naive understanding of the relationship between client and therapist. The inherent power hierarchy in the relationship, Volosinov argues, calls into question the nature of the dialogue that takes place and the nature of the representations made by both client and therapist.

2. Bakhtin's comments on empathy in *Toward a Philosophy of the Act* are helpful here. One cannot purely empathize with another, take another's position, feel another's pain. One can, nevertheless, have an interested *awareness* in another's position despite one's necessary distance from it.

3. Elbow's work, while considered subjective or expressivist, recently has taken on a more social flavor. See "Closing My Eyes as I Speak," *Embracing Contraries*, and *A Community of Writers* with Pat Belanoff.

4. I invoke the plural "voices" when referring to a Bakhtinian understanding of the term as polyphonous, heteroglossic. Like James Wertsch, who also opts for "voices," I find it a much more helpful term in representing the concept. In selecting "voices," Wertsch rejected Habermas's "role," in part because the notion of "voices" maintains a clear relationship between "social communicative processes and individual psychological processes" in a way "role" does not. See Wertsch, *Voices of the Mind* 13–14.

5. See Bator; Corder; Hairston, "Carl Rogers"; and Lunsford, "Aristotelian" for comments on these issues.

6. See Cherry, "Ethos versus Persona" for additional commentary on this distinction.

7. Stewart makes a similar comment, stating that the student wrote about something outside his own experience. Again, however, Stewart concludes that such writing is dishonest because a student expresses an opinion to please the teacher, but not his *true* opinion. Stewart remains unable to use the criteria he forwards to estimate the truthful-

ness of the student's writing beyond suggesting that true belief must run counter to popular (or, in this case, moralistic) belief.

8. See Thomas Kent, Greg Myers, and John Trimbur for additional critiques of Bruffee's understanding and construction of collaboration and community.

9. I do not doubt that there exist among college students at any given institution what might be called normal discourses. In fact, I am certain they exist, because the students in my writing courses use them. The normal discourses that writing students bring to college are not, however, the normal discourses of academia.

10. Helen Ewald and Irene Ward write on the work of Douglas Kent who, as an "externalist," argues (via Davidson in philosophy) against the need for discourse communities as a means of examining how language functions. Conventions, as defined by discourse communities, Kent argues, are merely a starting point, not a defining characteristic, of hermeneutics. Kent's arguments against discourse communities are compelling and warrant greater attention in composition studies.

11. In our ongoing research, Suellynn Duffey, Pam Engsinger-Antos, Jane Greer, and I have defined three tropes of collaboration—colonization, isolation, and integration—that define the ways that students work with and against their own and classmates' ideological positions during collaborative classroom activities.

12. David Bartholomae ("Study of Error," "Inventing," and "Tidy House"), Patricia Bizzell ("What Happens" and "William Perry"), and Min-zhan Lu ("Conflict" and "Redefining") offer the most comprehensive and compelling descriptions of this version of the writer and her relationship to the academy.

13. Bartholomae actually defines basic writers twice in this essay, first as those students who—through test scores, examination, or teacher referral—are placed in remedial or developmental writing courses, and second, as those "students who are refused unrestricted access to the academic community" ("Inventing" 136, 146). The second definition, which appears in a section devoted to Bizzell's work, is significantly more politicized. By "politicized" I mean to suggest that this latter definition recognizes the absolute complicity (and attendant right) of the institution in defining those who do or do not meet some standard of achievement or performance.

14. In effect, students develop "passing theories" (Kent) of academic discourse.

15. Thomas Recchio's article, "A Bakhtinian Reading of Student Writing," proves an interesting example of the way one instructor reads a student paper and the cultural commonplaces attending, informing, and constraining her reading.

16. See Goleman; Klancher; Recchio; Ritchie, "Beginning" for more on this.

17. Caroline Hudak is an undergraduate English major at Ohio State University. She has given her permission for the use of her writing here.

18. This quotation from Smith appears as an epigraph in Pamela Gay's *Developing Writers* (1).

19. This undergraduate, a student in the first-year expository writing course at Ohio State University, composed her remarks on a classroom electronic mail system and has given permission for their use.

20. Fiction writer Charles Baxter visited the Ohio State University English Department at the invitation of the Creative Writing and First-Year Writing Programs. As part of that visit, Baxter joined five other people in a panel on writing. The panel—which included Jennifer Cognard-Black, Vandana Gavaskar, Paul Hanstedt, Deborah Way, and me—was moderated by Suellynn Duffey.

21. I'm indebted to Jennifer Cognard-Black who cited this quotation from Michener at the Writers' Roundtable.

22. I choose Pamela Gay's and Peter Elbow and Pat Belanoff's texts because they are competent and representative examples of the practice in writing instruction to name students as writers. The reader is encouraged to browse through any writing text-book—including *A Brief Guide to Basic Writing*, which I coauthored with Roger Cherry—to determine the pervasiveness of this practice.

## 2. AUDIENCE, ADDRESSIVITY, AND ANSWERABILITY

1. Lunsford and Ede's retrospective on "Audience Addressed/Audience Invoked," "Representing Audience: Successful Discourse and Disciplinary Critique," questions several of the assumptions in the earlier article, particularly those that led them to "fail[ ] to explore . . . the ways in which audiences can not only enable but also silence writers and readers" (170).

2. I have not made much yet of "listener," the term Titunik uses in the English translation of "Discourse in Life and Discourse in Art." In many ways the issue is moot, for Volosinov notes that "every utterance in the business of life is an objective social enthymeme" ("Discourse in Life" 101). For compositionists, however, the distinction between listener and reader is critical and affects the ways that they read Bakhtinian commentary. I will continue to use—outside of quotations from texts that indicate "listener"—the broader term "audience."

3. Bakhtin also writes in "The Problem of Speech Genres" that social and economic class relationships and *"personal* proximity" of author and audience determine stylistic choices. He suggests that close personal proximity lends itself to a "certain *candor* of speech" not likely in discourses between people less closely bound (96–97).

4. In demonstrating that a listener must share elements of his apperceptive background with a speaker in order to understand an utterance, Volosinov turns to the simple utterance "Well!" spoken by one of two people sitting in a room. The second person does not respond. Volosinov uses the example to argue that the utterance is not meaningful to us as readers because we do not share context, knowledge, and disposition of the interlocutors. See "Discourse in Life" 99–100.

5. See also Todorov 41–42.

6. See Gregory Clark 1–32, for a discussion of Bakhtin's, Plato's, and Aristotle's theories of the functions of discourse.

7. Ede and Lunsford and Selzer suggest that synthesizing or eliding differences is the better pedagogical route. Selzer argues, for example, that because of the dynamism of audience and because audiences cannot be neatly parceled out (two points with which I agree), teachers would do well to "end by smoothing over the distinctions a bit" (172). While this might be useful advice in terms of audiences addressed and invoked, it is less satisfactory advice with respect the the teacher as evaluative audience.

8. This Bakhtinian construct might also usefully be compared to Prince's "virtual reader," Rabinowitz's "authorial audience," or even Riffaterre's "superreader." See Selzer 174n–75n on Rabinowitz, Prince, and Riffaterre.

9. Bakhtin comments on authorial representations in discourse when, in "The Problem of Speech Genres" he writes that "in addition to the actual author, there are also conventional and semiconventional images of substitute authors, editors, and various kinds of narrators" that might populate a discourse (98).

10. It bears repeating that although Park, Bakhtin, and Volosinov make interesting arguments regarding audience analysis and the relationship among speaker, listener, and subject, they still have not commented helpfully on the problematic nature of the teacher as an audience-behind-the-audience.

11. See also "The Problem of Speech Genres" (94ff) for another description of "active responsive understanding."

12. In her introduction, and in this quotation specifically, Shelley speaks of her own "invention," the story of Victor Frankenstein itself, having been influenced by Byron's and Percy Shelley's musings on Darwin and her own vision/dream of a "student of unhallowed arts" creating a living man.

13. If for this reason alone, I find Park's and Ward's (and others') arguments for writing for a real audience compelling. This strategy does not, of course, eliminate the ambiguous role of the teacher as the audience-behind-the-audience, but it clarifies one of the issues of audience I've raised in this chapter by creating a complete context for writing.

14. Arthur Applebee invokes the metaphor of conversation, for example, in *Curriculum as Conversation*.

15. See Bruffee, "Social Constructions" 783.

16. The gatekeeper metaphor, questioned in the 1970s by Mina Shaughnessy, is notorious now among compositionists for its assumptions about a teacher's role the educational enterprise. Teacher as initiator is not much better; the club metaphors and passwords are themselves very telling.

17. To refer to a writer gaining "control" or "power" over a text is problematic from a Bakhtinian perspective, which argues for a much more recognized and animated understanding of text and hero.

18. I thank the students in my English 467 class (Winter 1996) for encouraging my thinking on these various uses of audience.

19. We can never represent to ourselves precisely what the response of an audience would be to our text. In many cases, in fact, we cannot even approximate it. To suggest to students that having a firm sense of the demographics of an audience (e.g, 18-year-old males considering enlisting in the armed forces) and an accurate audience analysis (e.g., patriotic, athletic, aggressive) are enough to construct a viable text is misleading. The nexus of individual physical characteristics and psychic traits—even among a relatively homogeneous group—is not enough to account for (and cannot assume along with it) the variety of ideologies among that group. That is not the goal of a projected audience. Instead, the goal is to construct an audience that assists the writer as he writes.

20. Bizzell and Herzberg do not link their pedagogy explicitly to Bakhtin or the notion of intertextuality. Like Pratt, who writes of contact zones, Bakhtin understands intertextuality and the convergence of and conflict between texts as "zones of contact."

21. Students very often have immediate audiences even when their classrooms do not provide them. That is, students enrolled in a writing course that does not use peer groups often take their writing to other trusted readers (e.g., spouses, partners, roommates, friends) for an immediate response.

22. Kurt Spellmeyer's "Foucault and the Freshman Writer" addresses more specifically the role of the confession in first-year writing courses. His work, like that of Cooper and Selfe, uses the Foucauldian panopticon as a metaphor for repressive practices in the composition classroom—practices that Jerrie Cobb Scott, whom I mention shortly, demands we call into question.

### 3. THE SUBJECT AS "HERO," GENRE, AND AUTHORITY IN WRITTEN DISCOURSE

1. Ewald also argues that through externalism, which understands utterances as situational and dynamic, compositionists will come to better understand and utilize the notions of hero and answerability.

2. In most cases the texts I use here are not the most recent editions. Where I have chosen earlier editions or texts published prior to 1990, I do so to demonstrate the duration of the practice in composition studies to represent the subject as a static object rather than a generative coauthor of discourse.

3. For three related discussions of textbooks, pedagogy, and ideology, see Kathleen Welch's "Ideology and Freshman Textbook Production: The Place of Theory in Writing Pedagogy," and Bob Connors's "The Rise and Fall of the Modes of Discourse" and "Textbooks and the Evolution of the Discipline."

4. Jim Berlin describes the period from 1940–1960, during which time *The Technique of Composition* and *Writing with a Purpose* first appeared, as the "Communications Emphasis" in composition instruction. See Berlin, *Rhetoric and Reality* 92–119.

5. Karen Greenberg, like McCrimmon, encourages students to look to their own experiences to find topics. She then encourages them to keep their purposes and audiences in mind as they shape those topics.

6. Berlin dates the resurgence of classical rhetoric in composition studies at roughly 1960. See Berlin, *Rhetoric and Reality* 120–38.

7. A related metaphor of scientific inquiry and examination characterizes Pamela Gay's approach to invention and development: observe, reflect, interpret. I realize, of course, that scientific metaphors are themselves undergoing significant change as philosophers, sociologists, and scientists investigate the multivocality and contextualized nature of scientific inquiry. See, for example, Bruner, Geertz, Gilbert and Mulkay, and Polanyi.

8. An additional metaphor is one of ownership that appears even in Schuster's essay, "Mikhail Bakhtin as Rhetorical Theorist." Here, speakers "grasp" and "possess" words—problematic metaphors from a Bakhtinian perspective that eschews ownership of language. To his credit, Schuster recognizes the dialogic relationships inherent in the utterance as he characterizes "speakers struggl[ing] to replace alien meanings with their own semantic . . . intonations" (596).

9. Marilyn Cooper identifies the metaphor of participation in "Dialogic Learning Across Disciplines," but applies it more generally to language use. I extrapolate from her conclusions here.

10. Berlin cites this same passage from Young, Becker, and Pike in *Rhetoric and Reality* 172.

11. Kate Ronald and Hephzibah Roskelly include at the close of *Farther Along: Transforming Dichotomies in Rhetoric and Composition* an annotated "Bibliography of Works that Transform Dichotomies," which speaks to the rich interdisciplinary commentary on the social construction of knowledge and reality, see pp. 197–205.

12. I have chosen to employ the term "subject," as well as "hero" in my discussion—Volosinov and Bakhtin do this, as well—for "subject," like "hero," suggests an animate, dynamic element. Moreover, it is a term that already often represents the topic of discourse in composition studies. Finally, referring to the topic of a discourse as a "subject" places it more at the center of the utterance, because "subject" implies an agency absent in "object."

13. *Some* discourse forms (e.g., scholarly essays written *by* "authorized" academicians) have changed, perhaps even significantly, in the past two decades, a point I will discuss shortly. The forms that have *not* significantly changed are college essay assigned to and expected from student writers.

14. See, for example, Aronowitz and Giroux; Brodkey; Elbow, "Reflections"; Guerra; Lu, "Conflict"; Severino; and Spellmeyer, "A Common Ground."

15. See Berlin's *Rhetoric and Reality* for a discussion of the various forms of resistance pedagogies between 1960 and 1975 (145–55).

16. Bruffee adds a concluding paragraph to the students' essay task later in the process.

17. Hindman's argument is similar to Jerrie Cobb Scott's.

18. No one, of course, writes completely freely or without consequence. My point here is that the consequences for students and untenured faculty are analogous. A student working against dominant paradigms or a teacher's prescriptions risks failing a course. An untenured faculty member writing in non-traditional forms or expressing transgressive opinions risks termination.

19. Vitanza recognizes the paradox of his position. Having been asked to paraphrase for the "Octalog" (originally a panel at the 1988 Conference on College Composition and Communication) a statement regarding his views on history and historiography, Vitanza demonstrates that the *genre* of statement and paraphrase dictated by the event place him in an problematic position: to paraphrase his position is to lie, for his ideas must be performed.

20. Like Farmer, Jon Klancher constructs an assignment that I consider participative. Klancher briefly describes an assignment in which he asked students to "inventory the languages of the black civil-rights writers." Students found it difficult to name a single style or rhetorical form that would describe the writings of all of the writers, and, as a result, Klancher suggests that the students no longer viewed the civil rights movement as a "historical monolith" (94n). Because Klancher does not ask students to direct their gaze upon their own writing, however, his assignment is not as participative as Farmer's.

## 4. ACTIVE ENGAGEMENT AND PASSIVE RECEPTION: CRITICAL READING AND WRITING IN COMPOSITION

1. In addition to these general strategies, which appear in this same fashion in nearly every rhetoric textbook on the market, Axelrod and Cooper and Bazerman present annotations and reading journals (or short exploratory writing) as means of recording responses to texts, as methods of preserving first reactions. See Axelrod and Cooper, *Reading Critically* 3, 6; Bazerman 21–23, 27–34.

2. See Edlund and Cooper and Selfe for two examples of pedagogies that enact this sort of philosophy.

3. Welch implies in this description (by mentioning the possibility of silencing another's word) a form of Bakhtinian discourse that Cooper and Selfe describe as "discourse that doesn't matter" (859). Cooper and Selfe recognize, in other words, that readers do, and in fact must, make choices to ignore discourses. At the same time, however, readers must understand the consequences of ignoring or silencing others' discourses, naming them as insignificant or ineffectual.

4. Bakhtin distinguishes among four forms of understanding: (1) "Psychophysiologically perceiving a physical sign (word, color, spatial form). (2) *Recognizing* it (as familiar or unfamiliar). (3) Understanding its *significance* in the given context (imme-

diate and more remote). (4) Active-dialogic understanding (disagreement/agreement)" ("Toward a Methodology" 159; emphasis in original). Of these four, only the last may be characterized as internally persuasive. The third form, understanding the significance of the sign, does not entail engagement.

5. Welch extends the discussion of authoritative and internally persuasive discourses to teachers' responses to student writing, noting that even in this discursive form that writing teachers must consider carefully the power of their word as authoritative. See pp. 498–99.

6. Fetterley, of course, makes more specific claims with respect to gendered reading than those I represent here. For Fetterley, the relationship between reader and author is also a relationship between woman and man, female (reader) and male (author). I do not wish to ignore Fetterley's primary concern in *The Resisting Reader*; at the same time I wish to extend her arguments beyond issues of gender.

7. The converse is true, as well. No discourse is inherently or even eventually internally persuasive to all readers. Nor can we determine or control, as Cooper and Selfe argue, what texts students will engage internally persuasively.

8. For Kristeva, heteroglossia and dialogue characterize the general state of the world and provide room for feminism as a political, centrifugal movement. For Bauer, the male-dominated culture of American literature is counterpoised by the language and the ideology represented by subversive female characters. Such centripetal discourses are "monologic"; they position themselves above the milieu, pretending to be the "*ultimate word*" (Bakhtin, *Problems* 293; emphasis in original). Only through dialogue—through the intervention of alternative discourses (for Bauer in particular these are feminist discourses)—is the monologic, monolithic word questioned and new knowledge constructed.

9. See Mary Louise Pratt's "Arts of the Contact Zone" and M. H. Abrams's discussion of reader-response criticism.

10. Pamela Gay makes a similar statement but in the end argues for the ascendancy of critical reading. See p. 17.

11. Note that Belenky et al. include "Silence," a category that may be said to precede Perry's duality. Women characterized as silent perceive authorities as speaking not from a position of communal knowledge but from an individual and superordinate position. Silent subjects picture themselves as subservient to and completely controlled by authorities. The same may be said of members of minority or marginalized groups, including basic writers who, like the women about whom Belenky writes, find themselves facing responsibilities for which they feel unprepared. As a result of this insecurity, they become increasingly dependent on authority.

12. Programs of study like those of David Bartholomae and Anthony Petrosky and Kenneth Bruffee are constructed in such a way as to reduce an attitude of passive reception. Bruffee's, for example, allows students to formulate responses to texts based on their personal experiences rather than on academic or expert knowledge. This sort of methodology, as Klancher argues, allows students to investigate the dialogic nature of all discourse and realize that the words of a president, pastor, or professor are filled with the voices of myriad others. To this end, Klancher suggests a pedagogy that analyzes the ideological assumptions of various languages—he uses social languages of the 1960s—inviting students to investigate their own languages in a similar fashion.

13. By insisting on the existence of a "'real self' and 'real voice,'" however, Elbow continues to describe a monologic version of the psyche in which the loci of creation

and evaluation remain within the individual. As his work progresses over the years from *Writing Without Teachers* and *Writing with Power* to *Embracing Contraries* and *A Community of Writers* (with Pat Belanoff), the monologue is steadily replaced by a dialogue of doubting and believing within the self that relies on a "construct of internalized other . . . influenced by [the writer's] internalized social codes and values" (LeFevre 52). The internal dialogue relies on these elements of social codes and values, however, only insofar as they restrict and control—*constrain*—the writer's conscious choices, not in terms of their more basic constituative *generative* nature in unconscious choices. In *Writing with Power*, doubting and believing maintain their functions as tools for critique established in *Writing Without Teachers*, but in *Writing with Power* Elbow seemingly conceives the doubting game as sometimes desirable as believing. It can be, he argues, "equally powerful if everyone is up for it. Wrestling can lead to the truth" (271).

14. Doubting is not an activity reserved for the individual, as Elbow notes. Groups are just as capable as individuals of voicing doubt and striking out against a dominant or hegemonic community (*Embracing* 264).

15. Thomas Recchio, for example, distinguishes four "voices" in a student's essay on Freudianism and taboo. The student essay fails to present a successful reading of Freud, Recchio argues, because of the student's inability to work outside of the constraints placed on her by the discourses of pseudo-psychology and moralism. John Schilb critiques Recchio's representations of the student's writing as an example of scholarship that shows disdain for students. Welch critiques Recchio for his unwillingness to inquire into the student's confessional mode, arguing that Recchio undertakes the "kind of un-Bakhtinian reading that leads teachers to appropriate their students' texts and issue formal directives for 'coherence and continuity'" (502n).

16. Mutnick argues for a similar situated position for basic writing in the academy but does not articulate a fully dialogic or Bakhtinian understanding of writing instruction in the university.

17. Mutnick also uses authoritative and internally persuasive discourses as a hermeneutics for analyzing student writing and teacher response to that writing, examining the "processes of interpretation and identification" that take place as students and teachers write, read, and speak about writing. In her analyses, Mutnick examines "to what extent such processes [of interpretation and identification] situate students and teachers to become agents or passive recipients of their educational experiences" (xxiii).

18. Chris refers to the instructor as Jeff, a pseudonym. I quote here from a draft version of the paper because I feared that as the text continued to see the eyes of editors the tensions and inconsistencies in pronoun usage would be removed. The final version of the essay appears in Gail Tayko and John Tossani's *Sharing Pedagogies: Teachers and Students Respond to the English Curriculum*.

## 5. THE POLITICS OF REPORTED SPEECH AND THE IDEOLOGY OF FORM

1. See Berlin, *Writing Instruction*; Connors, "Thirty Years"; Crowley, *Methodical*; and Johnson, "Three Nineteenth" and *Nineteenth-Century Rhetoric*, for example.

2. See Crowley, *The Methodical Memory* 126, 18, 131. Crowley also acknowledges the contributions of Henry N. Day to current-traditional thought. His textbooks were, however, not as influential as Bain's, although she notes that they "enjoyed a popular-

ity that momentarily rivaled Bain's" (179n). She also suggests that Day's "complex but comprehensive system," had it held sway over Bain's, would have changed the face of current-traditional thought. See p. 180n. For a more detailed discussion of Day, see pp. 124–26, 128, 129.

3. Crowley offers much greater detail regarding the alterations made by Scott and Denney to Bain's theories. See pp. 128–32, 143. I am less concerned here with repeating her observations than with noting that Bain alone was not responsible for the representation of the paragraph in late-nineteenth- and early-twentieth-century composition textbooks.

4. This bit of circular reasoning is precisely the kind Crowley describes as characteristic of current-traditionalists, who advise that "[w]riters know that their paragraphs are complete when enough sentences have been supplied to support their topic sentence" (131).

5. This, too, has its roots in earlier current-traditional thought. Crowley argues that compositionists like Scott and Denney, who defined the paragraph as the fundamental discursive unit, were guided by a legitimate pedagogical concern. Because students could write more paragraphs than essays during a term, and because the paragraph was characterized as an essay in miniature (complete with thesis, development, and conclusion), it made pedagogical sense to substitute paragraphs for whole compositions in writing classrooms (131–32).

6. A related issue, instruction in topic sentences, has also undergone very little change in the last fifty years. McCrimmon in 1950, like Kennedy, Kennedy, and Holladay in 1996, define the topic sentence as summarizing (see McCrimmon 113) or "spell[ing] out the main idea of a paragraph (Kennedy, Kennedy, and Holladay 371). Both also discuss the placement of topic sentences at the head or close of a paragraph and acknowledge (but discourage students from writing) implied topic sentences. For more see McCrimmon 113, 123; Taft, McDermott, and Jensen 404–5. See also Harris and Cunningham 570, 609–12, and Hairston and Ruszkiewicz 147–48, for further examples of this same representation of the topic sentence in expository writing textbooks.

7. See Hairston and Ruszkiewicz 146–51 for a similar characterization.

8. Within the analytical, McCrimmon includes division and elaboration, and within elaboration, he includes exemplification, comparison (analogy), and contrast, see pp. 41–63.

9. Hairston and Ruszkiewicz do not entirely escape the practice of defining paragraph length in terms of readers' ability to process information, arguing that students should strive to produce "fairly short" ("no more than seven or eight sentences"), "reader friendly" paragraphs (160). They turn to convention as a determiner of paragraph length by defining formal, informal, and casual styles of writing in terms of paragraph length. See pp. 192, 193, 194 for more.

10. Even this shift in instruction is not discipline-wide. Some textbook authors merely dictate a rule—"The paragraphs in the body of a research paper ought to be about one-half page in length or longer" (Lester 168)—without articulating what considerations (beyond adequate development of the topic sentence) determine paragraph length.

11. Besides Harris and Cunningham, which appeared in 1993 in a "brief" edition, all other textbooks are in a fourth or eighth edition, suggesting that they have been well-enough received for publishers to continue to invest in them.

12. I agree that this paragraph could benefit from revision—but not on the basis of its length or the difficulty it might cause some readers. Rather, the paragraph introduces a complex series of voices and initiates some dialogue among them. It doesn't go far enough, however, in exploiting the dialogic nature of Chris's thinking on writing instruction.

13. Referred to as "documentation" in Taft, McDermott, and Jensen, quotation is relegated to matters of manuscript preparation—it follows "Appearance" and its subsections on materials (pens, papers), presentation (margins for titles, handwriting, and typewriting), and submission (page order and form). Instruction in documentation consists of advice on attribution, common knowledge, and plagiarism. Students are instructed in the proper use of quotation marks and conventions for proper quotation ("exact wording, spelling, and punctuation") (372). They're also instructed that quotations are not necessary when "another person's idea, but not his exact wording," is represented, and they are offered a few examples of "acknowledgements," and "explanatory" statements, and methods of introducing quotations (373). McCrimmon essentially ignores the question of quotation, limiting instruction to less than one page in the chapter on punctuation that outlines the details of quotation marks as a means of designating direct quotations, intentional use of slang expressions, and quoted passages (367).

14. It is not coincidental that as I present this information on quotations that I quote frequently from my sources.

15. For more, see Axelrod and Cooper, *Reading Critically* 428; Hairston and Ruszkiewicz 552; Reinking, Hart, and Von Der Osten 318.

16. See also Hairston and Ruszkiewicz 554; Kennedy, Kennedy, and Holladay 62.

17. Neither Volosinov nor Bakhtin relates authoritative and internally persuasive discourse with linear and pictorial forms of reported speech.

18. Volosinov also discusses "quasi-direct discourse," devoting an entire chapter in *Marxism* to its formulations in French and German. See pp. 141–59. I do not find quasi-direct discourse to be a necessary part of a pedagogy that introduces composition students to the notions of linear and ludic styles of reporting speech.

19. "Ludic" has an interesting etymology. It is related to *ludicrus* (Latin) and *ludus* (French), "game, play, sport"; akin to *ludere* (Latin), "to play"; *loidoros* (Greek), "abusive."

20. Spatt notes the euphemistic and ironic use of quotation marks—two additional forms of the ludic style of direct quotation that call upon selected words in reported discourses as a means of subversion. In the quotation, "The actor was joined by his 'constant companion'" (91), Spatt argues that the author is "both *calling attention to* and *distancing him- or herself from* the euphemism" (91), from the content of the reported discourse.

## 6. TOWARD A PEDAGOGY OF POSSIBILITY

1. hooks addresses academic discourse and domination in other passages in *talking back*. See pp. 29, 67, 77.

2. Joe Harris also critiques stances such as Bartholomae's and Bizzell's, arguing that they rely on sovereign notions of community like those outlined by Pratt.

3. Disciplinary discussions over the past several years have focussed more and more on the issues of critical pedagogy, and once again I find Bakhtinian work relevant to

this conversation. The content of education should not be empty and untested propaganda and slogans—the authoritative and monologic word of the oppressor—but the perceptions and concerns of the oppressed and their experiences with and comments upon the authoritative word made internally persuasive.

4. Here I am thinking, for example, of the effect of Mimi Orner's arguments regarding "voice" on our discussions of academic discourse.

5. Consider, for example, the varieties of academic discourse I have called upon in my own arguments in this text—Kurt Spellmeyer's *Common Ground*, Victor Villanueva's *Bootstraps*, Patricia Williams's *The Alchemy of Race and Rights*, or Jim Zebroski's *Thinking Through Theory*.

6. See "Personal and Public Authority in Discourse: Beyond Subjective/Objective Dichotomies," in which Kate Ronald and Hephzibah Roskelly define and elaborate upon the problematic nature of Berlin's taxonomy and his dismissal of expressivists.

7. Part of the difficulty compositionists face in discussing Bakhtin is a result of these taxonomies. That is, some Bakhtinian notions appear quite amenable to expressivist approaches to writing instruction. Frank Farmer suggests, for example, that the very helpful notion of *signature* (interpreted by some as "voice") is more amenable to expressivist pedagogies, which may cause some scholars to devalue or ignore it.

8. Although she calls upon Bakhtin in her final chapter, Ward does not discuss Bakhtin's work in any detail. She cites Bakhtin only three times, relying almost entirely on Don Bialostosky's "Liberal Education, Writing, and the Dialogic Self" for her interpretations of authoritative and internally persuasive discourse. See Ward 174–77.

9. My discussion of the linear style of quotation in chapter 5, for example, demonstrates a concern for proficiency because mastery of convention is a primary concern.

10. See Jeffrey T. Nealon's "The Ethics of Dialogue: Bakhtin and Levinas" for a more detailed discussion of Bakhtin's understanding of ethics.

11. Certainly exceptions to this observation exist. Fiore and Elsasser's pedagogy is one example. For the most part—and perhaps almost entirely—the American college classroom remains the province of the instructor. (Fiore and Elsasser, remember, worked with Bahamian women.)

12. I base a student-generated pedagogy on what little I know about Community Language Learning, a method of foreign language education in which students relate to the instructor what they wish to learn to say. The instructor then generates the phrase and the student repeats it. This process continues in a modified workshop format with students listening to one another. At the close of a session, the instructor reviews important linguistic, grammatical, or rhetorical features of those discourses.

13. See, for example, Linda Shaw Finlay and Valerie Faith, "Illiteracy and Alienation in American Colleges: Is Paulo Freire's Pedagogy Relevant?"

14. Klancher, in describing this process, argues that the goal of a writing class informed by Bakhtinian principles seeks to "empower students to *master* the monologues of which they have becomes hapless and usually ineffective reproducers" (86; emphasis added). I chose not to quote Klancher directly because his terminology is problematic in its understanding and treatment of the subject. In addition to its agonistic connotation, the notion of mastery is alien to a Bakhtinian understanding of discourse; a person cannot be said to "master" a discourse.

15. See Cooper and Selfe for a discussion of their computer-supported approach to "creatively adapt" others' discourses (866).

16. Jones refers to Jane Tompkins's "Pedagogy of the Distressed" as a useful essay

for this purpose. Tompkins suggests in that article that the classroom itself become an examined site. I used Tompkins's essay in a graduate course in feminist and critical pedagogies, and it did indeed initiate a thoughtful and exploratory discussion on the nature of discourse in the classroom. Among the topics raised in that class session were the constraints placed on the voices of gay and lesbian students and faculty who are not "allowed" to speak about their private lives in the same way heterosexual students and faculty are authorized to speak. Heterosexual students' experiences with partners or spouses are confirmed in and sanctioned by the culture and the discourses of the classroom in a way that gay and lesbian students' experiences with partners are not. Silence emerged as another significant issue in this class session, with both "voiced" and "silent" students speaking variously about the frustration, power, and protection of silence. For a discussion of silence, see Magda Gere Lewis's *Without A Word: Teaching Beyond Women's Silence*.

17. A disclaimer: Although I write here of students' complacency about their writing, these comments apply to any person who writes frequently. Novelists, academicians, journalists who don't explore, extend, and test their abilities, who do not exercise new muscles, as it were, also risk complacency: "No matter how adept a writer becomes, the activity of writing always entails a radical loss of certainty" (Spellmeyer, *Common Ground* 111).

18. To speak convincingly of proficiency, we must, of course, recognize the socially-constructed nature of proficien*cies*.

19. Kurt Spellmeyer also critiques courses in writing in the disciplines on similar grounds (*Common Ground* 107).

20. Maria Lugones's "world-travelling," Giroux's borders and border crossing, Mary Louise Pratt's "contact zones," Trin Mihn-Ha's "moving about," and Gloria Anzaldúa's "new mestiza": These constructs are informed (more or less) by poststructuralist and/or feminist notions of subjectivity and at the same time recognize (some better than others) the problem of "power as property" that presently informs discussions of academic discourse.

# WORKS CITED

Abrams, M. H. *Glossary of Literary Terms*. 6th ed. Fort Worth: Harcourt, 1993.

Annas, Pamela J. "Style as Politics: A Feminist Approach to the Teaching of Writing." *College English* 47.4 (1985): 360–71.

Anzaldúa, Gloria. *Borderlands/LaFrontera: The New Mestiza*. San Francisco: Aunt Lute, 1987.

Applebee, Arthur N. *Curriculum as Conversation: Transforming Traditions of Teaching and Learning*. Chicago: U of Chicago P, 1996.

Aristotle. *The Rhetoric*. Trans. Lane Cooper. Englewood Cliffs: Prentice-Hall, 1932.

Aronowitz, Stanley. "Notes from Underground: Mikhail Bakhtin Changes the Face of Criticism." *Voice Literary Supplement* 7 Mar. 1989: 22–24.

Aronowitz, Stanley, and Henry Giroux. *Education under Seige: The Conservative, Liberal, and Radical Debate over Schooling*. South Hadley: Bergin and Garvey, 1985.

Axelrod, Rise B., and Charles R. Cooper. *Reading Critically, Writing Well: A Reader and Guide*. 4th ed. New York: St. Martin's, 1996.

———. *The St. Martin's Guide to Writing*. 4th ed. New York: St. Martin's, 1994.

Bain, Alexander. *English Composition and Rhetoric*. 2 vols. New York: American Book, 1887. Appleton, 1888.

Bakhtin, Mikhail. "Art and Answerability." Bakhtin, *Art and Answerability*. 1–3.

———. *Art and Answerability: Early Philosophical Essays by M. M. Bakhtin*. Eds. Michael Holquist and Vadim Liapunov. Trans. Vadim Liapunov. Austin: U of Texas P, 1990.

———. "Author and Hero in Aesthetic Activity." Bakhtin, *Art and Answerability*. 4–256.

———. *The Dialogic Imagination: Four Essays by Mikhail Bakhtin*. Trans. Caryl Emerson and Michael Holquist. Ed. Michael Holquist. University of Texas Slavic Ser. 1. Austin: U of Texas P, 1981.

———. "Discourse in the Novel." Bakhtin, *The Dialogic Imagination*. 259–422.

———. "Forms of Time and Chronotope in the Novel." Bakhtin, *The Dialogic Imagination*. 84–258.

———. "From Notes Made in 1970–71." Bakhtin, *Speech Genres*. 132–58.

———. "The Problem of Speech Genres." Bakhtin, *Speech Genres*. 60–102.

———. "The Problem of the Text in Linguistics, Philology, and the Human Sciences: An Experiment in Philosophical Analysis." Bakhtin, *Speech Genres*. 103–31.

———. *Problems of Dostoevsky's Poetics*. Trans. and Ed. Caryl Emerson. Theory and History of Lit. 8. Minneapolis: U of Minnesota P, 1984.

———. *Rabelais and His World*. Trans. Helene Iswolsky. Cambridge: MIT P, 1968.

———. "Response to a Question from the *Novy Mir* Editorial Staff." Bakhtin, *Speech Genre*. 1–9.

———. *Speech Genres and Other Late Essays*. Trans. Vern W. McGee. Ed. Caryl Emerson and Michael Holquist. University of Texas Slavic Ser. 8. Austin: U of Texas P, 1986.

———. "Toward a Methodology for the Human Sciences." Bakhtin, *Speech Genres*. 159–72.

——. *Toward a Philosophy of the Act.* Trans. Vadim Liapunov. Eds. Michael Holquist and Vadim Liapunov. University of Texas Slavic Ser. 10. Austin: U of Texas P, 1993.

Bartholomae, David. "Inventing the University." *When A Writer Can't Write: Studies in Writer's Block and Other Composing-Process Problems.* Ed. Mike Rose. New York: Guilford, 1985. 134–65.

——. "The Study of Error." *College Composition and Communication* 31 (1980): 253–69.

——. "The Tidy House: Basic Writing and the American Curriculum." *Journal of Basic Writing* 12.1 (1993): 4–21.

Bartholomae, David, and Anthony Petrosky. *Facts, Artifacts, and Counterfacts: Theory and Method for a Reading and Writing Course.* Upper Montclair: Boynton/Cook, 1986.

——. *Ways of Reading: An Anthology for Writers.* 3rd ed. New York: Bedford-St. Martin's, 1993.

Bator, Paul. "Aristotelian and Rogerian Rhetoric." *College Composition and Communication* 31 (1980): 427–32.

Bauer, Dale M. *Feminist Dialogics: A Theory of Failed Community.* Albany: SUNY P, 1988.

——. "The Other 'F' Word: The Feminist in the Classroom." *College English* 52.4 (April 1990): 385–96.

Bauer, Dale M., and Susan Jaret McKinstry, eds. *Feminism, Bakhtin, and the Dialogic.* SUNY Series in Feminist Criticism and Theory. Albany: SUNY P, 1991.

Bazerman, Charles. *The Informed Writer: Using Sources in the Disciplines.* 4th ed. Boston: Houghton, 1992.

Belenky, Mary Field, Blythe McVicker Clinchy, Nancy Rule Goldberger, and Jill Mattuck Tarule. *Women's Ways of Knowing: The Development of Self, Voice, and Mind.* New York: Basic, 1986.

Bellanca, Mary Ellen. "Alien Voices, Ancient Echoes: Bakhtin, Dialogism, and Pope's 'Essay on Criticism.'" *Papers on Language and Literature* 30 (1994): 57–72.

Berger, Peter L., and Thomas Luckmann. *The Social Construction of Reality: A Treatise in the Sociology of Knowledge.* Garden City: Anchor-Doubleday, 1967.

Berlin, James. "Contemporary Composition: The Major Pedagogical Theories." *College English* 44 (1982): 765–77.

——. "Rhetoric and Ideology in the Writing Class." *College English* 50 (1988): 477–94.

——. *Rhetoric and Reality: Writing Instruction in American Colleges, 1900–1985.* Studies in Writing and Rhetoric. Carbondale: Southern Illinois UP, 1987.

——. *Rhetorics, Poetics, and Cultures: Refiguring College English Studies.* Urbana: NCTE, 1996.

——. *Writing Instruction in Nineteenth-Century American Colleges.* Studies in Writing and Rhetoric. Carbondale: Southern Illinois UP, 1984.

Berthoff, Ann E. *Forming/Thinking/Writing: The Composing Imagination.* Upper Montclair: Boynton/Cook, 1982.

Bialostosky, Don H. "Dialogics as an Art of Discourse in Literary Criticism." *PMLA* 101 (1986): 788–97.

——. "Liberal Education, Writing, and the Dialogic Self." *Contending with Words.* Eds. Patricia Harkin and John Schilb. New York: MLA, 1991. 11–22.

——. *Wordsworth, Dialogics, and the Practice of Criticism.* Cambridge: Cambridge UP, 1992.

Bizzell, Patricia. "Thomas Kuhn, Scientism, and English Studies." *College English* 40 (1979): 764–71.

——. "What Happens When Basic Writers Come to College?" *College Composition and Communication* 37.3 (1986): 294–301.

——. "William Perry and Liberal Education." *College English* 46 (1984): 447–54.

Bizzell, Patricia, and Bruce Herzberg. *Negotiating Difference: Cultural Case Studies for Composition*. Boston: Bedford-St. Martin's, 1996.

Blair, Catherine Pastore. "Only One of the Voices: Dialogic Writing Across the Curriculum." *College English* 50 (1988): 383–89.

Booth, Wayne. "Freedom of Interpretation: Bakhtin and the Challenge of Feminist Criticism." *Bakhtin: Essays and Dialogues on His Work*. Ed. Gary Saul Morson. Chicago: U of Chicago P, 1986. 145–76.

Breznau, Anne. "Writing and Self-Esteem in a Dialogic Classroom." Diss. U of Michigan, 1994.

Brodkey, Linda. *Academic Writing as Social Practice*. Philadelphia: Temple UP, 1987.

Bruffee, Kenneth. "Collaborative Learning and the 'Conversation of Mankind.'" *College English* 46 (1984): 635–52.

——. "Kenneth A. Bruffee Responds." Comment and Response. *College English* 48 (1986): 77–78.

——. *A Short Course in Writing: Practical Rhetoric for Teaching Composition Through Collaborative Learning*. 3rd ed. Boston: Little, 1985.

——. "Social Construction, Language, and the Authority of Knowledge: A Bibliographical Essay." *College English* 48 (1986): 773–90.

Bruner, Jerome. *On Knowing: Essays for the Left Hand*. Cambridge: Harvard UP, 1979.

Buitenhuis, Peter. "Present Imperative: New Directions in Canadian Literary Theory." Rev. of *Future Indicative: Literary Theory and Canadian Literature*, ed. John Moss. *College English* 50.8 (1988): 927–30.

Cherry, Roger D. "Ethos Versus Persona: Self-Representation in Written Discourse." *Written Communication* 5.3 (1988): 251–76.

Cherry, Roger D., and Kay Halasek. *A Brief Guide to Basic Writing*. New York: Harper, 1993.

Chiseri-Strater, Elizabeth. *Academic Literacies: The Public and Private Discourse of University Students*. Portsmouth: Boynton/Cook-Heinemann, 1991.

Clark, Gregory. *Dialogue, Dialectic, and Conversation: A Social Perspective on the Function of Writing*. Studies in Writing and Rhetoric. Carbondale: Southern Illinois UP, 1990.

Clark, Katerina, and Michael Holquist. *Mikhail Bakhtin*. Cambridge: Belknap-Harvard UP, 1984.

Cobley, Evelyn. "Mikhail Bakhtin's Place in Genre Theory." *Genre* 21 (Fall 1988): 321–38.

Comprone, Joseph J. "Textual Perspectives on Collaborative Learning: Dialogic Literacy and Written Texts in Composition Classrooms." *The Writing Instructor* 8 (1989): 119–28.

Connors, Robert. "The Rise and Fall of the Modes of Discourse." 1981. *The St. Martin's Guide to Teaching Writing*. 2nd ed. Eds. Robert Connors and Cheryl Glenn. New York: St. Martin's, 1992. 362–75.

——. "Textbooks and the Evolution of the Discipline." *College Composition and Communication* 37 (1986): 178–94.

——. "Thirty Years of *Writing with a Purpose*." *Rhetoric Society Quarterly* 11 (1981): 208–21.

Connors, Robert, and Andrea A. Lunsford. "Frequency of Formal Errors in Current

College Writing, or Ma and Pa Kettle Do Research." *College Composition and Communication* 39 (1988): 395–409.

Cooper, Marilyn. "Dialogic Learning Across Disciplines." *Journal of Advanced Composition* 14 (1994): 531–46.

Cooper, Marilyn, and Cynthia L. Selfe. "Computer Conferences and Learning: Authority, Resistance, and Internally Persuasive Discourse." *College English* 52 (1990): 847–69.

Corbett, Edward P. J. *Classical Rhetoric for the Modern Student*. New York: Oxford UP, 1971.

Corder, Jim. "Argument as Emergence, Rhetoric as Love." *Rhetoric Review* 3 (1985): 16–32.

Cross, Geoffrey A. "A Bakhtinian Exploration of Factors Affecting the Collaborative Writing of an Executive Letter of an Annual Report." *Research in the Teaching of English* 24.2 (May 1990): 173–203.

Crowley, Sharon. *Ancient Rhetorics for Contemporary Students*. New York: Macmillan, 1994.

———. *The Methodical Memory: Invention in Current-Traditional Rhetoric*. Carbondale: Southern Illinois UP, 1990.

———. *A Teacher's Introduction to Deconstruction*. Urbana: NCTE, 1989.

Day, Henry Noble. *Elements of the Art of Rhetoric*. Hudson: Skinner, 1850.

de Man, Paul. "Dialogue and Dialogism." *Poetics Today* 4 (1983): 99–107.

Dillon, George. "My Words of an Other." *College English* 50 (1988): 63–73.

Donahue, Patricia, and Ellen Quandahl, eds. *Reclaiming Pedagogy: The Rhetoric of the Classroom*. Carbondale: Southern Illinois UP, 1989.

Dunne, Michael. "Wild at Heart Three Ways: Lynch, Gifford, Bakhtin." *Literature/Film Quarterly* 23 (1995): 6–13.

Eco, Umberto. *The Role of the Reader: Explorations in the Semiotics of Texts*. Bloomington: Indiana UP, 1979.

Ede, Lisa A., and Andrea A. Lunsford. "Audience Addressed/Audience Invoked: The Role of Audience in Composition Theory and Pedagogy." *College Composition and Communication* 35 (May 1984): 155–71.

Edlund, John R. "Bakhtin and the Social Reality of Language Acquisition." *The Writing Instructor* 7.2 (Winter 1988): 56–67.

Elbow, Peter. "Closing My Eyes As I Speak: An Argument for Ignoring Audience." *College English* 49 (1987): 50–69.

———. *Embracing Contraries: Explorations in Learning and Teaching*. New York: Oxford UP, 1986.

———. "Reflections on Academic Discourse." *College English* 53 (1991): 135–55.

———. *Writing Without Teachers*. New York: Oxford UP, 1973.

———. *Writing with Power: Techniques for Mastering the Writing Process*. New York: Oxford UP, 1981.

Elbow, Peter, and Pat Belanoff. *A Community of Writers: A Workshop Course in Writing*. New York: McGraw Hill, 1995.

Ellsworth, Elizabeth. "Why Doesn't This Feel Empowering? Working Through the Repressive Myths of Critical Pedagogy." *Harvard Educational Review* 59.3 (August 1989): 297–324.

Emerson, Caryl. "The Outer Word and Inner Speech: Bakhtin, Vygotsky, and the Internalization of Language." *Bakhtin: Essays and Dialogues on His Work*. Ed. Gary Saul Morson. Chicago: U of Chicago P, 1986. 21–40.

Eno, Brian. *Fresh Air.* Interview. Natl. Public Radio. WCBE, Columbus. 13 Oct. 1995. Rbdcst. of 1990 Interview.

Ewald, Helen Rothschild. "Waiting for Answerability: Bakhtin and Composition Studies." *College Composition and Communication* 44 (1993): 331–48.

Faigley, Lester. "Competing Theories of Process." *College English* 48 (1986): 527–42.

Faigley, Lester, Roger D. Cherry, David A. Jolliffe, and Anna M. Skinner. *Assessing Writers' Knowledge and Processes of Composing.* Writing Research: Multidisciplinary Inquiries into the Nature of Writing. Series Ed. Marcia Farr. Norwood: Ablex, 1985.

Farmer, Frank. "The Dialogic Imagination: Vygotsky, Bakhtin and the Internalization of Voice." Diss. U of Louisville, 1991.

——, ed. *Landmark Essays on Bakhtin, Rhetoric, and Writing.* Mahwah: Lawrence Erlbaum, 1998.

——. "'A Language of One's Own': A Stylistic Pedagogy for the Dialogic Classroom." *Freshman English News* 19 (1990): 16–22.

Fetterley, Judith. *The Resisting Reader: A Feminist Approach to American Literature.* Bloomington: U of Indiana P, 1978.

Finke, Laurie. "The Dialogic Imagination and the Analytics of Power: Feminism and Bakhtin." Paper presented at Penn State Summer Seminar in Theory and Culture, "Working with Bakhtin Today." State College, PA, 26 July 1995.

——. *Feminist Theory, Women's Writing.* Ithaca: Cornell UP, 1992.

Finlay, Linda Shaw, and Valerie Faith. "Illiteracy and Alienation in American Colleges: Is Paulo Freire's Pedagogy Relevant." Shor 63–86.

Fiore, Kyle, and Nan Elsasser. "'Strangers No More': A Liberatory Literacy Curriculum." *College English* 44.2 (1982): 115–28.

Flower, Linda, and John Hayes. "A Cognitive Process Theory of Writing." *College Composition and Communication* 32 (1981): 365–87.

Flynn, Elizabeth A., and Patrocinio P. Schweickart, eds. *Gender and Reading: Essays on Readers, Texts, and Contexts.* Baltimore: Johns Hopkins UP, 1986.

Foerster, Norman, and J. M. Steadman Jr. *Writing and Thinking.* Boston: Houghton, 1931.

Fowler, H. Ramsey, Jane E. Aaron, and Kay Limburg. *The Little, Brown Handbook.* 5th ed. New York: Harper, 1992.

Freire, Paulo. *Pedagogy of the Oppressed.* Rev. ed. New York: Continuum, 1993.

Fulwiler, Toby. "Freshman Writing: It's the Best Course in the University to Teach." *The Chronicle of Higher Education* 5 Feb. 1986: 104.

Gardiner, Michael. *The Dialogics of Critique: M. M. Bakhtin and the Theory of Ideology.* 2nd ed. London: Routledge, 1992.

Gay, Pamela. *Developing Writers: A Dialogic Approach.* Belmont: Wadsworth, 1995.

Geertz, Clifford. *Local Knowledge.* New York: Basic, 1983.

Genung, John Franklin. *The Practical Elements of Rhetoric, with Illustrative Examples.* Boston: Ginn, 1885.

Gilbert, G. Nigel, and Michael Mulkay. *Opening Pandora's Box: A Sociological Analysis of Scientists' Discourse.* Cambridge: Cambridge UP, 1984.

Giroux, Henry. *Border Crossings: Cultural Workers and the Politics of Education.* New York: Routledge, 1993.

——. *Theory and Resistance in Education.* South Hadley: Bergin, 1983.

Glynn, Kevin. "Reading Supermarket Tabloids as Menippean Satire." *Communication Studies* 44 (1993): 19–37.

## Works Cited

Goleman, Judith. "The Dialogic Imagination: More than We've Been Taught." *Only Connect: Uniting Reading and Writing*. Ed. Thomas Newkirk. Upper Montclair: Boynton/Cook, 1986. 131–42.

Gore, Jennifer. "What We Can Do For You! What *Can* 'We' Do For 'You'? Struggling over Empowerment in Critical and Feminist Pedagogy." Luke and Gore 54–73.

Gradin, Sherrie L. *Romancing Rhetorics: Social Expressivist Perspectives on the Teaching of Writing*. Portsmouth: Boynton/Cook-Heinemann, 1995.

Greenberg, Karen. *Effective Writing: Choices and Conventions*. 2nd ed. New York: St. Martin's, 1992.

Guerra, Juan. "Bridging the Gap Between Home and Academic Literacies." *Purposes and Ideas: Readings for University Writing*. 2nd ed. Ed. David Jolliffe. Dubuque: Kendall-Hunt, 1991. 80–85.

Hairston, Maxine. "Carl Rogers's Alternative to Traditional Rhetoric." *College Composition and Communication* 27.4 (1976): 373–77.

———. *A Contemporary Rhetoric*. Boston: Houghton, 1974.

Hairston, Maxine, and John R. Ruszkiewicz. *The Scott, Foresman Handbook for Writers*. 4th ed. New York: Harper, 1996.

Halasek, Kay. "Back To Bakhtin: A Critique of Current Approaches to Rhetorical History." Rhetoric Society of America Meeting. Arlington, Texas. May 1988.

———. "Feminism and Bakhtin: Dialogic Reading in the Academy." *Rhetoric Society Quarterly* 22 (Winter/Spring 1992): 63–73.

———. "The Fully Functioning Person, the Fully Functioning Writing: Carl Rogers and Expressive Pedagogy." *Rogerian Perspectives: Communication, Writing, and Rhetoric*. Ed. Nathaniel Teich. Norwood: Ablex, 1992. 141–58.

———. "Mikhail Bakhtin and 'Dialogism': What They Have to Offer Composition." *Composition Chronicle* 3.4 (May 1990): 5–8.

———. "Of Reeling and Writhing; Or, Mixed Up Metaphors in the Teaching of Writing." *CCTE Studies* 54 (September 1989): 20–27.

———. "Starting the Dialogue: What Can We Do about Bakhtin's Ambivalence Toward Rhetoric?" *Rhetoric Society Quarterly* 22.4 (Fall 1992): 1–9.

Hale, Dorothy J. "Bakhtin in African American Literary Theory." *ELH* 61 (1994): 445–71.

Harkin, Patricia, and John Schilb. *Contending with Words: Composition and Rhetoric in a Postmodern Age*. New York: MLA, 1991.

Harrington, Michael. *The Other America: Poverty in the United States*. New York: Penguin, 1981.

Harris, Jeanette, and Donald H. Cunningham. *The Simon and Schuster Guide to Writing*. Englewood Cliffs: Prentice-Hall, 1993.

Harris, Joseph. "From the Editor: Writing from the Moon." *College Composition and Communication* 45.2 (May 1994): 161–63.

Harris, R. Allen. "Bakhtin, *Phaedrus*, and the Geometry of Rhetoric." *Rhetoric Review* 6 (1988): 168–76.

Henderson, Mae Gwendolyn. "Speaking in Tongues: Dialogics, Dialectics, and the Black Women Writer's Literary Tradition." *Changing Our Own Words: Essays on Criticism, Theory, and Writing by Black Women*. Ed. Cheryl A. Wall. New Brunswick: Rutgers UP, 1991. 16–37.

Hill, Carolyn Ericksen. *Writing From the Margins: Power and Pedagogy for Teachers of Composition*. New York: Oxford UP, 1990.

Hindman, Jane E. "Reinventing the University: Finding the Place for Basic Writers." *Journal of Basic Writing* 12.2 (1993): 55–76.

Hohne, Karen, and Helen Wussow, eds. *A Dialogue of Voices: Feminist Literary Theory and Bakhtin*. Minneapolis: U of Minnesota P, 1994.

Holquist, Michael. *Dialogue: Bakhtin and His World*. New Accents. London: Routledge, 1990.

———. "Introduction: The Architectonics of Answerability." Bakhtin, *Art and Answerability*. ix–xlix.

hooks, bell. "Bell Hooks Speaking About Paulo Freire—The Man, His Work." *Paulo Freire: A Critical Encounter*. Eds. Peter McLaren and Peter Leonard. New York: Routledge, 1993. 146–54.

———. *talking back: thinking feminist, thinking black*. Boston: South End, 1989.

———. *Teaching To Transgress: Education as the Practice of Freedom*. New York: Routledge, 1994.

Hoy, Mikita. "Bakhtin and Popular Culture." *New Literary History* 23 (1992): 765–82.

Hunt, Alina C. "Toward an Unfinalizable Dialogue: Robert Musil's Essayism and Bakhtinian Dialogism." *College Literature* 22 (1995): 116–24.

Hunt, Russell. "Speech Genres, Writing Genres, School Genres, and the Computer." *Learning and Teaching Genre*. Eds. Aviva Freeman and Peter Medway. Portsmouth: Boynton/Cook-Heinemann, 1994. 243–62.

Johnson, Nan. *Nineteenth-Century Rhetoric in North America*. Carbondale: Southern Illinois UP, 1991.

———. "Three Nineteenth-Century Rhetorics: The Humanist Alternative to Rhetoric as Skills Management." *The Rhetorical Tradition and Modern Writing*. Ed. James J. Murphy. New York: MLA, 1982.

Jones, Robin. " . . . Mah Tongue is in Mah Friend's Mouf ': The Effects of Bakhtin in Classroom and Text." *Studies in the Humanities* 18 (1991): 12–24.

Kennedy, X. J., Dorothy M. Kennedy, and Sylvia A. Holladay. *The Bedford Guide for College Writers with Reader, Research Manual, and Handbook*. 4th ed. Boston: Bedford-St. Martin's, 1996.

Kent, Thomas. "Hermeneutics and Genre: Bakhtin and the Problem of Communicative Interaction." *The Interpretive Turn*. Eds. David R. Hiley, James F. Bohman, and Richard Shusterman. Ithaca: Cornell UP, 1991. 282–303.

Kinneavy, James. "*Kairos*: A Neglected Concept in Classical Rhetoric." *Rhetoric and Praxis: The Contribution of Classical Rhetoric to Practical Reasoning*. Ed. Jean Dietz Moss. Washington: Catholic U of America P, 1986. 79–105.

———. "The Relation of the Whole to the Part in Interpretation Theory in the Composing Process." *Linguistics, Stylistics, and the Teaching of Composition*. Ed. Donald McQuade. Akron: L&S, 1979. 1–23.

———. *A Theory of Discourse: The Aims of Discourse*. New York: Norton, 1971.

Klancher, Jon. "Bakhtin's Rhetoric." *Reclaiming Pedagogy: The Rhetoric of the Classroom*. Eds. Patricia Donahue and Ellen Quandahl. Carbondale: Southern Illinois UP, 1989. 83–96.

Knoblauch, C. H. "Rhetorical Constructions: Dialogue and Commitment." *College English* 50 (1988): 125–40.

Knoblauch, C. H., and Lil Brannon. *Critical Teaching and the Idea of Literacy*. Portsmouth: Boynton/Cook-Heinemann, 1993.

Knoper, Randall. "Deconstruction, Process, Writing." Donahue and Quandahl 128–43.

*Works Cited*

Kozol, Jonathan. *Illiterate America*. Garden City: Anchor-Doubleday, 1985.

Kristeva, Julia. "Word, Dialogue and Novel." *The Kristeva Reader*. Trans. Alice Jardine, Thomas Gora, and Léon S. Roudiez. Ed. Toril Moi. New York: Columbia UP, 1986. 34–61.

Laib, Nevin. "Conciseness and Amplification." *College Composition and Communication* 41 (1990): 443–59.

Lamb, Catherine. "Beyond Argument in Feminist Composition." *College Composition and Communication* 42 (1991): 11–24.

Lather, Patricia Ann. *Getting Smart: Feminist Research and Pedagogy with/in the Postmodern*. New York: Routledge, 1991.

LeFevre, Karen Burke. *Invention as a Social Act*. Studies in Writing and Rhetoric. Carbondale: Southern Illinois UP, 1987.

Leith, Dick, and George Myerson. *The Power of Address: Explorations in Rhetoric*. London: Routledge, 1989.

Lensmire, Timothy J. "Writing Workshop as Carnival: Reflections on an Alternative Learning Environment." *Harvard Educational Review* 64 (1994): 371–391.

Lester, James D. *Writing Research Papers: A Complete Guide*. 8th ed. New York: Harper, 1996.

Lewis, Magda Gere. *Without a Word: Teaching Beyond Women's Silence*. New York: Routledge, 1993.

Lodge, David. *After Bakhtin: Essays on Fiction and Criticism*. London: Routledge, 1990.

Longfellow, Brenda. "Eccentric Subjects: Feminist Film Theory and Its Others." Diss. York U [Canada], 1993.

Lu, Min-Zhan. "Conflict and Struggle: The Enemies or Preconditions of Basic Writing?" *College English* 54.8 (December 1992): 887–913.

———. "Redefining the Legacy of Mina Shaughnessy: A Critique of the Politics of Linguistic Innocence." *Journal of Basic Writing* 10.1 (1991): 26–39.

Lugones, Maria C. "Playfulness, 'World'-Traveling, and Loving Perceptions." *Haciendo Caras, Making Face, Making Soul: Creative and Critical Perspectives by Women of Color*. San Francisco: Aunt Lute, 1990. 390–402.

Luke, Carmen, and Jennifer Gore. *Feminisms and Critical Pedagogy*. New York: Routledge, 1992.

Lunsford, Andrea A. "Aristotelian vs. Rogerian Argument: A Reassessment." *College Composition and Communication* 30 (1979): 146–51.

———. "Composing Ourselves: Politics, Commitment, and the Teaching of Writing." *College Composition and Communication* 41 (1990): 214–20.

Lunsford, Andrea, and Lisa Ede. "Representing Audience: 'Successful' Discourse and Disciplinary Critique." *College Composition and Communication* 47.2 (May 1996): 167–79.

———. *Singular Texts/Plural Authors*. Carbondale: Southern Illinois UP, 1990.

Lynn, Steven. "Reading the Writing Process: Toward a Theory of Current Pedagogies." *College English* 49 (1987): 902–10.

Mader, Diane C. "What Are They Doing to Carl Rogers?" *ETC: A Review of General Semantics* 37 (1980): 314–20.

Martin, Jane Ronald. *Reclaiming a Conversation: The Ideal of the Educated Woman*. New Haven: Yale UP, 1985.

Mason, Theodore O., Jr. "Walter Mosley's Easy Rawlins: The Detective and Afro-American Fiction." *Kenyon Review* 14 (1992): 173–83.

McCrimmon, James M. *Writing with a Purpose: A First Course in College Composition.* Boston: Houghton, 1950.

McLaren, Peter, and Colin Lankshear. "Critical Literacy and the Postmodern Turn." *Critical Literacy: Politics, Praxis, and the Postmodern.* Eds. Colin Lankshear and Peter McLaren. Albany: SUNY P, 1993. 379–419.

Medvedev, Pavel N. *The Formal Method in Literary Scholarship: A Critical Introduction to Sociological Poetics.* Trans. Albert J. Wehrle. Cambridge: Harvard UP, 1985.

Middendorf, Marilyn. "Bakhtin and the Dialogic Writing Class." *Journal of Basic Writing* 11.1 (Spring 1992): 34–46.

Miller, Susan. *Textual Carnivals: The Politics of Composition.* Carbondale: Southern Illinois UP, 1991.

Min-Ha, Trin. *Woman/Native/Other: Writing Postcoloniality and Feminism.* Bloomington: Indiana UP, 1989.

Mirskin, Jerry. "Writing as a Process of Valuing." Diss. U Wisconsin-Madison, 1992.

Moi, Toril. *Sexual/Textual Politics: Feminist Literary Theory.* New Accents. London: Routledge, 1985.

Monas, Sidney. "'The Word with a Sidelong Glance': On Mikhail Bakhtin." *Encounter* 66 (1986): 30–35.

Morgan, Bob. "Three Dreams of Language; Or, No Longer Immured in the Bastille of the Humanist Word." *College English* 49 (1987): 449–58.

Morrison, Toni, ed. *Race-ing Justice, En-gendering Power: Essays on Anita Hill, Clarence Thomas, and the Construction of Social Reality.* New York: Pantheon Books, 1992.

Morson, Gary Saul, ed. *Bakhtin: Essays and Dialogues on His Work.* Chicago: U of Chicago P, 1986.

Morson, Gary Saul, and Caryl Emerson. *Mikhail Bakhtin: Creation of a Prosaics.* Stanford: Stanford UP, 1990.

———, eds. *Rethinking Bakhtin: Extensions and Challenges.* Evanston: Northwestern UP, 1989.

Moss, Beverly. *A Community Text Arises.* Cresskill: Hampton, forthcoming.

Murray, Donald M. *A Writer Teaches Writing: A Practical Method of Teaching Composition.* Boston: Houghton, 1968.

Mutnick, Deborah. *Writing in an Alien World: Basic Writing and the Struggle for Equality in Higher Education.* CrossCurrents Series. Ed. Charles I. Schuster. Portsmouth: Boynton/Cook-Heinemann, 1996.

Myers, Greg. "Reality, Consensus, and Reform in the Rhetoric of Composition Teaching." *College English* 48 (1986): 154–74.

Nealon, Jeffrey T. "The Ethic of Dialogue: Bakhtin and Levinas." *College English* 59 (1997): 129–48.

North, Stephen M. *The Making of Knowledge in Composition: Portrait of an Emerging Field.* Upper Montclair: Boynton/Cook, 1987.

Nystrand, Martin. "Rhetoric's 'Audience' and Linguistic's 'Speech Community': Implications for Understanding Writing, Reading, and Text." *What Writers Know: The Language, Process, and Structure of Written Discourse.* Ed. Martin Nystrand. New York: Academic, 1982. 1–28.

Nystrand, Martin, Stuart Green, and Jeffrey Wiemelt. "Where Did Composition Studies Come From?: An Intellectual History." *Written Communication* 10.3 (July 1993): 267–333.

"Octalog: The Politics of Historiography." *Rhetoric Review* 7.1 (1988): 5–49.

Olson, Gary A. "Social Construction and Composition Theory: A Conversation with Richard Rorty." *Interviews: Cross-Disciplinary Perspectives on Rhetoric and Literacy.* Eds. Gary A. Olson and Irene Gale. Carbondale: Southern Illinois UP, 1991. 227–35.

Ong, Walter, S. J. "The Writer's Audience Is Always a Fiction." *PMLA* 90 (1975): 9–21.

Orner, Mimi. "Interrupting the Calls for Student Voice in 'Liberatory' Education: A Feminist Poststructuralist Perspective." Luke and Gore 74–89.

Park, Douglas B. "Analyzing Audiences." *College Composition and Communication* 37.4 (1986): 478–88.

Pattison, Robert. *On Literacy.* Oxford: Oxford UP, 1982.

Percy, Walker. "The Loss of Creature." *Ways of Reading: An Anthology for Writers.* Ed. David Bartholomae and Anthony Petrosky. Boston: Bedford-St. Martin's, 1987. 393–410.

Perry, William G., Jr. *Forms of Intellectual and Ethical Development in the College Years: A Scheme.* New York: Holt, 1970.

Plato. *Theatetus.* Trans. Robin A. H. Waterfield. New York: Penguin, 1987.

Polanyi, Michael. *Personal Knowledge: Toward a Post-Critical Philosophy.* Chicago: U of Chicago P, 1962.

Pratt, Mary Louise. "Arts of the Contact Zone." *Profession 91.* New York: MLA, 1991. 33–40.

Prince, Gerald. "Introduction to the Study of the Narratee." *Poetique* 14 (1973): 177–93.

Quantz, Richard A., and Terence W. O'Connor. "Writing Critical Ethnography: Dialogue, Multivoicedness, and Carnival in Cultural Texts." *Educational Theory* 38.1 (Winter 1988): 95–109.

Rabinowitz, Peter. "Truth in Fiction: A Reexamination of Audience." *Critical Inquiry* 4 (1977): 121–41.

Recchio, Thomas E. "A Bakhtinian Reading of Student Writing." *College Composition and Communication* 42.4 (Dec. 1991): 446–54.

Reinking, James A., Andrew W. Hart, and Robert von der Osten. *Strategies for Successful Writing: A Rhetoric, Research Guide, and Reader.* 4th ed. Upper Saddle River: Prentice Hall, 1996.

Richter, David H. "Bakhtin in Life and Art." Rev. of *Mikhail Bakhtin,* by Katerina Clark and Michael Holquist, and *Mikhail Bakhtin: The Dialogical Principle,* by Tzvetan Todorov. *Style* 20 (1986): 411–19.

———. "Dialogism and Poetry." *Studies in the Literary Imagination* 23 (1990): 9–27.

Riffaterre, Michael. "Describing Poetic Structures: Two Approaches to Baudelaire's 'Les chats.'" *Yale French Studies* 36–37 (1966): 200–42.

Ritchie, Joy S. "Beginning Writers: Diverse Voices and Individual Identities." *College Composition and Communication* 40 (1989): 152–74.

———. "Confronting the 'Essential' Problem: Reconnecting Feminist Theory and Pedagogy." *Journal of Advanced Composition* 10.2 (Fall 1990): 249–73.

Rogers, Carl. *Freedom to Learn.* Columbus: Charles Merrill, 1969.

Rohmann, D. Gordon, and Albert O. Wlecke. *Pre-Writing: The Construction and Application of Models for Concept Formation in Writing.* U. S. Office of Education Cooperative Research Project no. 2174. East Lansing: Michigan State U, 1964.

Ronald, Kate. "Personal and Public Authority in Discourse: Beyond Subjective/Objective Dichotomies." Ronald and Roskelly, *Farther Along* 25–39.

Ronald, Kate, and Hephzibah Roskelly, eds. *Farther Along: Transforming Dichotomies in Rhetoric and Composition.* Portsmouth: Boynton/Cook-Heinemann, 1990.

Rorty, Richard. *Philosophy and the Mirror of Nature*. Princeton: Princeton UP, 1979.

Rose, Mike. *Lives on the Boundary: A Moving Account of the Struggles and Achievements of America's Educational Underclass*. New York: Penguin, 1989.

——. "Narrowing the Mind and Page: Remedial Writers and Cognitive Reductionism." *College Composition and Communication* 39.3 (1988): 267–302.

——. *Possible Lives: The Promise of Public Education in America*. New York: Penguin, 1995.

Rosenblatt, Louise. *The Reader, the Text, the Poem*. Carbondale: Southern Illinois UP, 1978.

Roth, Robert G. "The Evolving Audience: Alternatives to Audience Accommodation." *College Composition and Communication* 38.1 (1987): 47–55.

Sabatini, Arthur. "Mikhail Bakhtin and Performance." Diss. New York U, 1994.

Schilb, John. *Between the Lines: Relating Composition Theory and Literary Theory*. Portsmouth: Boynton/Cook, 1996.

Scholes, Robert. *Protocols of Reading*. New Haven: Yale UP, 1989.

Schultz, Emily A. *Dialogue at the Margins: Whorf, Bakhtin, and Linguistic Relativity*. Madison: U of Wisconsin P, 1990.

Schuster, Charles. "The Ideology of Illiteracy: A Bakhtinian Perspective." *The Right to Literacy*. Eds. Andrea A. Lunsford and James Slevin. New York: MLA, 1990. 225–32.

——. "Mikhail Bakhtin as Rhetorical Theorist." *College English* 47 (1985): 594–607.

Schweickart, Patrocinio P. "Reading Ourselves: Toward a Feminist Theory of Reading." Flynn and Schweikart 31–62.

Schweickart, Patrocinio P., and Elizabeth A. Flynn. Introduction. Flynn and Schweickart ix–xxx.

Scott, Fred Newton, and Joseph Villiers Denney. *Paragraph-Writing: A Rhetoric for Colleges*. 3rd ed. Boston: Allyn, 1893.

Scott, Jerrie Cobb. "Literacies and Deficits Revisited." *Journal of Basic Writing* 12.1 (1993): 46–56.

Selzer, Jack. "More Meanings of *Audience*." *A Rhetoric of Doing: Essays on Written Discourse in Honor of James L. Kinneavy*. Eds. Stephen P. Witte, Neil Nakadate, and Roger D. Cherry. Carbondale: Southern Illinois UP, 1992. 161–77.

Severino, Carol. "Where the Cultures of Basic Writers and Academia Intersect: Cultivating the Common Ground." *Journal of Basic Writing* 11.1 (1992): 4–15.

Shapiro, Marianne. "Dialogism and the Addressee in Lyric Poetry." *University of Toronto Quarterly* 61 (1992): 392–413.

Shaughnessy, Mina P. "Diving In: An Introduction to Basic Writing." *College Composition and Communication* 27.3 (October 1976): 234–39.

Shelley, Mary. *Frankenstein, Or the Modern Prometheus*. New York: Signet Classics, 1965.

Shor, Ira, ed. *Critical Teaching and Everyday Life*. Chicago: U of Chicago P, 1987.

——, ed. *Freire for the Classroom: A Sourcebook for Liberatory Teaching*. Portsmouth: Boynton/Cook-Heinemann, 1987.

Silverman, David, and Brian Torode. *The Material Word: Some Theories of Language and Its Limits*. London: Routledge, 1980.

Sipiora, Phillip. "Rearticulating the Rhetorical Tradition: The Influence of A Theory of Discourse." *Journal of Advanced Composition* 8 (1988): 123–36.

Soliday, Mary. "From the Margins to the Mainstream: Reconceiving Remediation." *College Composition and Communication* 47.1 (February 1996): 85–100.

Sontag, Susan. *On Photography*. New York: Farrar, 1966.

Souris, Stephen. "'Only Two Kinds of Daughters': Inter-monologue Dialogicity in *The Joy Luck Club*." *MELUS* 19 (1994): 99–123.

Spatt, Brenda. *Writing from Sources*. 4th ed. New York: St. Martin's, 1996.

Spellmeyer, Kurt. *Common Ground: Dialogue, Understanding, and the Teaching of Composition*. Prentice Hall Studies in Writing and Culture. Englewood Cliffs: Prentice Hall, 1993.

———. "A Common Ground: The Essay in the Academy." *College English* 51 (1989): 262–76.

———. "Foucault and the Freshman Writer: Considering the Self in Discourse." *College English* 51.7 (November 1989): 715–29.

Stewart, Donald. "Prose with Integrity: A Primary Objective." *College Composition and Communication* 20 (1969): 223–27.

Taft, Kendall B., John Francis McDermott, and Dana O. Jensen. *The Technique of Composition*. 3rd ed. New York: Rinehart, 1946.

Tayko, Gail, and John Tossani, eds. *Sharing Pedagogies: Teachers and Students Respond to the English Curriculum*. Portsmouth: Boynton/Cook, 1996.

Thomas, Gordon P. "Mutual Knowledge: A Theoretical Basis for Analyzing Audience." *College English* 48.6 (1986): 580–94.

Titunik, I. R. "The Formal Method and the Sociological Method (M. M. Baxtin, P. N. Medvedev, V. N. Volosinov) in Russian Theory and Study of Literature." *Marxism and the Philosophy of Language*. Trans. Ladislav Matejka and I. R. Titunik. Cambridge: Harvard UP, 1973. 173–200.

Todorov, Tzvetan. *Mikhail Bakhtin: The Dialogical Principle*. Trans. Wlad Godzich. Theory and History of Literature 13. Minneapolis: U of Minnesota P, 1984.

Tompkins, Jane. "Me and My Shadow." *New Literary History* 19 (1987): 167–78.

———. "Pedagogy of the Distressed." *College English* 52.6 (Oct. 1990): 653–60.

Trimbur, John. "Collaborative Learning and Teaching Writing." *Perspectives on Research and Scholarship in Composition*. Ed. Ben W. McClelland and Timothy R. Donovan. New York: MLA, 1985. 87–109.

Villanueva, Victor. *Bootstraps: From an American Academic of Color*. Urbana: National Council of Teachers of English, 1993.

Volosinov, Valentin N. "Discourse in Life and Discourse in Art (Concerning Sociological Poetics)." Volosinov, *Freudianism* 93–116.

———. *Freudianism: A Critical Sketch*. Trans. I. R. Titunik. Ed. I. R. Titunik with Neal H. Bruss. Bloomington: Indiana UP, 1976.

———. *Marxism and the Philosophy of Language*. Trans. Ladislav Matejka and I. R. Titunik. Cambridge: Harvard UP, 1973.

Vygotsky, Lev S. *Mind in Society: The Development of Higher Psychological Processes*. Eds. Michael Cole, Vera John-Steiner, Sylvia Scribner, and Ellen Souberman. Cambridge: Harvard UP, 1978.

———. *Thought and Language*. Trans. and Ed. Alex Kozulin. Cambridge: MIT P, 1986.

Ward, Irene. *Literacy, Ideology, and Dialogue: Towards a Dialogic Pedagogy*. SUNY Series, Teacher Empowerment and School Reform. Eds. Henry A. Giroux and Peter L. McLaren. Albany: SUNY P, 1994.

Welch, Kathleen. "Ideology and Freshman Textbook Production: The Place of Theory in Writing Pedagogy." *College Composition and Communication* 38.3 (1987): 269–82.

Welch, Nancy. "One Student's Many Voices: Reading, Writing, and Responding with Bakhtin." *Journal of Advanced Composition* 13.2 (Fall 1993): 494–502.

*Works Cited*

Wendell, Barrett. *English Composition*. New York: Ungar, 1963.

Wertsch, James V. *Voices of the Mind: A Sociocultural Approach to Mediated Action*. Cambridge: Harvard UP, 1991.

White, Hayden. *Metahistory: The Historical Imagination in Ninteteenth-Century Europe*. Baltimore: Johns Hopkins, 1973.

Williams, Patricia J. *The Alchemy of Race and Rights: Diary of a Law Professor*. Cambridge: Harvard UP, 1991.

Winkler, Anthony, and Jo Ray McCuen. *Rhetoric Made Plain*. 5th ed. San Diego: Harcourt, 1988.

Young, Richard E., Alton L. Becker, and Kenneth L. Pike. *Rhetoric: Discovery and Change*. San Diego: Harcourt, 1970.

Zebroski, James Thomas. *Thinking Through Theory: Vygotskian Perspectives on the Teaching of Writing*. Portsmouth: Boynton/Cook-Heineman, 1994.

KAY HALASEK attended Georgetown College, Northern Arizona University, and the University of Texas at Austin. She is currently an associate professor of English at Ohio State University, where she also serves as the director of the First-Year Writing Program.